Approaching Deliberative Democracy:

Theory and Practice

edited by
Robert Cavalier

Approaching Deliberative Democracy:

Theory and Practice

edited by
Robert Cavalier

Carnegie Mellon University Press
Pittsburgh 2011

Photo: Robert Cavalier, Editor (copyright © Ken Andreyo)

Cover: Pictures from deliberative polling events and community
conversations (copyright © Robert Cavalier)

Library of Congress Number 2010930074
ISBN 978-0-88748-537-4
Copyright © 2011 by Robert Cavalier
All rights reserved
Printed and bound in the United States of America.

10 9 8 7 6 5 4 3 2 1

To

Liz Style

Wife, Friend, and

Local Community Hero

Contents

The Conversational Turn in Political Philosophy

Robert Cavalier

Liberal democracies of the kind we see forming around the world are only the beginning of what Benjamin Barber has called strong democracies.[1] Thin, liberal democracies provide the constitutional essentials of universal suffrage, freedom of press and assembly, etc., but this in no way guarantees that the citizens of these societies will see themselves as any more than isolated individuals who periodically vote (if they choose to do so). Recent work in "Citizenship Theory" has made clear that "the health and stability of a modern democracy depends, not only on the justice of its basic institutions, but also on the qualities and attitudes of its citizens."[2] These qualities and attitudes are often highlighted by proponents of deliberative democracy and emphasize the role of the citizen in becoming a truly informed and engaged individual, a person willing to listen to all sides and willing to let the force of the better argument (in all its richness) become a guide to opinion formation.

Over the past 20 years, the concept of deliberative democracy has emerged as a major contribution to democratic theory. With philosophical foundations in the later writings of Jürgen Habermas and John Rawls, the concept has also received considerable attention within the social sciences.[3] Put briefly, the citizens of the modern

---

[1] See Barber, *Strong Democracy: Participatory Politics for a New Age* (Berkeley: University of California Press, 2000 [1984]).

[2] Will Kymlicka, *Contemporary Political Philosophy: An Introduction* (Oxford: Oxford University Press, 2002), 285.

[3] See Habermas, *The Structural Transformation of the Public Sphere*, trans. Thomas Burger (Cambridge: The MIT Press, 1991) and *Between Facts and Norms: Contributions to a Discourse of Law and Democracy*, trans. William Rehg (Cambridge: The MIT Press, 1996), along with John Rawls, *Political Liberalism* (New York: Columbia

liberal state manifest an irreducible plurality of visions of the good that encompass all but the most basic principles of justice. In turn, the principles of justice that make up the "constitutional essentials" ensuring "life, liberty and the pursuit of happiness" provide the political horizon wherein diverse visions of the good can be pursued. Much of the theoretical work of Habermas and Rawls is devoted to defending the rational foundation of liberal constitutional democracies through arguments revolving around notions of "normative validity" and "overlapping consensus." Fundamental to both of their arguments is what Habermas calls "Dialogical Reason." In this view, political reason moves through conversations characterized by the fact of plurality and the richness of perspectives. Ideally, it reaches consensus on "constitutional essentials" through the uncoerced conversation of rational beings pursuing the stronger argument or the overlapping interests of diverse populations in their desire to live their lives in the light of their own comprehensive worldviews.[4]

"Open and informed" conversations on the part of the citizenry are essential to the concept of deliberative democracy. "Openness" refers to the ability of all perspectives to be allowed a voice in the discussion, and "informed" refers to the need for the discussion to

---

University Press, 1993), and "The Idea of Public Reason Revisited" in *The Law of Peoples* (Cambridge: Harvard University Press, 1999). The relation of deliberative democratic theory to the social and decision sciences can be seen by contrasting the works of Habermas with standard rational choice and social choice approaches to democratic theory: See Joseph Heath, *Communicative Action and Rational Choice* (Cambridge: The MIT Press, 2003). See also Dryzek and List, "Social Choice Theory and Deliberative Democracy: A Reconciliation," *British Journal of Political Science* 33, no. 1, 2003, pp. 1-28.

[4] Borrowing from the later Rawls and Habermas, one can view "the citizen" as a complex person capable of being (1) "rational" in the sense of being able to use means/ends reasoning in a self-interested way and (2) "reasonable" in the sense of being able to compromise on self-interested calculations if it seems that others have alternate views that are worth supporting or at least acknowledging. For example, I may accept a higher rate of property tax if you convince me that an extended bike trail may bring a good quality of life to others, even if I don't benefit from these trails, or I may assent to the policies that others adopt even though I opposed them with my vote. Furthermore, I follow Rawls in ascribing to this person two "moral powers": (1) a sense of reciprocity/fairness (and, I would add, empathy) and (2) the capability of generating a vision of the good. The latter accounts for a significant part of "pluralism" and can be seen, for example, in the different political platforms of the American Democratic and Republican parties.

be based upon the best information and arguments available. These broad requirements of practical reason have been adopted by advocates of deliberative democracy with the goal of achieving a strategy for democratic decision-making on a range of practical political problems.[5] And while there is considerable debate within the literature over the appropriate scope and epistemological nature of these conversations, there is general agreement about the Deweyan belief in social intelligence and the hope that we "think best when we think together."

The Land of Middle Democracy

To approach the field of deliberative democracy, it will be helpful to follow a line of argument found in Amy Gutmann and Dennis Thompson's *Democracy and Disagreement* (1996). In the first chapter of their book, Gutmann and Thompson distinguish three models of democracy: procedural, constitutional, and deliberative. For these authors, the first two models provide seeds that can grow into the third, thus showing how deliberative democracy can be seen as a synthesis of the previous models. We distinguish their approaches from the broader, theoretical descriptions above since they move us closer to the actual practice of deliberative democracy.

Procedural Democracy

Procedural democracy is characterized by the equality of each vote and a respect for majority outcomes. With some basic protections for minority rights, it is a form of majoritarianism and describes a very common notion of democracy. The legitimacy of this system is based on the fairness of the procedures that allow for the vote (and for opportunities of more votes in the future). As a vote-centric model of democracy, it looks to the total aggregation of votes to determine social choice (or the will of the people). Critiques

---

[5] For an overview of perspectives on deliberative democracy, see Samuel Freeman, "Deliberative Democracy: A Sympathetic Comment," *Philosophy and Public Affairs* 29, no. 4 (2000): 371–418, *Deliberative Democracy*, eds. Bohman and Rehg (Cambridge: The MIT Press, 1997), and *Debating Deliberative Democracy*, eds. Fishkin and Laslett (Indianapolis: Wiley-Blackwell, 2003). Iris Young's *Inclusion and Democracy* (Oxford: Oxford University Press, 2002) adds valuable insight into the diverse forms of argument and persuasion evident in different communities and socio-economic strata.

of this model abound, from the paradoxes of voting theory to the media manipulation of voters to the fairness of the outcomes. For example, there are those who distinguish between democratic procedures and democratic values, and here situations can arise where the former (each person has one vote) violates the latter (a segment of the population is treated unjustly). This appeared to many to be the case with the 2008 California referendum on same-sex marriage. Criticisms like this lead us to consider substantive constitutional values outside of the purely internal democratic values held by strict proceduralists (e.g., freedom of assembly, universal suffrage).

Constitutional Democracy

Constitutional democracy, best exemplified in the literature by John Rawls' *Theory of Justice* (1971), seeks to provide "moral constraints based on nonprocedural considerations."[6] Modern "welfare democracies" like those found in Europe embed in their basic laws concerns for what Rawls calls "fair equality of opportunity" and provide foundations for public policies governing healthcare and marriage and so forth. But Rawls' method of arriving at these basic principles of justice was limited by the monologue of a rational, but somewhat ghostly individual behind a veil of ignorance. The abstractness of this approach as well as the generality of constitutional principles fail to address "at a level of specificity sufficient to resolve the conflicts they manifest" the diverse interpretations and moral arguments that abound when considering concrete proposals for healthcare reform or the legalization of same-sex marriages. This is where the rubber hits the road and where the hard work of democracy goes on. It is what Gutmann and Thompson call "middle democracy."

> This is the land of everyday politics, where legislators, executives, administrators, and judges make and apply policies and laws, sometimes arguing among themselves, sometimes explaining themselves and listening to citizens, other times not. Middle democracy is also the land of interest groups, civic associations, and schools, in which adults and children develop political un-

---

[6] Amy Gutmann and Dennis Thompson, *Democracy and Disagreement* (Cambridge: Harvard University Press, 1996), 33-39.

derstandings, sometime arguing among themselves and listening to people with differing points of view, other times not.[7]

Here both proceduralism and its development into constitutionalism need to be buttressed by the third model: deliberative democracy.

Deliberative Democracy

In these everyday workings of our public discussions about "What we ought to do," deliberation has a number of advantages over the previous approaches.[8] First is that we often confront a scarcity of resources and hard choices have to be made. For example, our public libraries are facing cutbacks due to a lack of funding. Should they close some libraries or seek support from state tax revenues? By finding ways to bring stakeholders and the public into a forum for discussing the necessary tradeoffs, final decisions will achieve a level of legitimacy since the process included a broad range of perspectives and the opportunity to hear from all sides (including those affected by the closings).

A second advantage of the deliberative approach is that the very act of engaging in these kinds of public forums helps one shift perspective from one's private preference ("I don't want my tax dollars going to these non-profits") to a form of public judgment ("Even though I may not personally want this, I understand how it might be necessary"). Gutmann and Thompson quote John Stuart Mill with approval, noting how a citizen is "called upon . . . to weigh matters not his own; to be guided, in case of conflicting claims, by another rule than his private partialities; to apply at every turn, principles and maxims which have for their reason of existence the common good."[9]

The third and fourth advantages of a more deliberative approach relate to disagreements over fundamental values and stress the impor-

---

[7] Gutmann and Thompson (1996), 40.

[8] For Gutmann and Thompson, the deliberative principles guiding the discourse of middle democracy are 1) the sense of reciprocity (respect, public reasoning), 2) the value of publicity (public forums), and 3) the scope of accountability (citizens and public officials accountable to each other for political actions). *Democracy and Disagreement* (Cambridge: Harvard University Press, 1996), 52.

[9] Gutmann and Thompson 42.

tance of what members of the dispute mediation community call active listening, brainstorming and conflict resolution. In fact, new ideas and "win-win" situations arise precisely because of the deliberative process, where sometimes unexpected perspectives and new metaphors emerge. Even within the strains of the abortion debate, citizens can agree that teenage pregnancies are to be avoided and can seek to support community organizations that work in this area.

Compromise need not leave parties dissatisfied if the process has gone well. It's not that each side gets only a half an orange when they initially wanted the whole orange, it's that after talking they found out that one side wanted it for the juice and the other for the rind. Henry Richardson goes further and suggests that deliberation can lead to "deep compromise" of the kind that involves reevaluating one's ends. For Richardson, this is "a change in one's support of policies or implementing means that is accompanied and explained or supported by a changes in one's ends that itself counts as a compromise."[10] This certainly happened to many senators and ordinary citizens during the civil rights era and may be happening today with regard to the issue of "civil marriages" for same-sex couples.

The more we talk, the more we learn—about each side's concerns and aspirations. The more we talk, the more we see—and the better we can judge "what we ought to do." As Iris Young argues, the process of democratic discussion not only allows participants to express their opinions, but it can actually transform "the preferences, interests, beliefs, and judgments of participants. Through the process of public discussion with a plurality of differently opinioned and situated others, people often gain new information, learn of different experiences of their collective problems, or find that their own initial opinions were founded on prejudice or ignorance, or that they have misunderstood the relation of their own interests to others."[11]

For Young, these conversations are not only characterized by arguments but often by storytelling. In line with the work of philosophical writings of Martha Nussbaum and the work in cognitive science by Mark Johnson, we are not so much *Homo economicus* as

---

[10] Henry Richardson, *Democratic Autonomy: Public Reasoning about the Ends of Policy* (New York: Oxford University Press, 2003), 147.

[11] Iris M. Young, *Inclusion and Democracy* (Oxford: Oxford University Press, 2002), 26.

Homo narrans. It is through life stories that we come to cognitively grasp the lifeworld of others and are imaginatively able to get into their shoes.

> Narrative thus exhibits the situated knowledge available from various social locations, and the combination of narratives from different perspectives produces a collective social wisdom not available from any one position. By means of narratives expressed in public with others differently situated who also tell their stories, speakers and listeners can develop the 'enlarged thought' that transforms their thinking about issues from being narrowly self-interested or self-regarding about an issue, to thinking about an issue in a way that takes account of the perspectives of others.[12]

Not to be a Pollyanna here—those on the front lines know the challenges and the fault lines, they know how things can falter and fall apart. Democracy is the second best form of government and deliberation is imperfect. There can be deliberative trouble when those who agree with an ideological perspective raise their own rhetoric and move toward extremes and there can be unforeseen conflict and discomfort (imagine Steve Carell of the television show *The Office* trying to hold a dialogue on race).[13]

Social scientists who observe community meetings often confuse examples of grassroots participatory democracy with the thoughtful practice of deliberative democracy. And writers who focus on "oppositional political perspectives" as the paradigm of "political talk," miss the detailed tasks of real world citizen deliberators. In *Hearing the Other Side* (2006), for example, Diana Mutz emphasizes and studies "real world" political talk and downplays "specially orchestrated forums." But the heart of deliberative practice as it has been evolving in the United States is in the design of well-structured environments that allow diverse groups of people to come together to discuss rather specific issues confronting them as members of

---

[12] Young 78.

[13] See Cass Sunstein "Deliberative Trouble? Why Groups Go to Extremes," *Yale L.J.* 71 (2000): 71-119. Gerry Mackie's chapter in this volume alludes to the kinds of situations in which deliberation can lead to conflict.

a larger community.[14] Thus, when people from all over Northeast Ohio came together to discuss regional issues—and to see themselves as part of a region—they did not discuss "politics." The background materials provided them with information about the region's geography and the cities and counties of the region as well as briefed them on the economies of the region and the challenges and opportunities that faced the region. In roundtable sessions, they were asked to locate themselves within the region (a large map allowed participants to mark where they lived and worked, where they traveled for recreation). They were then to discuss how they thought about the region and what they believed were its strengths and weaknesses. As a large screen in the auditorium displayed the features of the region that were being identified, people used their "clickers" to select the top three in one area for further discussion. Sitting at one of the tables that day, I observed that there were no Republicans or Democrats talking, just people "rolling up their sleeves and working on a problem."[15]

Here the practice of deliberative democracy can be seen as a kind of craft and democracy itself as a design problem.[16] Young,

---

[14] See Mutz 60. As valuable as her study is, to the extent that she defines away the actual practice of such settings, her analyses miss the mark. Mutz also argues that organized and structured deliberative events are artificial and non-scaleable. One could counter that it is the 'participatory distortion' of activist politics that is artificial (non-representative) and that the problem of scale will take care of itself as deliberative practices become more ingrained at the local and regional level. And while we may never witness a National Deliberation Day, one could imagine a brand name polling group conducting two or three national deliberative polls on issues of interest to the country as a whole (with the issue-focused discussions and issue-focused results influencing the talk of the news media).

[15] AmericaSpeaks "Voices and Choices" (www.americaspeaks.org/). A central distinction between the 21st Century Town Hall meetings developed by Carolyn Lukensmeyer and Deliberative Polls developed by James Fishkin revolves around sampling techniques, where the former relies on convenience samples to achieve a large audience that is demographically representative and the latter relies on random samples that contain attitudinal representation as well as demographic representation (Fishkin, *When the People Speak*, 111-112). Both have their usefulness depending on the circumstances and it is possible to imagine initiatives that can combine strategies (Cavalier, *Democracy for Beginners*, 96-99).

[16] These techniques have flourished and many groups and organizations adopt and adapt them in varied settings across the country. The National Coalition for Dialogue & Deliberation, for example, has compiled nineteen "Engagement Streams" that

for instance, highlights the role of "greeting" in the initial stages of a discussion.[17] Add to this well-designed and accessible background information on an issue and trained moderators to facilitate the discussion. Slowly there arises in middle democracy inclusive, informed, structured conversations about "What we ought to do"— be it national healthcare or neighborhood development. In America the practice of deliberative democracy has come from the ground up—from citizen juries to deliberative polls; from the learning circles of Everyday Democracy to the 21st Century Town Hall meetings of AmericaSpeaks.[18]

Approaching Deliberative Democracy

This collection begins with a reflection on certain aspects of 20th Century intellectual history leading up to Rawls' embrace of deliberative democracy. In her previous work, *Rationalizing Capitalist Democracy* (2003), S.M. Amadea's analysis of the Cold War origins of Rational Choice Liberalism reveals many of the assumptions behind social choice theory from Joseph Schumpeter through William Riker to the early work of John Rawls. In many ways, these "economic theories of democracy" and the libertarian ideals that many proponents espouse have led to foreign and domestic policies that have become problematic during the first decade of the 21st century. Taking this into consideration, Amadea clears the path for a more "deliberative" democracy in her essay on Buchanan, Rawls and Democratic Governance.

Some readers may not immediately appreciate the preparatory nature of this philosophical survey, but ideas espoused by Schum-

---

include Citizen Choicework, Exploration and Conflict Transformation Models, Appreciative Inquiry, and Consensus Conferences.

[17] "Such gestures do not offer information or further arguments directly by giving reasons or criticisms. But without such spoken moments of politeness, deference, acknowledgment of the particular perspective of others, their goodwill and contribution to the collective, the discussion itself would often break down." (Young 2002), 60.

[18] See *The Deliberative Democracy Handbook: Strategies for Effective Civic Engagement in the Twenty-First Century* edited by John Gastil and Peter Levine (San Francisco: Jossey-Bass, 2005) for articles by leading practitioners on the implementation of the principles of deliberative democracy.

17

peter, Downs, Riker and Buchanan have dominated political science curriculum. And graduates of such programs have become the kinds of "political consultants" that have turned American politics into a "win at all costs" battlefield.

In *Strong Democracy* (2004 [1984]), Benjamin Barber argued for a more participatory democracy wherein citizens see themselves as judges of the common good as opposed to individuals with private preferences. In ways that expand upon Amadea's intellectual history, he explores the cultural and global contexts of these ideas in *Consumed* (2007), where the market paradigm filters into the very soul of the individual in both his private and civic life. In "From Citizen to Consumer and Back Again: Deliberative Democracy and the Challenge of Interdependence," he addresses a broad audience with this thesis and provides us with the background and overview necessary to grasp the larger picture before moving on to the more specific studies that follow. Originally a keynote address, it is both provocative and edifying.

Gerry Mackie worked for years as a political organizer and this experience informs his understanding of both the scope and limits deliberative democracy. His major work, *Democracy Defended* (2003), also established him as a keen critic of certain aspects of social choice theory, especially the kind represented by Riker in *Liberalism against Populism* (1982). In "Deliberation, but Voting Too," he reviews the political and personal framework of deliberation, pointing out that short of Habermasian Ideal Speech Situations, discussions can benefit not only from organizational structure but also majority voting. It brings closure to the conversation and moves us toward action.[19] It is wrong, he argues, for "deliberationists" to separate talk-

---

[19] See James S. Fishkin, *Democracy and Deliberation.* (New Haven: Yale University Press, 1991): "An ideal of deliberation . . . would take us ultimately to something like the 'ideal speech situation' of Jürgen Habermas—a situation of free and equal discussion, unlimited in its duration, constrained only by the consensus which would be arrived at by the 'force of the better argument.'" Anticipating Mackie's concerns, Simone Chambers notes that "the more public debate conforms to the ideal of discourse, the less useful it is as a tool of democratic decision making. Discourse involves a trade-off between efficiency and the goal of mutual understanding. The more our conversations are directed at mutual understanding, the less efficient they are in producing a determinate outcome that can be acted upon"(241). See Chambers, "Discourse and Democratic Practices," in *The Cambridge Companion to Habermas*, ed. Stephen K. White (Cambridge: Cambridge University Press, 1995), 233-262.

centric from vote-centric models of democracy. Toward that end, Mackie offers an empirical and normative account of voting that actually advances the deliberative goals of filtering out self-interest and including public interest in social choice matters. Mackie further notes that a change in voting models for counties like Papua New Guinea, from plurality rule to alternate vote, can have consequences not seen by deliberation alone.[20] The need for further research into democratic voting practices to complement the need for further research into democratic deliberation is essentially a call for further research in the field of political theory itself.

A number of initiatives discussed in the next set of chapters make use of a particular instantiation of deliberative democracy called a Deliberative Poll®. Developed by James Fishkin, a deliberative poll gathers a representative sample of the community to discuss and respond to questions on pressing local, regional or national issues. While traditional public opinion polls solicit "intuitive" responses from people who are not well-informed on the topic,[21] a "deliberative opinion poll models what the electorate would think if, hypothetically, it could be immersed in an intensive deliberative process." [22]

Formally, the protocols of a face-to-face deliberative poll entail a random sample of the population who receive ahead of time materials that represent the topics to be discussed; an opportunity for those citizens to gather in moderated, small group discussions; an opportunity for the small groups to generate and pose questions to an expert panel in a plenary session; a second set of deliberations and then a survey designed to gauge the considered opinions

---

[20] Peter Emerson also sees the problems that certain majoritarian voting procedures can cause and suggests his own version of a Modified Boda Count as an alternate way of introducing deliberation and conflict resolution into the broader activity of decision-making. See *Beyond the Tyranny of the Majority: Voting Methodologies in Decision-Making and Electoral Systems* (Belfast: The De Borda Institute, 1998). For an accessible overview of voting theory and its practical applications, see William Poundstone, *Gaming the Vote* (New York: Farrar, Straus and Giroux, 2008).

[21] Fishkin reviews studies by Eugene Harty and Philip Converse in this regard. He also refers to a study in *Public Opinion Quarterly* that sought opinions on the "Public Affairs Act of 1975." Despite the fact that there was no such act, about one-third of the respondents offered opinions (Fishkin 1995, 80-84).

[22] Fishkin, *The Voice of The People: Public Opinion and Democracy* (New Haven: Yale University Press, 1995), 81.

resulting from the day's deliberation. While Vincent Price and Peter Neijens note that the results and meaning of these kinds of polls still call for further research, initial studies by Shanto Iyangar, Robert Luskin, and others are promising.[23]

Christian List has been a collaborator with Fishkin in analyzing empirical data from national deliberative polling events. In 2009 he co-authored a paper seeking to analyze the effects of deliberative polling in the context of the formal face-to-face setting.[24] The issue here involves two areas of concern to the citizens of New Haven, Connecticut: regional tax sharing and a proposal to expand the local airport. Using data from a randomized field experiment within a deliberative poll, the authors analyze the effects of deliberation on policy attitudes as well as on the extent to which ordinal rankings (1st, 2nd, 3rd . . . n) of such policy options approach single-peakedness. The latter refers to a combination (along, say, an x, y axis) of individual preference ordering such that there exists at least one left-right alignment of ordering (e.g., decrease the size of the airport, maintain current size, expand the airport) and each participant has a 'most preferred' position on that axis while preferring the alternatives less (e.g., expand, maintain, decrease). In "Learning Democratic Communication through Deliberative Polling," he is joined by Anne Sliwka in another investigation of single-peakedness, this time in the context of student discussions of a number of issues relating to the German Education Policy. Although this was a limited field test, the

---

[23] Price and Neijens raise a number of important methodological concerns in their article "Deliberative Polls: Toward Improved Measures of 'Informed' Public Opinion?" *International Journal of Public Opinion Research* 10 (Summer 1998): 141-176. While hopeful that these kinds of deliberative polls might actually contribute to better public opinion, they argue for more social science research into the area, research that will seek to isolate the various effects that occur in the deliberative process so as to demonstrate the virtues of the process more accurately. For empirical studies that can be seen to address these concerns, see Luskin et al., "The Deliberative Voter" at the Center for Deliberative Democracy (cdd.stanford.edu/ research/papers/2006/deliberative-voter.pdf). This study exams the effects of a deliberative poll on voters' ability to distinguish the personality of the candidates from the policy positions of the candidates.

[24] See Cynthia Farrar et al., "Disaggregating Deliberation's Effects: An Experiment within a Deliberative Poll," *British Journal of Political Science* (2009). Here researchers also used controls to verify that the observed effects in the study could be attributed to group deliberation rather than to some other cause.

authors cast their study as one addressing some notorious paradoxes of aggregative voting theory. They propose that deliberative polling can structure problem fields in ways that allow participants to achieve a meta-consensus on, for example, the ideological dimension underlying a given decision problem and that individual preferences of the participants can be systematically arranged to achieve a degree of single-peakedness. While agreeing on the structuring of the decision problem does not imply agreement on the solution, it does allow one to overcome the "cycling" problem posed by voting theorists such as Kenneth Arrow.

Within the field of deliberative democracy, theory and practice often cross-fertilize. Theory helps guide practice and practice can inform and deepen theory. Mackie, List and Sliwka have done this to varying degrees and so will the authors of the next three chapters. Julie Marsh is a Policy Researcher at RAND specializing in research on school-community collaboration, policy implementation, district-level educational reform, and accountability. Drawing on three years of field research, her chapter describes the ways in which power, deliberative values, organizational climates, and trust shaped face-to-face deliberations and actions in two California school districts. As she demonstrates, those deliberative practices that are well-structured, open, and have the commitment of all stakeholders are more likely to have outcomes considered more helpful and legitimate than those efforts that lack these elements despite their claims to be deliberative.

In many ways, the failure of one school district's approach is as instructive as the success of the other district. From the perspective of deliberative theory, it highlights the challenge posed by the "face of power"—those dynamic forces that often determine who initiates a deliberative process, who sets the agenda and who determines the spectrum of choices to be discussed.[25] At the same time, Marsh's analysis of the more positive outcome shows how deliberative practices can overcome or at least be sensitive to such a challenge. To paraphrase Dewey, the problems of deliberation can be solved through better deliberative practice.

In the 1980s the City of Pittsburgh suffered from the decline of its industrial past. Loss of jobs led to a decline in population and,

---

[25] See Ian Shaprio, *The State of Democratic Theory* (Princeton University Press, 2003) for a forceful delineation of this challenge.

with that, a decline in the quality of life in number of its many neighborhoods. The nine neighborhoods that comprised a "hilltop" area in Pittsburgh's District Three, for example, suffered from vacant houses and a rise in crime associated with drug use and prostitution. In his chapter, "Civic Renewal and the Practice of Deliberative Democracy," Gregory J. Crowley combines the complementary models of deliberative democracy and participatory strategic planning to show how this community was brought together in a "Community Conversation" and how this conversation contributed to the development of a "Hilltop Alliance" in the City of Pittsburgh.

In parallel accord with the recommendations suggested by Julie Marsh, the Coro Center for Civic Leadership and the Southwestern Pennsylvania Program for Deliberative Democracy worked with private foundations and the Federal Weed and Seed Program to create a sense of community and a commitment to pursue common goals over time. The event that brought steering committee members, stakeholders and a randomized sample of the neighborhood community together for a day-long conversation has been recognized by participants and city officials as an essential catalyst in the creation of the Hilltop Alliance and without which there would be no such Alliance today.

As a partner of Crowley in this endeavor, I have seen the positive ways that one can use the principles of deliberative democracy literally to build communities and create a newly engaged citizenry.[26]

---

[26] From Anthony's Downs's deduction of 'Rational Ignorance' to Russell Hardin's attempt to retrieve a modicum of engagement through "An Economic Theory of Knowledge," in *How Do You Know? The Economics of Ordinary Knowledge* (Princeton: Princeton University Press, 2009) writers in the tradition of Social Choice Theory, even if they don't intend to, dull what I call the 'civic imagination' and, as a consequence, the possibility of civic engagement. See Downs' (1957) "Deductions from the Citizen-Rationality Hypothesis": Prop. 12: "Because nearly every citizen realizes his vote is not decisive in each election, the incentive of most citizens to acquire information before voting is very small" and Prop. 13: "A large percentage of citizens—including voters—do not become informed to any significant degree on the issues involved in elections, even if they believe the outcomes to be important." But data show that, for example, Deliberative Polls *do* motivate "a microcosm of the entire population to overcome the incentives for rational ignorance and to engage in enough substantive face to face discussion to arrive at informed judgments— informed about the issues and the main competing arguments about them that other citizens would offer" (Fishkin 2003).

I have seen, in other words, how the thoughtful practice of deliberative democracy can be structurally connected to the "qualities and attitudes of citizens," as noted by Kymlicka above.

In "From Student Senate to State Senate: Deliberative Polling in Pennsylvania," Jayna Bonfini, Michael Bridges and Joanna Dickert discuss deliberative democracy initiatives at Carnegie Mellon University (CMU). Going beyond the summer study of List and Sliwka, Joanna Dickert has integrated the practices of deliberative democracy at the institutional level, through Carnegie Mellon's Office of the Dean of Student Affairs. Michael Bridges worked with the CMU program on a statewide deliberative poll involving a proposed Marriage Protection Amendment and Jayna Bonifini developed a follow-up survey to measure participant attitudes three months after the event.

Commentators on deliberative democracy have pointed out the importance of linking conversations to outcomes, i.e., that the deliberations should have an influence on the policy matters being discussed. In 2005 a Student Senator suggested that the campus adopt the Student Bill of Rights developed by the conservative David Horowitz. The Student Senate decided to use the techniques of a deliberative poll to ascertain student and faculty support for this initiative. Initially, 49% of those polled in a pre-survey opposed the proposal. After deliberation (and after becoming aware of CMU's own policy on student rights), 78% of the participants opposed the bill. The Student Senate considered this supermajority sufficient to table the proposal. In light of this, the study can be considered a paradigm example of how these kinds of deliberations lend legitimacy to the very outcomes they influence.

As discussed in this chapter, initial results from the statewide deliberative poll showed that nearly 70% of the Pennsylvania voters who participated support the legal recognition of same-sex relationships, either through marriage or civil unions. Among those who supported legal recognition of same-sex relationships, participants split with approximately 35% supporting same-sex marriage and 35% supporting a version of civil union. Interestingly, participant data also showed approximately 50% support for the Pennsylvania Marriage Protection Amendment as it relates to the definition of marriage. This is because up to 70% of those supporting civil unions were conservative in their opinion regarding a change in name. Nevertheless, since that group did support civil unions, support for the current phrasing of the amendment (which precludes recognition of civil unions) would drop back to 35% based on the analysis of our data.

Unlike referenda, deliberative polls only have consulting power; they can inform but not determine policy. But they also deliver more nuanced information on public opinion and this can be used to influence policy discussion. It is interesting to note that Pennsylvania now has a Senate Bill that would allow for what could be called "civil marriages" for same-sex couples. Framed this way, it turns out that this bill could garner more support from our participants than the one seeking to ban same-sex marriage. Results of this poll appeared in media throughout the state, a fact that did not go unnoticed by the State Senator offering this bill. This situation reflects another element in linking these discussions to outcomes, namely, the importance of an "echo" effect, so that those not involved in the deliberations can become informed about the deliberations.

Finally, this volume addresses the use and assessment of online environments supporting what could be called "Deliberative E-Democracy" (as opposed to more standard concept of "e-democracy"). This section begins with Vincent Price, Steven H. Chaffee Professor of Communication and Political Science at the University of Pennsylvania'a Annenberg School for Communication. Price analyzes a series of innovative online field experiments designed to explore the contours and effects of citizen discussion, set against normative standards of deliberative theory. I complete the volume by contributing a chapter on the origin, use, and evolution of Project PICOLA (Public Informed Citizen Online Assembly), in which he considers how its design could serve as a model for the next generation of online tools for deliberation. Both Price and I show how data-gathering features enable online tools to become "microscopes" for social science research. Data generated from this kind of software is used to address and confront the thesis advanced by John Hibbing and Elizabeth Theiss-Morse in *Stealth Democracy* (2002).

For many, both inside and outside the deliberative community, the surveys developed and the data analyzed by the authors of *Stealth Democracy* pose one of the most pointed arguments against the theory of deliberative democracy.[27] Relying on the services of a Gal-

---

[27] While critical of the inferences that Hibbing and Theiss-Morse draw, their polling data and analyses do provide an insight into the 'off the top' opinions and

lup opinion poll and eight 2-hour focus group sessions consisting of 6-12 participants each, they probed Americans' opinions about how government should work. "In a perfect world," reads the focus group script, "what would the ideal government be? If you were designing a system from scratch, what would it look like?"[28]

In response to these kinds of questions, the authors discover that most Americans want a political process that works well and for the most part "in the background." They want decision makers to care about them and the issues that matter and to do so in a non-self-interested way. County government, for instance, should take care of the business of serving the region, making sure that streets are salted and plowed when necessary and that taxes are used wisely. They are perfectly happy to have "elites" work on these matters and do not want to be involved in the minutia of policy discussions nor do they want to engage in disagreeable arguments with others over these matters.

All things being equal, this is not an unreasonable expectation. Except for political junkies in the blogosphere, most people probably do expect a kind of stealth democracy, a normal democracy where, say, county government works reasonably well and does so quietly, on a daily basis. But there are certainly times when counties and their municipalities encounter a crisis—for example, over budget deficits caused by commitments to employee pension funds. Discussions by county officials and local city governments might lead to discussions of a functional consolidation of services. Oth-

---

preferences that the public does seem to have. For those familiar with the uneven and fragile nature of typical town hall meetings or community-based organizations (including block-watches and neighborhood development steering committees), personal conflict, groupthink, squeaky wheels that become broken wheels, frustration and alienation give scant empirical hope for a new Athens. But rather than tell their readers not to "rub the noses" of Americans in deliberative forums, the authors should make room for more structured, moderated environments of the kind indicated in this Introduction.

[28] *Stealth Democracy*, 252. A question later on solicits opinions on participatory governance by saying "Some people advocate moving toward a total direct democracy where people vote directly on important political decisions and we wouldn't even need to have elected officials anymore. Much like a large New England town meeting, the American people would be making all of the decisions themselves. What do you think of this idea?" One wonders how questions like these shaped the responses of the focus groups.

ers might argue for a kind of structural consolidation, where the city government would merge with county government. Yet doing so would dissolve, for example, the very district that is the focus of Greg Crowley's chapter.

These are precisely the kinds of hard decisions that would benefit from some kind of well-structured deliberative loop. Voters would need to be educated on a number of topics (What role can Councils of Government play in leveraging the cost of salt for winter road maintenance? What happens when the police force for a small township can no longer afford its three officers?). Policy makers would need to hear of the concerns that people throughout the county have and what suggestions they might make in the course of their discussions. Both public education and public input are formally required during this kind of process but the current model of 'public hearings' is hardly up to the task. Like the way that the issue of healthcare burst upon the scene in 2009, crises break through the processes of normal democracy on a rather regular basis and middle democracy is constantly in flux.

Contrary to the normative claims that Hibbing and Theiss-Morse make, when tapped to participate in well-structured, informed discussions of issues with clear choices or focus, conversations that stakeholders agree to take seriously in terms of policy implementation, Americans show a remarkable degree of interest and engagement. This data comes from surveys and reports of actual deliberative events.[29] It is remarkable that the authors of *Stealth Democracy* did not themselves study these kinds of fora. Instead, their empirical data relied on a standard poll (already suspect from the perspective of deliberative democrats) and some 85-90 quota-like sampled citizens in focus groups. Viewed from the trenches of deliberative practice, their study only produces, unless properly qualified, an army of straw men.

In many ways the idea for this book grew out of my own practical experience in deliberative democracy as founder and Co-Director of the Southwestern Pennsylvania Program in Deliberative Demococ-

---

[29] See, for example, the final reports behind the case studies of Chapter 6 (caae. phil.cmu.edu/caae/dp/polls/spring07/) and Chapter 7 (caae.phil.cmu.edu/caae/dp/polls/fall08/). For more systematic empirical studies "defending deliberative democracy," see the research resources available at Stanford's Center for Deliberative Democracy (cdd.stanford.edu/research/).

racy. It also arose as a result of organizing a year-long Lecture Series sponsored by Carnegie Mellon's Humanities Center. The series allowed me to contact leading figures in the field and invite them to participate in the program and in this book project. I also recruited Julie Marsh from RAND and my colleagues Jayna Bonfini, Mike Bridges and Joanna Dickert to fill out the topics to be covered. The text itself benefits from comments made by early reviewers and from the collegial environment provided by the Center for the Advancement of Applied Ethics and Political Philosophy, housed in the Philosophy Department at Carnegie Mellon. Finally, I want to thank Tim Dawson, Adam Howard, and Avery Wiscomb for their work on the manuscript along with the editors at Carnegie Mellon University Press for supporting this effort.

BIBLIOGRAPHY

Amadae, S.M. *Rationalizing Capitalist Democracy: The Cold War Origins of Rational Choice Liberalism.* Chicago: University of Chicago Press, 2003.

Barber, Benjamin. *Strong Democracy: Participatory Politics for a New Age*, 20th anniversary edition. Berkeley: University of California Press, 2004.

—. *Consumed: How Markets Corrupt Children, Infantilize Adults, and Swallow Citizens Whole.* New York: W. W. Norton and Company, 2007.

Bohman, James and William Rehg, editors. *Deliberative Democracy.* Cambridge: MIT Press, 1997.

Cavalier, Robert. "E-Democracy and the Structural Transformation of the Public Sphere." In *Computing and Philosophy in Asia,* edited by Soraj Hongladarom. Cambridge: Cambridge Scholars Press, 2007.

—. *Democracy for Beginners.* Danbury: For Beginners, LLC, 2009.

Chambers, Simone. "Discourse and Democratic Practices." *The Cambridge Companion to Habermas.* Edited by Stephen K. White, 233-262. Cambridge: Cambridge University Press, 1995.

Downs, Anthony. *An Economic Theory of Democracy.* New York: Harper and Row, 1957.

Dryzek, John and List, Christian "Social Choice Theory and Deliberative Democracy: A Reconciliation," *British Journal of Political Science* 33, no. 1, 2003, pp. 1-28.

Emerson, Peter. *Beyond the Tyranny of the Majority: Voting Methodologies in Decision-Making and Electoral Systems.* Belfast: The De Borda Institute, 1998.

Farrar, Cynthia, James Fishkin, Donald Green, Christian List, Robert Luskin and Elizabeth Levy Paluck "Disaggregating Deliberation's Effects: An Experiment within a Deliberative Poll," *British Journal of Political Science* (2009).

Fishkin, James. *Democracy and Deliberation.* New Haven: Yale University Press, 1991.

—. *The Voice of The People: Public Opinion and Democracy.* New Haven: Yale University Press, 1995.

—. "Who Speaks for the People? Deliberation and Public Consultation." *Public Participation and Local Governance*, edited by J. Font. Barcelona: Institut de Ciències Polítiques i Socials, 2003.

—. *When the People Speak: Deliberative Democracy and Public Consultation.* New York: Oxford University Press, 2009.

—, and Peter Laslett, editors. *Debating Deliberative Democracy*. Indianapolis: Wiley-Blackwell, 2003.

Freeman, Samuel. "Deliberative Democracy: A Sympathetic Comment." *Philosophy and Public Affairs* 29, no. 4 (2000).

Gastil, John, and Peter Levine, editors. *The Deliberative Democracy Handbook: Strategies for Effective Civic Engagement in the Twenty-First Century*. San Francisco: Jossey-Bass, 2005.

Gutmann, Amy, and Dennis Thompson. *Democracy and Disagreement*. Cambridge: Harvard University Press, 1996.

Habermas, Jürgen. *The Structural Transformation of the Public Sphere: An Inquiry into a Category of Bourgeois Society*, trans. Thomas Burger. Cambridge: MIT Press, 1991.

—. *Between Facts and Norms: Contributions to a Discourse Theory of Law and Democracy*. Cambridge: MIT Press, 1996.

Hardin, Russell. *How Do You Know? The Economics of Ordinary Knowledge*. Princeton: Princeton University Press, 2009.

Hibbing, John R. and Elizabeth Theiss-Morse. *Stealth Democracy: Americans' Beliefs about How Government Should Work*. Cambridge: Cambridge University Press, 2002.

Kymlicka, Will. *Contemporary Political Philosophy: An Introduction*. Oxford: Oxford University Press, 2002.

Price, Vincent, and Peter Neijens. "Deliberative Polls: Toward Improved Measures of 'Informed' Public Opinion?" *International Journal of Public Opinion Research* 10, no. 2 (Summer 1998): 145-176.

Rawls, John. "The Idea of Public Reason Revisited" in *The Law of Peoples* Cambridge: Harvard University Press, 1999.

—. *Political Liberalism*. New York: Columbia University Press, 2005.

Richardson, Henry. *Democratic Autonomy: Public Reasoning about the Ends of Policy*. New York: Oxford University Press, 2003.

Riker, William. *Liberalism Against Populism*. Long Grove: Waveland Press, 1998.

Young, Iris M. *Inclusion and Democracy*. Oxford: Oxford University Press, 2002.

CHAPTER 1

James M. Buchanan, John Rawls, and Democratic Governance

S.M. Amadae

> Our world may have never before been so ruthlessly divided along the lines of extractive power between those with and those without access to productive means. And yet never before has the dominant ideology [of] . . . mainstream economics, and by association game theory . . . been so successful at convincing most people that there are no systematic social divisions; that the poor are mostly undeserving and that talent and application is all the weak need in order to grow socially powerful.
>
> —Shaun P. Hargreaves Heap and Yanis Varoufakis[1]

> In a strictly personalized sense, any person's ideal situation is one that allows him full freedom of action and inhibits the behavior of others so as to force adherence to his own desires. That is to say, each person seeks mastery over a world of slaves.
>
> —James M. Buchanan[2]

The financial crisis of 2008 provoked a lively discussion of its causes. For some, the collapse of the housing market stemmed from "progressive" attempts in the 1990s to make housing more affordable for the less well-off. For others, it was due to "neo-liberal" desires to relax government regulation of the free market.[3] Whatever the explanation, the amount of the bailout was approximately the

---

[1] Shaun P. Hargreaves Heap and Yanis Varoufakis, *Game Theory* (London: Routledge, 2004), 262-3.

[2] James Buchanan, *Limits of Liberty* (Indianapolis: Liberty Fund, Inc., 1975), 92.

[3] For a critique of "neo-liberal" policies, see Pierre Bourdieu, *Acts of Resistance: Against the Tyranny of the Market*, trans. Richard Nice (Oxford: Polity Press, 1998).

amount that the top one percent of American income-earners accumulated in the prior decade.[4] This outcome may be interpreted as the instantiation of a new guiding principle of privatizing profits and socializing debt.[5] Underneath these public policy decisions lie deep currents of political theory and, ultimately, of differing models of who we are and how we choose to be governed.

This chapter will look at two of these philosophies through the works of political theorist John Rawls, and political economist James M. Buchanan. Along the way, it will point out some ironies of recent neo-liberal views on the market and gesture toward a more deliberative way to address many of the problems that confront our society and the state that governs it.

If the progressive view of the 1930s was a combination of Keynesianism and welfare state socialism, we may identify today's neo-liberalism by the following tenets: First, private ownership is the way to solve the world's ills; second, redistribution is a form of theft; and third, no income or wealth-status disparity can be too great.[6] There is a set of arguments underlying these tenets: (1) Private ownership solves the tragedy of the commons by providing incentives for agents to use resources "efficiently." (2) Because interpersonal comparisons of individuals' satisfaction cannot be based in scientific analysis, economists' only criterion for assessing people's welfare is "Pareto efficiency," or the idea that a community is better off if at least one person is made better off and no one is made worse off, regardless of distributional consequences.[7] (3) No individual's free-

---

[4] United States Senator Bernie Sanders reports on an Online Op-Ed column that the wealthiest 400 American citizens had a wealth increase of $670 billion over the past eight years (http://www.sanders.senate.gov/news/ record.cfm?id=303313, posted Sept. 19, 2008). These figures are consistent with the US Bureau of Census 2002 Current Population Survey figures used by Robert Rector and Rea Hederman, Jr. in "Two Americas: One Rich, One Poor; Understanding Income Inequality in the US," *The Heritage Foundation*, posted Aug. 24, 2004; for recent adroit commentary, see "Workingman's Blues," *The Economist*, posted July 24, 2008.

[5] For commentary see "I Want Your Money," *The Economist*, Sept. 27, 2008, 17; and "World on the Edge," *The Economist*, Oct. 4, 2008, 11.

[6] "A Question of Justice?: The Toll of Global Poverty is a Scandal. But Deploring Economic 'Injustice' is no Answer," *The Economist*, March 13, 2004, 13.

[7] Daniel M. Hausman and Michael S. McPherson, "Economics, Rationality, and Ethics," *The Philosophy of Economics an Anthology*, 2nd ed., ed. Daniel M. Hausman (Cambridge: Cambridge University Press, 1993), 252-78.

dom is thwarted by the increase of another individual's wealth.

The writings of James Buchanan can serve to give us access to these ideas. *Calculus of Consent* (1962) argues that beginning with the premise of rational self-interest, individuals can design a constitution that at least minimally serves everyone's interests by building on virtually unanimous agreement.[8] This view eventually cohered with libertarian confidence that the government that governs least, governs best. My book *Rationalizing Capitalist Democracy* (2003) was an attempt to demonstrate step-by-step the series of moves that went into rebuilding the theoretical underpinning of this version of capitalist democracy as a direct US Cold War response to communism, Marxism, and totalitarianism.[9]

Historically, however, as the 1960s gave way to the 1970s, the major theme on Buchanan's mind was that of social anarchy expressed in student protests, and what he took to be a general breakdown of social decorum. *Limits of Liberty* (1975) is a response to this latter problem of social order. Buchanan articulates his main theme on the first prefatory page: "'Law,' in itself, is a 'public good,' with all of the familiar problems in securing voluntary compliance. Enforcement is essential, but the unwillingness of those who abide by law to punish those who violate it, and to do so effectively, must portend erosion and ultimate destruction of the order we observe."[10] Buchanan intimates that we live in a dark world in which the only force sustaining social concourse is the sword.

Thus the turbulent and undisciplined 1960s and early 1970s are as important to assessing the origins of contemporary neoliberalism as was the threat of communism and authoritarianism during the 1950s' reconceptualization of classic liberal principles. The Enlightenment era political economy of Adam Smith was predicated on the voluntary renunciation of any claims on others' personhood, property, and contracts, in keeping with sympathetic and impartial judgment of third-party injuries, personal conscience, and the legitimate rule of law. The central unifying

---

[8] James M. Buchanan and Gordon Tulluck, *The Calculus of Consent* (Ann Arbor: University of Michigan Press, 1962).

[9] S.M. Amadae, *Rationalizing Capitalist Democracy* (Chicago, Chicago University Press, 2003).

[10] James Buchanan, Limits of Liberty (Indianapolis: Liberty Fund, Inc., 1975), ix.

theme was that of "negative liberty," or the "no-harm principle": each should be free to do as she pleases, so long as no
one violates the integrity of another person or his possessions.
The belief was that given the rule of law, restricted to commuta-
tive justice and banned from mandating redistribution, prosperity would emerge. Each person, in improving private affairs, will
necessarily add to the joint stock comprising a nation. Voluntary
consent was thought to be the basis of interactions in the market
place, and subsequently also that of individuals' social contract
with government, as the franchise continued to increase throughout the nineteenth and twentieth centuries. By contrast, the neo-
liberal justification of government is predicated on an analysis
of individuals' partially-aligned and partially-conflictual private
preferences over social outcomes. An individual's identity is formulated in terms of one's logically-ordered preferences over all
conceivable states of the world and one's actual opportunities,
instead of by the legal attributes of one's personhood, property
and contractual obligations. The predominant operating theme
of this new relationship between the individual and government
is contained in the "Prisoner's Dilemma."

Since its invention by two game theorists working at the Santa
Monica-based RAND Corporation in the 1950s, a voluminous literature has amassed discussing this thought experiment's paradoxical
nature that seems to indicate the limitations of instrumental rationality. In their classic game theory textbook, Duncan Luce and Howard set forth the decision problem confronting two conspirators:

> Two suspects are taken into custody and separated. The district
> attorney is certain that they are guilty of a specific crime, but he
> does not have adequate evidence to convict them at a trial. He
> points out to each prisoner that each has two alternatives: to
> confess to the crime the police are sure they have done, or not
> to confess. If they both do not confess, then the district attor-
> ney states he will book them on some very minor trumped up
> charge such as petty larceny and illegal possession of a weapon,
> and they will both receive minor punishment; if they both con-
> fess they will be prosecuted, but he will recommend less than
> the most severe sentence; but if one confesses and the other

does not, then the confessor will receive lenient treatment for turning state's evidence whereas the latter will get "the book" slapped at him.[11]

The *Prisoner's Dilemma,* as this type of scenario is now referred to, is sometimes introduced as though each inmate faces the quandary of whether to be loyal to his former ally, risking a terrible outcome if the other does not take reciprocal action, or whether to protect himself by preemptively betraying his former partner. It may seem that the dilemma is about which action each agent should take, raising the question of whether to betray the other. However, this is not the bind the two individuals face because each prefers to cheat the other, regardless of what the other will do.

Consider a routine single-meeting bargaining situation, say, on the western frontier with one individual who has a gold coin, and another who has a horse. We may conceive of each hoping to secure both the horse and the gold coin for himself, but each also worrying about receiving the 'sucker's payoff' of personal injury and no goods. If both would-be-traders cooperate, they achieve an amicable exchange; if they both renege, the coin is lost, and the horse runs away. According to the logic of game theory, any rational individual caught in such a situation will necessarily not cooperate, thereby achieving a worse outcome than would be possible if the two were able to cooperate. Game theorists believe that rational individuals have no means to circumvent this mutually-impoverishing outcome, unless external penalties are introduced to induce each to cooperate.

The shift to a game theoretic universe of economic and political competition defines a rupture from classic and neoclassical economics of unproblematic and voluntary exchange within the context of a system of justice as stipulated by Adam Smith and Immanuel Kant. Michel Foucault's work on modern governmentality tightly intersects with this narrative because the efficiency supposedly characterizing market interactions bears a conceptual resemblance to mechanical efficiency. Allocating scarce resources efficiently was the automatic

---

[11] Duncan Luce and Howard Raiffa, *Game and Decisions* (New York: Wiley, 1957), 95. Mathematicians Merrill Flood and Melvin Dresher invented the game; for discussion see William Poundstone, *Prisoner's Dilemma: John von Neumann, Game Theory, and the Puzzle of the Bomb* (New York: Doubleday, 1992).

coordinating principle of modern economics and modern governmentality. Government ruled as a set of disciplinary tactics dedicated to establishing and maintaining norms of conduct in accordance
with a central theme of social welfare.[12] The rule of law was justified
because it served individuals' interests, and it was obeyed because
individuals preferred to live in a law-governed state rather than in a
chaotic state of nature.

As we turn the corner from neoclassical economics as voluntary, mutually-beneficial exchange presupposing the role of government in sanctifying the legal integrity of property rights, to the
late twentieth-century coalescence of governing all transactions via
incentives, the Prisoner's Dilemma becomes the Rosetta Stone for
comprehending human interrelations. This transition is the most
evident in contrasting Friedrich Hayek's description of trade as occurring between two primitive tribes who find that by leaving surplus
goods on their boundary, others naturally reciprocate, with the new
view that any and all exchange is subject to the Prisoner's Dilemma.
By the latter account, in any exchange transaction, each party has
the incentive to cheat the other party, thereby achieving a "mutual
defection" instead of a "mutual cooperation" outcome. Trade itself,
because individuals are incapable of forming binding agreements by
consent, must be encased within government threatening sanctions
to ensure that no one selects to cheat the other. This leads to a great
irony: if we are to have a minimal state in which the unfettered market thrives, then that state needs to be able to at least monitor (not
regulate) that market. At the same time that the "public" was eroded
as a meaningful corporate body, so privacy has become eviscerated
of specific content.

Solving the Prisoner's Dilemmas abounding throughout society requires pervasive inspections of individuals' activities. Employees' phone
conversations are routinely recorded; trucks are marked: "How's my
driving, call 1-800-555-1212 to report." No one is trusted to do her job
as it is assumed all will cut any corner they can get away with.

Despite the strangeness of this notion, the idea of the Prisoner's
Dilemma has been discussed as though its form of governmentality

---

[12] Michel Foucault, *Discipline and Punish: The Birth of the Prison*, (New York: Random
House, 1979), 135-69.

is co-extensive with all of human history.[13] The problem of achieving social order out of anarchy has been and will always be, so the story goes, a Prisoner's Dilemma. Therefore, it is not surprising that in the rational choice appropriation of canonical political theory, Thomas Hobbes' *Leviathan* is the favorite point of departure; it is maintained that all exchange is subject to a Prisoner's Dilemma and that the solution to the problem of social order must be that of government via sanctions to prevent, or punish if necessary, defection in transactions ranging from one-off exchanges to more complex multi-party interactions. The claim then can be put forward that the Buchanan's fascination with a maximal security state was anticipated by the seventeenth-century Hobbes, who astutely understood the impossible Prisoner's Dilemma bind we all find ourselves in when we attempt to cooperate with each other. This account, of course, is readily sounded in his choice of a subtitle to *Limits of Liberty: Between Anarchy and Leviathan.*

The rational choice fixation on the Prisoner's Dilemma and its resolution with a *Leviathan*-like state may give us pause to begin with, but as long as it seems like a strand of an earlier form of argumentation already bequeathed to us by Hobbes and amended by Smith as well as by Kant, this does not seem so significant or problematic by itself. However, once we realize that even Hobbes spoke of rights, duty, consent, and mutual forbearance, we can make a case that Hobbes' analysis of the problem of social order, and that of neoliberalism, are not equivalent.[14] Indeed, as game theorists themselves seem aware, the new mode of governmentality predicated on the inmate's dilemma requires a maximal and not a minimal security state:

> While Hobbes thought that the authority of the State should be absolute so as to discourage any cheating on "peace," he also thought the scope of its interventions in this regard would be quite minimal. In contrast much of the modern fascination with

---

[13] See, for example, Ken Binmore's *Natural Justice* (New York: Oxford University Press, 2005). Note that Binmore focuses on the repeated Prisoner's Dilemma, which is solved by each individual personally threatening the other with defection in future rounds of play.

[14] For an insightful discussion, see Edward F. McClennen, "The Tragedy of National Sovereignty," in *Nuclear Weapons and the Future of Humanity*, ed. Avner Cohen and Steven Lee (Totowa, NJ: Rowman and Allanheld, 1986), 391-406.

the *Prisoner's Dilemma* stems from the fact that it seems such a ubiquitous feature of social life. For instance, it lies plausibly at the heart of many problems which groups of individuals (for instance, the household, a class, or a nation) encounter when they attempt a collective action. . . . This is important for Liberal political theory because it seems to suggest that the State . . .will be called upon to police a considerable number of social interactions in order to avoid the sub-optimal outcomes associated with this type of interaction.[15]

These game theorists are fully aware that somewhere between the absolutism of Hobbes and latter-day rational choice theory, we have made a transition from providing minimal security to policing virtually all transactions. The authors concur that in a game theoretic world typified by the Prisoner's Dilemma, "the boundaries of the State . . .will be drawn quite widely."[16] This pervasive state is conceptually linked to *laissez faire* capitalism, as no voluntary barter is deemed safe without a punitive guarantor. As well, this transition directly relies on the Prisoner's Dilemma for its rationale of intrusive governmentality. Individuals themselves are incentivized to actively participate. Thus, a private company in the airport security industry is licensed to give priority to passengers who pay for their service of personal identification through fingerprinting or iris scanning.[17]

Buchanan's Prisoner's Dilemma-based analysis to the problem of social order in *Limits of Liberty* precisely demarcates the moment of adoption of this new logic of governmentality. Conveniently, it is over this point that Buchanan and public choice, not to mention much rational choice scholarship, diverge from John Rawls' approach to justice and good governance. The point of schism is that of Buchanan's proposal that government and law is inseparable from incentives and sanctions on the one hand, and, on the other, Rawls' view that mutual consent and mutual forbearance are a mandatory basis for maintaining a civil society. This point of division is not just that between Buchanan and Rawls, but it is indicative of a much greater disagreement regard-

---

[15] Hargreaves Heap and Varoufakis (2004), 175.

[16] Ibid.

[17] Flyer from "Flyclear.com" picked up at Washington Dulles International Airport.

ing the bases of civil society: the neo-liberal practice of government relies on the Prisoner's Dilemma assessment of the problem of social order that is mutually exclusive of legitimacy through consent. In traditional democratic theory, law is bequeathed its legitimacy from due process entailing the participatory deliberation of its citizens. However, once one accedes to the central applicability of the Prisoner's Dilemma to analyze many human interactions, and once one accepts that it provides an ahistoric analysis of human governmentality, then there is not much left to debate.

Another way to review this argument is to compare John Rawls' *Theory of Justice* (1971) with James Buchanan's *Limits of Liberty*. It is a relevant fact that even though Rawls wrote his *Theory of Justice* to be wholly consistent with the underlying premises of rational choice theory, in 1985 he split with rational choice-informed philosophers and social scientists over the reasonableness of "fair play." As is well-known in game theory, it is a standard formulation of rational action that each individual will cheat whenever the calculable consequences are superior to the costs of compliance.[18] It is accepted across the board by game theorists that the concept of "fair play," or upholding a set of behavioral standards one personally consented to, carries no weight in a decision-theoretic calculation. Rawls, at this juncture exhibiting what to some appeared to be a Kantian influence, broke with the rationality program to advocate a notion of the "reasonable" in contradistinction to the "rational."[19] One way to view this difference hinges on whether an agent will adhere to law as a matter of voluntary obligation in accordance to agreeing with its rationale, or whether the agent solely upholds law out of fear of sanctions.[20]

Of course, the means by which law may be said to be conditioned by "right," and not solely by "might," has been a central problem of western political philosophy at least since Hobbes' *Leviathan*, which some commentators take to imply "the subjugation of individual men to a sovereign master, with the latter empowered to en-

---

[18] Gregory Kavka, "The Toxin Puzzle," *Analysis* 43, no.1 (1983): 33.

[19] John Rawls, "Justice as Fairness: Political Not Metaphysical," *Philosophy and Public Affairs* 14, no. 1 (1985): 223-51.

[20] For further discussion see Joseph Heath, *Communicative Action and Rational Choice* (London: MIT Press, 2001), esp. 129-72.

force 'law' as he sees fit."[21] Neo-liberalism, in some form advocated by Buchanan, reaches a new adjudication of the problem of social order adopting total adherence to rational egoism that has been defined to exclude a consent-based approach to political legitimacy. As Buchanan acknowledges in identifying our current moment of civilization as post-constitutional, in which individual alienation and disaffection from state-prescribed laws is the norm, "Once this stage is reached, the individual abides by existing law only because he is personally deterred by the probability of detection and subsequent punishment."[22] Thus, even if American law had the semblance of legitimacy in the late eighteenth century, it is harder for many today to either be so sanguine, or to marshal an argument for a practical return to semi-transparent legitimacy given our distance to the constitutional moment.

Buchanan acknowledges that he and Rawls share their concerns with this predicament, and although their analyses are similar, they each reach a different position on governance. In brief, Buchanan believes that the social anarchy of the American 1960s and 1970s was a function of the lack of will to enforce rights through punishment. On the other hand, Rawls concludes that "[e]nforcement may not be possible unless the prevailing distribution meets norms of justice . . .notably those summarized in the difference principle."[23] For Rawls, individuals' compliance to social law is not maintained by force, but rather through hypothetical consent to the terms of government. This hypothetical consent, which serves to acknowledge that most of us do not actually agree to the rules that govern us, must at least be conceivable in principle for one's government to have a degree of legitimacy, and thus a display of "right" over merely "might." In the rational choice world, there is no test to differentiate between valid and invalid law, because individuals will seek to break the law when it serves their private interest in any and all cases.

This assumption that everyone is a cheater is a sly means of eradicating the distinction between the concerns of efficient use of resources to generate wealth, and the distribution of resources.

---

[21] Buchanan (1975), 130.

[22] Ibid., 96.

[23] James M. Buchanan, "A Hobbesian Interpretation of the Rawlsian Difference Principle," *Kyklos* 29 (1976): 23.

Here two recognizable forms of criminality are conflated: a form of criminality that is encouraged by lack of inclusion within the social contract, and a form of criminality that preys on the social contract, even though the individual in question is already well-poised to gain fruits from the social contract. The distinction may be illustrated by contrasting the Enron executive with the homeless person who shoplifts motivated by hunger. In the first case an individual cheats despite the rule of law required to produce fruit in the first place; in the second case, an individual cheats because there is insufficient fruit to be gained by upholding the rule of law. Early modern political philosophers were keen to draw this distinction. Locke was the clearest and Hobbes not far behind: when an individual's self-preservation is at stake, the rule of nature prevails over the rule of law regardless of whether or not one is in a civil society.

The Prisoner's dilemma is definitive of neo-liberalism and captures its central paradox: if free trade is so obviously in each individual's interest, then why the need for police, enforcement, and sanctions? It makes more sense to expect a system that is so obviously in each person's interest to be sufficiently self-enforcing so as not to require microscopic policing. To restate my position, neo-liberalism is coextensive with the Prisoner's Dilemma rationale for governance; the same central paradox governs both systems. We are familiar with the "ruthless logic" of the Prisoner's Dilemma: each can see that "cooperate-cooperate" is a better individual and collective outcome than "defect-defect," but each of us has the ever-present incentive to cheat in pursuit of unilateral, if benighted, success. Therefore, given that we are all cheaters by the mere fact that we are rational actors, the only means by which we can achieve mutual cooperation is via the imposition of sanctions on all transactions. This resolution of the problem of social order is obviously at least as paradoxical as Jean Jacques Rousseau's observation that we must be "forced to be free": the role of government is to guarantee by force that populations of individuals can achieve the "Pareto optimal" cooperate-cooperate result. Throughout this analysis, agreement to the terms of trade or governance is irrelevant. As long as the terms are better than those achieved by mutual defection, any arrangement of provisions may be enforced.

In the hands of Buchanan, the Prisoner's Dilemma analysis of social order grows in mytho-poetic proportions. In developing his Hobbesian-like narrative, Buchanan deviates from Hobbes, and other Enlightenment-era thinkers, holding that humans are naturally unequal, and that even prior to the establishment of civil society, a status quo inegalitarian distribution will result because some are more capable, talented, and strong. Notwithstanding this disparity in status quo allocation based on objectively observable merit, trade occurs, supposedly under the traditional neoclassical logic that Pareto optimality will result no matter what the initial endowment of goods. To quote Buchanan:

> The gains from trade that are potentially achievable by an agreement on rights are realized by all parties through the disinvestment in socially wasteful effort devoted to both predatory and defense activity. An agreed-on assignment will not normally be stable in one particular sense.[24]

However, notwithstanding the self-evident quality of exchange to achieve mutual gain, Buchanan observes that "Once reached, one or all parties may find it advantageous to renege on or to violate the terms of contract."[25] Essentially, according to Buchanan, even though it is obvious that mutual cooperation (even given inegalitarian original distribution) is superior, still each has the ever-present incentive to rob the other.

To make clear that this "state of nature" problem is that of the Prisoner's Dilemma, Buchanan continues,

> Within the setting of an agreed-on assignment of rights, the participants in social interaction find themselves in a genuine dilemma, familiarized under the "prisoners' dilemma" rubric in modern game theory. All persons will find their utility increased if all abide by the "law," as established. But for each person, there will be an advantage in breaking the law, in failing to respect the behavioral limits laid down in the contact.[26]

To make headway with Buchanan's formulation of the problem

---

[24] Buchanan, 26.

[25] Ibid.

[26] Ibid.

of social order, it is necessary to be fully aware of the differences between his analysis and Hobbes'. For Buchanan, as for libertarian philosopher Robert Nozick, rights are prior to civil society, and they therefore provide the point of origin for a "naturally just" initial distribution.[27] The role of the state is only to objectively referee transactions as a matter of protection, and not to adjudicate matters of distribution.[28]

All of this sounds uncannily like classic political economy with its night-watchman state. The analysis, in fact, is developed to resemble traditional liberalism. However, it departs from classic political economy in its inability to locate a normative pole external to the central logic of rational self-interest. It is true that both Adam Smith and Immanuel Kant advocated a minimal security state. However, for both these philosophers, justice has normative purchase external to rational self-interest. For Smith the basis of justice resides in non-utilitarian sympathy; for Kant the basis for justice resides in transcendental practical reason.[29] Buchanan himself acknowledges that the basic premises upon which public choice theory is built makes it impossible to locate any source of normativity for so basic a concept of mutual respect, or for treating individuals as ends and not solely as means.[30] The Prisoner's Dilemma, and its premise of ubiquitous cheating in the absence of sanctions, appears to be the dual result of accepting some version of moral relativism and realism about human nature. As is typical for rational choice theorists, the suggestion that individuals could be motivated by a sense of duty, or of mutual forbearance, or of compliance with one's word, evokes the ready rejoinder, *"that's so naive!"* Buchanan is clear that his political philosophy is one that embraces a community of devils, and does

---

[27] Robert Nozick, *Anarchy, State, and Utopia* (Oxford: Basil Blackwell, 1974), 8-11; 23-26.

[28] Ibid., 95.

[29] For the normative basis of Smith's system of justice, see S.M. Amadae, *Rationalizing Capitalist Democracy* (Chicago: University of Chicago Press, 2003), 193-219; see S.M. Amadae, "Impartiality, Utility, and Induction in Adam Smith's Jurisprudence," *Adam Smith Review* 4 (2008); see also Immanuel Kant's *Metaphysical Elements of Justice*, 2nd ed., trans. John Ladd (1797; Indianapolis: Hackett Publishing Company, 1999).

[30] Amadae, *Rationalizing Capitalist Democracy*, 151-2.

not optimistically assert or require a community of angels.[31]

The rational choice insistence on not assuming that individuals bring any type of moral qualities to decision-making is what resulted in John Rawls' break with both rational choice theory and his earlier claim in *Theory of Justice* that justice is the most important aspect of a theory of rational choice. Subsequently, Rawls proposed the idea of "the reasonable" that pivots on the concept of fair play: "if the participants in a practice accept its rules as fair, and so have no complaint to lodge against it, there arises a prima facie duty . . . of the parties to each other to act in accordance with the practice when it falls upon them to comply."[32] In Rawls' post-1985 assessment, it is reasonable to be committed to rules of conduct that one consented to, despite the fact that one's personal payoffs for doing so in each and every instance may not calculably be to one's advantage. At this juncture, rational choice theorists ceased being interested in what they took to be Rawls' self-professed Kantianism and its attendant idealism. Instead, they upheld their canonical assertion that defection, when it is demonstrably in one's interest, is always the rationally sanctioned norm.

The assumption that we are all naturally born cheaters, which requires notions of consent, duty or legitimacy to be irrational, serves a particular function in neo-liberal governmentality[33]: it permits the conflation of forms of crime that prey on the legally sanctioned system and forms of crime that exist despite the system. Public Choice theorists, Buchanan included, are of course savvy about calculating each individual's rewards for acting in one way versus another. Therefore, it is a first principle in Buchanan's assessment that each individual benefits from participating in a civil society *regardless of distributional concerns.* His dedication to this assumption is manifest in his quasi-inter personally comparable rendition of the Prisoner's

---

[31] Buchanan's position is already evident in *Calculus of Consent.*

[32] John Rawls, "Justice as Fairness," in *John Rawls: Collected Papers*, ed. Samuel Freeman (Cambridge: Harvard University Press, 1999), 60.

[33] For discussion, see Anatol Rapoport's early book co-authored with Albert M. Chammah, *Prisoner's Dilemma: A Study in Conflict and Cooperation* (Ann Arbor: University of Michigan Press, 1965); see also Martin Hollis, *Trust within Reason* (Cambridge: Cambridge University Press, 1998).

Dilemma at the heart of the social contract.[34] No matter how small one's share is, mutual cooperation is superior to mutual defection. Similarly, and this is key, no matter what one's share is *it is in each individuals' equal interest to defect*. Buchanan clearly articulates this point: "Once reached, one or all parties may find it advantageous to renege on or to violate the terms of contract. This applies to *any* assignment [of goods] that might be made."[35] Accepting the ubiquity and rationality of defection is so important that Buchanan clarifies: "the tendency toward individual violation is not characteristic of only some subset of possible agreements."[36] In other words, it is a crucial starting point for rationalizing neo-liberal governance that no matter what the distribution of rights, all are alike in their motives to cooperate or to defect from that system of rights. Within this narrative, there is no categorical distinction between the poor individual with few legitimate opportunities and the wealthy banker: each alike has the ever-present incentive to cheat the system; each alike finds mutual cooperation to be superior to mutual defection.

The focus of Buchanan's discussion in *Limits of Liberty*, and his "A Hobbesian Interpretation of the Rawlsian Difference Principle" (1976) is on the social disruption caused by rule-breakers. In the latter article, he observes, "Honest assessment of life about us should suggest that there has been an erosion in the structure of legal order, in the acknowledged rights of persons, and that, indeed, modern society has come to be more and more vulnerable to disruption and the threat of disruption."[37] Buchanan finds that Rawls' difference principle, that strives to guarantee that all society's institutions which are structured in accordance with inegalitarian distribution of resources must provide some benefit to society's least advantaged members, is an attempt by Rawls to ensure that pockets of disaffected individuals do not arise. Therefore, the difference principle is read by Buchanan as being Hobbesian, because it strategically aids in securing social order by staving off disaffection.

However, ultimately, Buchanan recognizes that Rawls' solution is different from his own, because it assumes that compliance with

---

[34] Buchanan, 27.

[35] Buchanan, 26.

[36] Ibid.

[37] Buchanan, 21.

the system can be maintained through inclusion and through sharing the spoils of mutual cooperation. Buchanan is quite open in the
different conclusions he and Rawls reach: "Parts of . . .[Rawls'] argument may be read to suggest that individuals *should not* abide by the
distribution of rights assigned in the existing legal order unless this
distribution conforms to the norms for justice. And persons in the
original position *should not* agree on a set of social arrangements that
are predicted to place strains on individual norms of adherence and
support."[38] For Rawls' compliance and the duty to comply is wedded
to one's sense of commitment to the social system; complicity in
society demonstrates allegiance to its overriding principles.

Buchanan, however, reaches the Machiavellian conclusion that:

> The difference principle can be identified as emerging from con-
> tractual agreement in the initial position only if the participants
> make the positive prediction that least-advantaged persons and/
> or groups will, in fact, withdraw their cooperation in certain sit-
> uations and that the threat of this withdrawal will be effective.[39]

Thus Buchanan unequivocally differs from Rawls in his assertion that in order to maintain social order, enforcement is all that is
necessary. Buying-in potentially disaffected parties via adherence to
the difference principle is necessary only when enforcement fails. In
his view, the potential gains of mutual cooperation, despite disparate
distribution, should be sufficient to secure cooperation, when sanctions are used for enforce contracts. He writes,

> My own efforts have been directed toward the prospects that gen-
> eral attitudes might be shifted so that all persons and groups come
> to recognize the mutual advantages to be secured from a renewed
> consensual agreement on rights and from effective enforcement
> of these rights. Rawls may be, in one sense, more pessimistic about
> the prospects for social stability. [For Rawls,] enforcement may not
> be possible unless the prevailing distribution meets norms of jus-
> tice, and notably those summarized in the difference principle.[40]

---

[38] Buchanan, 23.

[39] Ibid.

[40] Ibid.

Buchanan decisively concludes, "Whereas I might look upon the breakdown of legal enforcement institutions in terms of a loss of political will, Rawls might look on the same set of facts as a demonstration that the precepts of a just society are not present."[41] Whereas Rawls argues that consent and duty are necessary to maintaining political stability via an ongoing process of inclusion guaranteed by the difference principle, Buchanan looks to force to maintain law and social order without considerations of the distribution of individuals' entitlements.

What is missing from the neo-liberal view of governance is the crucial role that agreement to terms has traditionally played in legitimizing both free-trade and democratic government. It is well-known that Enlightenment liberalism did not encourage the state to play a role in redistributing resources. However, classic liberalism did rest on the firm assumption that in any contract setting, individuals' consent to the terms of the agreement provides a rationale for their ensuing compliance with the contract. In neo-liberalism, agreement does not play a role in motivating action. Therefore, the content of terms, apart from as generated by the respective bargaining power of the participants, is immaterial. In fact, virtually any terms may be enforced with sufficient force or "political will."

One can appreciate the hope to study the interactions of self-interested agents, without assuming that they have concern for each other, as contemporary societies largely operate on faceless interactions. The Prisoner's Dilemma construed as a multi-party problem seems well-suited to describe large joint actions in which it appears gratuitous to suggest that each acts to further others' interests, as well as his own. However, the stakes in this debate are high. According to one view of the individual and society, each of us acts to maximize expected utility regardless of the effects on others. Law steps in as a "public good" that realizes prospects for joint gain when myopic self-interest would otherwise leave everyone worse off; law motivates by imposing penalties on would-be cheaters. According to Gary Becker and Richard Posner, who work within this rational choice tradition, the purpose of law and justice is to make social interactions efficient such that they generate the most wealth, regard-

---

[41] Ibid.

less of how that wealth is distributed.[42] Agreement to terms carries no weight, as was evident in the unprecedented 2004 United States Supreme ruling in *Kelo vs. City of New London,* which mandated that private property may be seized not just for public use, but also for private ownership and use, if the recipient is able to make better economic use of it; the US Federal Government allows that "private property is forcibly relinquished to new private use."[43] The content of law can be determined by performing cost-benefit analyses of how to best satisfy individuals' preferences. Wealthy individuals, who have proven their value to society by meriting high-paying jobs, have a higher economic value and have justifiably higher compensation packages.[44] Deliberation is superfluous to this public policy process as it may only serve to be a potentially inflammatory distraction.

In the supergame of life, there is no necessity to live, but there is a subjectively felt necessity to live well. According to the rational choice view, "living well" means maximizing expected utility by making consistent decisions throughout one's lifetime. Supposedly, rational choice can encompass any conception of "the good life." According to the alternative view championed by critical and deliberative democratic theorists, living well entails realizing one's goals in the company of others. An agent's relation to herself is predicated on internal dialogue, just as are relations to others. Deliberation punctuates one's inner psyche, especially in reaching decisions, just as it regulates human activities.[45] Understanding of one's own identity, and its inter-

---

[42] Gary Becker, *The Economic Approach to Human Behavior* (Chicago: University of Chicago Press, 1976); Richard Posner, "The Law and Economics Movement," *American Economic Review* 77 (1987): 1-13; and "Wealth Maximization and Judicial Decision-Making," *International Review of Law and Economics* 4 (1984): 131-5.

[43] See opinion of Supreme Court of the United States, October Term, 2004; quote is from J. O'Connor, dissenting, p. 10; see also p. 8. Available at www4.law.cornell.edu/supct/pdf/04-108P.ZD.

[44] As a practical example of the logical conclusion of this reasoning, consider the World Trade Center Victim Compensation Fund that unprecedentedly allocated resources according to expected earnings potential. See Elizabeth Kolbert, "How Kenneth Feinberg Determines the Value of Three Thousand Lives," *The New Yorker*, Nov. 25, 2002.

[45] See Jürgen Habermas on the relationship between internal dialogue and intersubjective communication, "The Paradigm Shift in Mead and Durkheim: From Purposive Activity to Communicative Action," in *The Theory of Communicative Action*, vol. 2, trans. Thomas McCarthy (Boston: Beacon Press, 1987), 1-112. See also Margaret

dependence with historical facts, present circumstances, and others' presence, is crucial to having goals and pursuing them rationally.

Whereas the rational choice perspective insists that it is consistent with any and all facets of deliberative democracy and active citizenry, we must acknowledge that the two traditions reach abruptly distinct appraisals of law. For the deliberativist, understanding the law, and voluntarily consenting to its validity, at least in principle, provides a rationale for following the law and is therefore behaviorally motivating. Similarly, agreeing to the terms of an exchange is tantamount to committing oneself to carry them out, even if it were feasible to stab the other in the back upon leaving the bargaining table. Given that consent to the terms of a rule or bargain has grounded the twin Enlightenment era traditions of democratic government and the free market, it seems that undermining its cogency as a social practice would signal that classic liberalism has more in common with deliberation than with a rational computation of personal interests constrained only by one's ability to dominate outcomes.

Both classic liberalism and neo-liberalism are dedicated to a view of the state whose role should be that of providing a framework for individuals to pursue their self-construed life plans. However, classic liberalism provides two avenues to prevent self-interested individuals from simply asserting their will over others to whatever extent is feasible given reigning power relations. On the one hand, classic liberalism recognizes the fundamental interdependence and mutuality of citizens, and therefore mandates that a condition for the pursuit of one's livelihood is that of respecting others' like claims. On the other hand, the content of law, if it is to be just and not whimsical, must be understandable as a guide to action that makes sense to those whom it governs. "Making sense" connotes conveying a motivation for action that may be at odds with personal expected utility calculations: "It makes sense to stop at red traffic lights because overall in our nation traffic accidents will be lowered by everyone following this rule, even though I am tempted to run red lights in order to get to work on time." The Prisoner's Dilemma logic recommends to the contrary that rational individuals stop at red lights because they calculate the cost of getting a traffic citation, or of getting in an accident, against

---

Gilbert, *A Theory of Political Obligation: Membership, Commitment, and the Bonds of Society* (Oxford: Clarendon Press, 2006).

the cost of running several minutes behind.[46]

Interestingly, Rawls himself came to see the limits of his earlier ideas and wrote in 1985 that "it was an error in *Theory* (and a very misleading one) to describe a theory of justice as part of a theory of rational choice."[47] By the time we get to his Idea of Public Reason in the late-90s, he is explicit about his general acceptance of deliberative democracy: "I am concerned only with a well-ordered constitutional democracy . . . understood also as a deliberative democracy."[48] The other essays in this volume will advance the idea that democratic government is predicated on participatory deliberation and voluntary consent manifested in appropriate collective decision-making procedures, rather than merely an amalgamation of individuals' private preferences over state of affairs.

---

[46] This philosophy is articulated in Gary Becker, *The Economic Approach to Human Behavior* (Chicago: University of Chicago Press, 1978).

[47] Rawls "Justice and Fairness: Political, not Metaphysical," *Philosophy and Public Affairs* 14, no. 3 (summer 1985): 223-51 and see Amadae (2003), 270-273.

[48] Rawls, "The Idea of Public Reason Revisited," first published in 1997 and contained in *The Law of Peoples with "The Idea of Public Reason Revisited"* Harvard University Press, 1999. Gutmann and Thompson appraise the kind of deliberation that Rawls has in mind when he characterizes himself as a deliberative democrat. "In his later writings Rawls moves significantly further toward deliberative democracy . . . " but he "says little about the role of actual deliberation in non-ideal conditions" *Democracy and Disagreement* (38-39).

BIBLIOGRAPHY

"A Question of Justice?: The Toll of Global Poverty is a Scandal. But Deploring Economic 'Injustice' is No Answer." *The Economist*, March 13, 2004.

Amadae, S.M. "Impartiality, Utility, and Induction in Adam Smith's Jurisprudence." *Adam Smith Review* 4 (2008).

—. *Rationalizing Capitalist Democracy.* Chicago: Chicago University Press, 2003.

Becker, Gary. *The Economic Approach to Human Behavior.* Chicago: University of Chicago Press, 1976.

Binmore, Ken. *Natural Justice.* New York: Oxford University Press, 2005.

Bourdieu, Pierre. *Acts of Resistance: Against the Tyranny of the Market*, translated by Rich ard Nice. Oxford: Polity Press, 1998.

Buchanan, James M. "A Hobbesian Interpretation of the Rawlsian Difference Principle." *Kyklos* 29 (1976): 23.

—, and Gordon Tulluck. *The Calculus of Consent.* Ann Arbor: University of Michigan Press, 1962.

—. *Limits of Liberty.* Indianapolis: Liberty Fund, Inc., 1975.

Foucault, Michel. *Discipline and Punish: The Birth of the Prison.* New York: Random House, 1979.

Gilbert, Margaret. *A Theory of Political Obligation: Membership, Commitment, and the Bonds of Society.* Oxford: Clarendon Press, 2006.

Gutmann, Amy and Dennis Thompson. *Democracy and Disagreement.* Cambridge: Harvard University Press, 1996.

Habermas, Jürgen. "The Paradigm Shift in Mead and Durkheim: From Purposive Activity to Communicative Action." In *The Theory of Communicative Action*, vol. 2, translated by Thomas McCarthy. Boston: Beacon Press, 1987.

Hargreaves Heap, Shaun P., and Yanis Varoufakis. *Game Theory: A Critical Text*, 2nd ed. London: Routledge, 2004.

Hausman, Daniel M., and Michael S. McPherson. "Economics, Rationality, and Ethics." *The Philosophy of Economics: an Anthology*, 2nd ed., edited by Daniel M. Hausman. Cambridge: Cambridge University Press, 1993.

Heath, Joseph. *Communicative Action and Rational Choice.* London: MIT Press, 2001.

Hollis, Martin. *Trust within Reason.* Cambridge: Cambridge University Press, 1998.

"I Want Your Money." *The Economist*, Sept. 27, 2008.

Kant, Immanuel. *Metaphysical Elements of Justice*, 2nd ed., translated by John Ladd. 1797; Indianapolis: Hackett Publishing Company, 1999.

Kavka, Gregory. "The Toxin Puzzle." *Analysis* 43, no. 1 (1983): 33.

Kolbert, Elizabeth. "How Kenneth Feinberg Determines the Value of Three Thousand Lives." *The New Yorker*, Nov. 25, 2002.

Luce, Duncan, and Howard Raiffa. *Game and Decisions*. New York: Wiley, 1957.

McClennen, Edward F. "The Tragedy of National Sovereignty." In *Nuclear Weapons and the Future of Humanity*, ed. Avner Cohen and Steven Lee. Totowa, NJ: Rowman and Allanheld, 1986.

Nozick, Robert. *Anarchy, State, and Utopia*. Oxford: Basil Blackwell, 1974.

Posner, Richard. "The Law and Economics Movement." *American Economic Review* 77 (1987).

—. "Wealth Maximization and Judicial Decision-Making." *International Review of Law and Economics* 4 (1984).

Poundstone, William. *Prisoner's Dilemma: John von Neumann, Game Theory, and the Puzzle of the Bomb*. New York: Doubleday, 1992.

Rapoport, Anatol and Albert M. Chammah. *Prisoner's Dilemma: A Study in Conflict and Cooperation*. Ann Arbor: University of Michigan Press, 1965.

Rawls, John. *A Theory of Justice*. Cambridge: Harvard University Press, 1971.

—. "Justice as Fairness." In *John Rawls: Collected Papers*, ed. Samuel Freeman. Cambridge: Harvard University Press, 1999.

—. "Justice as Fairness: Political Not Metaphysical." *Philosophy and Public Affairs* 14, no. 1 (1985).

Rector, Robert and Rea Hederman, Jr. "Two Americas: One Rich, One Poor; Understanding Income Inequality in the US." *The Heritage Foundation*, Aug. 24, 2004.Sanders, Bernie. Op-Ed, Sept. 19, 2008. www.sanders.senate.gov/news/record.cfm?id=303313.

Shapiro, Stewart. *Thinking About Mathematics*. Oxford: Oxford University Press, 2000.

Wittgenstein, Ludwig. *Remarks on the Foundations of Mathematics*, edited by G. H. von Wright, R. Rhees, and G.E.M. Anscombe, translated by G.E.M. Anscombe.Cambridge: MIT Press, 1996.

"Workingman's Blues." *The Economist*, July 24, 2008.

"World on the Edge." *The Economist*, Oct. 4, 2008.

Wright, Crispin. *Wittgenstein on the Foundations of Mathematics*. Cambridge: Harvard University Press, 1980.

CHAPTER 2

From Citizen to Consumer and Back Again: Deliberative Democracy and the Challenge of Interdependence[1]

Benjamin Barber

Democracy's history unfolds in stages and reveals that, in fact, we really shouldn't talk about the history of *democracy*, but about *democracies* in the plural. There is no such thing as democracy: one model, one place, one time, one country. Instead, when we look across time, across cultures and across frontiers, we see that democracy describes a variety of systems that have something in common but in many ways are deeply differentiated one from the other. So we really need to think about democracy in the plural rather than the singular. When we do that and go back to the origins of democracy, at least in the West, we go back to our foundational courses in liberal arts and philosophy and political theory, to the ancient Greeks. There it is evident that democracy starts as a regime of public life in a self-governing entity known as the *polis*. Democracy was born in a place that was characterized by very modest dimensions, both geographically and in terms of numbers of people, by a relatively homogenous population that spoke a single language, shared common beliefs, had a common history and common values.

Much of the value conflict we face in our society today was foreign to early democracy because, in fact, it was assumed that democracy would only work in a place with homogenous, consistent values, where people shared the same religion, the same ethnicity. In ancient Greece, people who did not share such values and ethnicity were regarded as "barbarians," as outsiders, not just to the Greek way of life but, as Aristotle had suggested, to some extent to the human way of life. In short, democracy was born as a form of self-

---

[1] Adapted from my Keynote Address, "The Decline of Capitalism and the Infantilist Ethos" (Carnegie Mellon University, September 21, 2006).

government, in the belief that we could govern ourselves, but only under those very strict conditions of a limited territory, a modest population, probably not more than 20,000-30,000 citizens at any one time, and, most importantly, with a great deal of natural consensus. We say nowadays democracy is about dealing with conflict; but in the ancient *polis*, while of course there were some conflicts, some disagreements about war and peace, and about how to spend revenue, on the whole the sorts of deep value and cultural conflicts that are the essence of say American or Iraqi politics today simply were not present then.

It's not clear if anyone could or would have contemplated a democratic, self-governing regime in a system that didn't have that kind of homogeneity, consistency, fluid unity, and natural consensus. To some degree, democracy as a search for common ground was born in a place with a lot of common ground to start with, so it wasn't a very demanding search.

In early Rome, the Greek model persisted but evolved. The early Roman Republic was homogenous, small, limited to the territories of the city of Rome and around Rome. By the time of the Roman Empire, it expanded greatly, becoming one of the first great multicultural empires on Earth—developments that led to the end of Roman democracy and the Roman Republic. Most theorists from that time on down to the end of the 18th century (say Montesquieu) argued that the moment a nation acquires a large territory, a multi-ethnic, multi-cultural identity, that's the end of democracy: a large scale society can be governed only by a regime of empire—monarchy, unilateral government and strong central rule.

By the 18th century, we witnessed the emergence of the second stage of democratic thought. Beginning in the 17th century with Bodin, Hobbes, Grotius and Locke, and then into the 18th century with Rousseau and the philosophers of the Enlightenment, the new question became: "Is it possible that there is a form of democracy that can work in the new large-scale nation states?" Although we have called them nation states, they were to some degree multi-cultural, multi-ethnic states. The idea of a French people, as Jeanne D'Arc understood, actually went beyond the ethnicities of particular provinces. Similarly, the War of the Roses in England suggested that English citizenship was actually an accretion on top of what had been local citizenship in the shires and counties of medieval England. The so-called nation states, though we look back upon France and England today as being relatively pure nationalities, were already divided, multi-cultural and, to some degree, divided confessionally (the sectarian wars among Protestants and Catholics).

By the 18th century democracy had a new face; it was no longer a system for manifesting the natural consensus of a homogenous people living in a very limited territory but had become a mechanism for dealing with the conflicts of people who lived in an extended territory and had distinctive interests organized around religious confession, ethnicity and, in time, economic class, including the interests of the city versus the interests of the land and the interests of agriculture against the interests of commerce and industry. In this second phase, democracy became a way not of expressing commonality but of dealing with difference.

At the same time, the democratic ideal of citizenship underwent radical alteration. In the early stages of democracy, in the time of the Greek *polis* and Roman Republic, citizenship was seen as an expression of active participation in governance. The result was that citizenship had a strongly deliberative flavor to it: the people gathered to debate their values, interests and goals. But by the 18th century, the citizen was no longer a deliberating, active participant in governance. Rather, in the language of the Enlightenment, he was a rights bearing individual with autonomous interests who found himself in conflict with other rights bearing individuals with other interests. Democracy became not a way for them to find commonality but to deal with and adjudicate the differences that grew out of their distinctive interests and backgrounds.

Citizenship had become a much less deliberative and much more concerned with the aggregation of interests, the adjudication of conflict and mechanisms like representation and the majority vote that allowed people to determine what to do when they didn't agree. In the ancient *polis*, when people couldn't reach consensus, they would ideally sit together in a forum that met every ten or twelve days and have it out until they could agree. By the 18th century it became clear that what was required was a way to deal with the fact that people couldn't and wouldn't agree, that interests were radically divergent. The task of the democratic process was to deal with and adjudicate those differences and come up with voting mechanisms that determined winners and losers in a system of self-interest. Citizens were now defined by interest, by their differences rather than their similarities.

Rousseau, who talked about a *General Will* and the need for all citizens to participate in its making, believed that many of the new mechanisms supposedly bringing democracy into the new era were not democratic at all. He thought that without direct participation in governance and the making of laws, there could be no reconciliation of liberty and sovereignty or of the individual and the community. Representing will was not an option; common willing was necessarily participatory. Unless people could discern their common values and interest, there could be no general willing. And without that, there was neither democracy nor the legitimacy that democracy conveyed. By the 18th century, then, there was both a new understanding of democracy as representative government and interest adjudication and a critique of that understanding by critics like Rousseau, critics who insisted democracy had to entail the preservation of the autonomy of citizens through the participation of citizens in self-legislation. Though Rousseau sometimes gets blamed for the application of the idea of the General Will to the Jacobins' regime of terror, he himself warned precisely against such a development. He prophesized that if you try to apply the General Will in a large, urban setting defined by difference, you're going to have a disaster. The French Revolution yielded that disaster.

The most telling moment in this second phase of the history of democracy came in the new United States of America. Even in the 18th century, America was expressly a multi-cultural, multi-ethnic land, with economic interests that diverged across city and country. With a plantation economy in the south, a new industrial economy in the northern cities, the nation was riven by differences. In the attempt to establish democracy on a continental scale most people believed could only support Empire, the Americans seized on the new democratic device of representative government and employed it to save deliberation, but ironically by taking it away from the people.

In a large-scale society with differing interests and a multitude of citizens, not everybody can be engaged in seeking some minimal common ground. What's required is a representative assembly in which the various interests of vastly divergent populations are represented and in which not ordinary citizens but the wise delegates they choose are the ones who engage in deliberation and decision-making. Politicians become democracy's only real citizens.

Madison spoke about the "filter" of representation, suggesting that the American people were no longer capable of deliberation, and that democracy could only refer to their right to choose the deputies who were capable of deliberation. Even the democratic task of choosing representatives might in the name of prudence be filtered. The electors were not necessarily the people themselves, with their whims and prejudices, but those the people chose (or allowed to be appointed) to do the choosing, as happened in the early electoral assemblies and the electoral college by which Senators and the President were chosen. The aim was to bring the best men together so that they might deliberate and seek common ground in a way that those they represented could not.

The American Compromise was seductive and provocative because it saved democratic deliberation by delegating it in a rather undemocratic way to electors and chosen delegates. They would be able to use their wisdom and prudence to find consensus, whereas the imprudent people they represented, divided by interests, would not.

Ironically, today, the relationship between prudent moderation and representation have been almost reversed. There is more polarization, less deliberativeness, and less civility among our politicians and the media than the American people. Many polls have shown that the American people are far less divided than the politicians or the media suggests. Recognizing this, the 2008 Presidential campaign was contested by two candidates who, at least rhetorically, spoke against polarization and for unity, courting independents and crossover voters in the American center. This is the very opposite of what Madison thought would be the case, that somehow the unwashed masses couldn't get it together but their politicians could. The result of a Madisonian representative system was a regime far less deliberative than the ancient polis, but in which deliberation was nonetheless to some extent salvaged at the political level, especially in the Senate.

The third phase has come more recently, and defines our own times. That's the phase in which neither the *polis* nor the nation state are the primary theater for the playing out of powers and interests in the country, but rather the international, globalized domain. If Rousseau asked how can democracy survive the large-scale nation-state, we must ask whether democracy can survive a globalized, interdependent world in which neither representation nor deliberation seem very feasible.

In the new interdependent world we live in, most of the forces that determine our destiny are beyond the control of sovereign nation states. Indeed, sovereignty itself as a principle is quickly eroding; within nation-states, privatization and the neo-liberal ideology have stolen much of government's force and marketized many functions that were once public. Moreover, privatizing power and turning it over to markets is not really a shifting of sovereignty from the political to the economic, but its destruction as a source of collective, legitimate power.

And, of course, globally, there is no sovereignty at all, hence no democracy, no law, and no political legitimacy. Yet most of the forces that concern us unfold in the global setting. In a certain sense World War II with the new United Nations system, the move to a common market in Europe, and the new hegemony of international trade, spelled the end of the classical nation-state. That doesn't mean that the nation state does not continue to play a prominent role in our lives. In terms of the history of democracy, however, it is morphing in ways that challenge both democracy and deliberation. Three hundred years of warfare between nation states, particularly in Europe, turned sovereignty into a principle by which nations destroyed one another. Europe emerged sixty years ago from a half century of aggression, world war, genocide and holocaust with the acknowledgement that French sovereignty or the German nation-state could no longer be foundations for equity or justice, let alone for peace and security.

As a consequence, after World War II, the United Nations was established and the kernel of the European Union was established in a European Steel and Coal Community. For the first time, jealous sovereign entities that had been making war on one another joined together, pooled their sovereignty, and created a supra-national entity larger than any one of them. It wasn't just the wars; what was also happening, just as Adam Smith and later Marx and Engels and Lenin had predicted, was that capitalism itself had escaped the boundaries of nation states and was dragging states reluctantly with it so that they could continue to try to control it. From the 16th- and 17th-century mercantilist economies of the European monarchies through the early 20th-century global trading economy, nation states had controlled not just their territory and their people, but also their markets in labor, goods and finance. Even before World

War I, something like 13-14% of world's economy was grounded in world trade, although that was mostly in traditional natural resources and manufactured goods. But in the period after World War II, even more of that world's economy eluded the grasp of nation states, and trade was now in information, technology, services and other forms of capital that were by definition global rather than national.

Presidents and politicians, including Barack Obama, still talk about American sovereignty, and bringing the jobs back home, and respecting the sovereignty of other nations. Yet America's hegemonic government cannot stop one job, one dollar—let alone whole industries and billions in financial capital—from finding their way around the world as they will. It is not just that Washington cannot control the American economy; there is no such thing as the American economy or an American firm. When President Hu of China came to the United States, he stopped and talked to the American sovereign. No, not American President Bush in Washington, but Microsoft President Bill Gates in Seattle, on his way to Washington. Only after a conversation with Bill Gates did he proceed to Washington to chat briefly with George Bush.

As for the classical all-American companies: Coca-Cola does over seventy percent of its business outside the United States. Nike does seventy five percent of its business abroad. These so-called American brands aren't really American at all. They're part of a global economy in which the United States can't really meddle. Even the Bill and Melinda Gates Foundation has become more important than American foreign aid in battling disease in Africa. Some think that Bill Clinton is more 'powerful' as the head of his foundation than he ever was as president. What is true for companies is true for labor markets too. Yet the fustian American government is building a wall along the Mexican-American border, as if it could wall off the flow of labor, as if the issue is one of national law ('illegal immigrants") rather than global markets ("go where the jobs are!").

We are talking about a global economy in which labor moves in accord with global market forces, and for such forces borders and frontiers are irrelevant. Even as we build the wall, farmers in the west are asking "Who will pick the fruit and vegetables? if they cut off the flow of 'illegals,' we can't put food on America's dinner tables." Moreover, it is not just immigrants coming to America in search of jobs, but American farmers and factory owners searching for workers. The market is global and it answers to that call. The "sovereignty" of the United States is simply not relevant to the conversation, which is why reviewing immigration laws in Washington or listening to Lou Dobbs rant about illegal immigration is wasted time. Former foreign minister Louis Derbez of Mexico said over and over again, "We need a solution that looks at labor and industry and jobs throughout the hemisphere." The frontier between Mexico and the United States is no more porous than the frontier between Mexico and Guatemala and its other southern neighbors. There are as many people trying to get into Mexico (in part to come through Mexico up to the United States) as come from Mexico to the United States—and the Mexicans, with more draconian measures that the United States has taken, has had little success in stemming the flow. The situation is the same in Morocco. All of Africa tries to get into and traverse Morocco in order get into Spain and the borderless European Union. Sovereign law is not the cure to porous borders because it is the failure of sovereign law that is the symptom of why borders have become so porous.

What is true for markets is true for drugs, crime, technology, the environment, terrorism and most of the other afflictions of the 21st century. Interdependence is the rule. Nothing the United States does in Japan, Canada, or Mexico will ensure a safe environment if it does not approve the Kyoto protocol and then cooperate with others in going far beyond it. There is no such things a clear air in Dallas unless there is clear air in Mexico City and Calgary. Global Warming is global. The same with technology. It's not the Weehawken wide web but the world-wide web. The West New York flu has been overtaken by the West Nile virus, and safe public health in one country now depends safe public health everywhere. And as Americans learned the hard way on 9/11, terrorism is neither local nor global but a perverse combination of both. The terrorists, although "foreigners," did not come from abroad but had been living in the U.S. for years. They used not foreign rockets that a "sovereign defense force" might have defended against, but box cutters and hijacked airplanes to do their mayhem. It was neither an "inside job" nor an "outside job" because in an interdependent world the very distinction between inside and outside no longer holds.

In this third stage of democracy then, with markets and war and technology and environment all global issues, it would seem that we either have to democratize globalization or globalize democracy or we will not have a democracy capable of dealing with the problems. But surely we then have a right to ask "What might global democracy look like?" How do we democratize globalization when it was hard enough to democratize the Greek *polis*, to keep the Roman *republic* democratic, to find ways to save democracy in the 18ᵗʰ-century nation-state where, in every case, one had entities that were homogenous, territorially-limited, and consensual. Today, in the third phase of democracy, the whole world is the stage and there is not multiculturalism but omni-culturalism, omni-ethnicity, omni-religion and not a hint of consensus. No political regime, let alone a democracy, was designed to deal with the world as a whole, incorporating and encompassing peoples as divergent as those who populate the globe today. Yet that is the challenge. It's hard enough, skeptics will complain, to get Democrats and Republicans in Albany on the same page once and awhile. Now we're supposed to get Wahabbist Muslims and radical Hindu nationalists and secular Buddhists and enlightenment rationalists with different skins and rival interests and conflicting ideologies and put them in a room and do . . . what? a "deliberative poll?" A town-hall debate? A vote that allows six billion people to take a common decision? For many democrats, the challenge of the third phase of democracy is not yet to globalize democracy or democratize globalization but also to make democracy work within corrupt and failing nation-states where it has not yet taken hold, or has lost its vigor. You're not going to globalize democracy when a lot of the world's nations are not yet themselves really democratic.

But democratizing emerging nations is not just a matter of overthrowing a tyranny, as President Bush seemed to believe. While that administration was correct in believing democracy within nations is a prerequisite to a stable, working international system, the experience in Iraq suggests it did not have a clear idea of what democratization means, or the 'rules' that guide the development of democratic practices.

Let me just suggest briefly what a few of those rules for democracy are—and then offer ten rather specific proposals for globalizing democratic civil society. In doing so, we need to remember we're talking about democracies in the plural, not "democracy." There's not one model; it's not that every nation must look like Switzerland or America or Great Britain. It does mean, however, there has to be an element of deliberative participation in which people control some part of the power within the nation that determines their lives. That's a minimal, and not a very hard definition. One easy way to understand the rules for democratization is to look at what United States has done in Iraq—let's assume out of the best of motives—and conclude "Don't do that." Which is to say, the very first rule is you cannot bring democracy to another people by force of arms. It's possible to overthrow tyranny by force, but overthrowing tyranny and establishing democracy are two completely different processes requiring quite different strategies. It sometimes seems as if President Bush and his neo-conservative democratizers thought democracy in Iraq was a lawn ready to bloom but that the weeds of tyranny sown by Saddam Hussein had first to be removed. Removing them, overthrowing Hussein by force, would allow the lawn to spring forth: and there'd be democracy. The historical truth is that applying herbicide to a lawn that has only weeds (overthrowing tyranny) kills the weeds but yields a desert, not a lawn. We overthrew what was a tyrannical regime but also the only stabilizing force in that part of the world, without creating the foundations for a new democracy. What ensued was not democracy but anarchy, instability, and disorder, which bred conflict and violence and years later still risks, insurgency, civil war, and renewed tyranny. That's the old Aristotelian cycle: overthrow tyranny with anarchy and after a while anarchy breeds a new form of tyranny.

The German example to which President Bush so often resorted did not really apply. The work done to overthrow the Nazis was unrelated to the work done to establish German democracy. That work took ten to fifteen to twenty years: a Marshall plan, billions of dollars, reeducation, new schooling, a retooled economy and a whole world around it of democratic regimes that it could imitate. And of course a new democratic Europe to which Germany would belong (and help lead). Defeating Germany in World War II didn't create German democracy any more than defeating Saddam in Iraq will create Iraqi democracy.

This first rule that you can't impose democracy by force is actually a subset of another principle: that you can't import democracy from the outside, not by force but also not by good will or persuasion. America can't export democracy and the Iraqis can't import it. You can't FedEx the Bill of Rights to Cambodia and think it will receive freedom. You don't send over a constitution by parcel post and assume a republic is created. The constitutional lawyer Noah Feldman wrote a constitution for the Iraqis. Nice. But a constitution, our own founders reminded us, is nothing but a piece of paper, and it's no better than the civic competence, the social capital, the civic foundations on which it rests, and without those capacities it's nothing more than parchment.

There is no country that has become free that hasn't sought and struggled for its own freedom. Freedom can never be a gift of strangers. The English didn't give the Americans their freedom; we seized it from them. Nor did the French come in and liberate us from the English. Liberation is a task of citizens and patriots working from within.

If democracy must come from the inside out, it also must come bottom up rather than top down. The third rule of democratization is that a constitution is the capstone for civic and democratic work already done. It is the culmination not the beginning of the democratization process. Think of the United States: superficial history teachers will lecture their students that American democracy began with a Declaration of Independence in 1776, a Constitution in 1789. But it didn't. We had a hundred years of local practice habituating ourselves to self-governance in the townships and in the commonwealths, so that in fact the Declaration of Independence was the culmination of a hundred years of learning citizenship and practicing democracy. The success of the American experiment was grounded as much on what came before the famous documents as on the ingenuity of those documents. And of course the lessons had not really been fully learned since only a few white, propertied males were citizens in the beginning. Real democracy would take another hundred years of struggle, including a bloody civil war. But what success the early Americans had came bottom up—citizens first, civil society second and a constitution last. It was what people learned in the New England townships and the southern assemblies that allowed them after the Declaration of Independence to provide something like wise government. When Alexis de Tocqueville visited America in the 1830s, democracy was something he discovered in the towns and municipalities, not in the federal capital. "Liberty," he said, "is local and municipal."

And what this means is that democracy takes patience, creating citizens time. The Swiss began their experiment in autonomous self-government in 1291; that's more than seven hundred years ago. Magna Carta decreed the rights of nobleman against the crown in 1215 and it was not until the Glorious Revolution of 1688 and then the extension of the franchise to all males in 1832 that something resembling democracy came into view. In France a "democratic" Revolution raged in 1789 but democracy took another hundred years. In short, the old established democracies have been at it for hundreds of years, in some case four or five or even seven hundred years, and still haven't really got it right. Yet in Iraq and Afghanistan pessimists worry it might take three or even four years to realize democracy while optimists assure them it can be done in six months.

Democracy takes time, and pushing fast is likely to lead to failure, as happened in the French Revolution. Learning democratic habits and civic skills—engaging in what Tocqueville called "the apprenticeship of liberty"—is a gradual process that works only from the bottom up. A democratic constitution has to rest on a democratic civic culture, and what sociologists call social capital, the civic assets on which democratic citizens depend in governing themselves prudently. Sara Evans and Harry Boyte of the University of Minnesota wrote a book called *Free Spaces* (1992) in which they described how Americans learn the habits of democracy. Not simply by voting once in a while. They learn citizenship in the union halls and school, in their churches and synagogues. They learn it on the floor of the plants in which they work and in the PTAs and philanthropies and other civic associations that comprise their daily lives. Robert Bellah's book *Habits of the Heart* (1985) takes the same Tocquevillean insight and demonstrates that democracy rests in attitudes and behaviors that precede democratic institutions and that help them function. Crucial is developing a democratic demeanor, a democratic outlook.

Democracy cannot exist without civil society, civil society cannot exist without a civic culture, and civic culture cannot exist without civic education—general education, liberal education, education in citizenship. We forget that the term "liberal arts" is rooted in the old idea of the arts of liberty, what citizens must know to become and remain free! That is to say what makes democracy work is not constitutions but citizens, and citizens have to be created. We may be born free, but we are not born citizens. To become citizens takes a life of practice, learning, and engagement. People are born knowing what they want and what they desire; they are not born deliberative. The capacity to deliberate and reflect takes time, education, and work. Neither the rights bearing individual of the Enlightenment and the bundle of desires that is the modern market consumer is yet the deliberative, thoughtful, competent, engaged citizen. Citizenship does not merely require deliberation: citizenship *is* deliberation, and the citizen is the individual who has learned to deliberate, because to deliberate means to take your own desires and interests and put them in the context of the interests of the community. One must see herself through the lens of her neighbors needs and think not just of "me," but of "us." That's not altruism or saying, "I'm not important"; it's saying, "I am part of a community and my interests are also the community interests."

We all know that we have some interests that are solely our own and some interests we share with our family, and still other interests that we share not with our family but with our neighbors and a more extended community. Deliberation is how we figure out which are which. We grasp that we're not putting some "selfish me" aside in favor of family or neighborhood or country, but we are incorporating a sense of who we are as "me's" into the greater sense of family, neighborhood, and country. Deliberation is how we figure out the difference between what I want and what the community that I belong to needs (note that I also want that!). Deliberation is how we go from the sphere of my interests to the more encompassing sphere of our interests—even "the public interest." It is how we move from the private to the public, from the individual to the individual-embedded-in-the-community.

Failing to make distinctions like these has led us in the developed West (but also in "liberated" Russia or places like Iraq or Afghanistan), to believe that to be a citizen in a modern, large-scale democracy it is enough to be a consumer; to believe that as consumers spending our dollars, euros or yen, we can influence and shape the public realm—that through what we do as shoppers and consumers we can make public policy and be good citizens. That is a deeply false understanding of the nature of citizenship because it leads us to think that by pursuing private interests, preferences, and desires we can somehow achieve public ends.

Take a concrete example: you travel to LA, and look move around. It may seem you have endless choice because in LA you can choose between 223 different kinds of automobile in all price ranges. Get yourself a Kia for $11,000 on a great four-year deal; you'll only pay $99/month. Get yourself a Mercedes and pay $800/month, or pick up a Chrysler, a Toyota, or a Hummer. That's freedom! But there is one choice not on the menu: *public* transportation. A one-line subway, local buses, but finally, you have no choice but to drive. Through other earlier decisions in which you did not participate, Los Angeles has basically taken away what is the most fundamental choice in transportation: the choice between public and private transportation. What seems to be endless choice is actually constrained choice. He who contrives the menu of choices has the real power (and hence the real freedom), while you have only apparent choices within what is an extremely narrow ranges of choices—the kind of car you will drive. This turns out to be a problem particularly for the poor who can't afford the sticker price of a car, or the costly gas, and truly need efficient and inexpensive public transport. What starts out looking like freedom is anything but, and ends up skewing society and reinforcing inequalities. Is that really liberty?

Sure, as consumers we have endless choices, but private choices made one by one by individual consumers cannot create public goods, period. It's the fundamental difference between public and private judgment, between public and private choosing, and the failure to understand the difference is deeply disempowering.

Consumerism not only deprives us of public liberty and access to public goods, it also leaves deliberation out. Most polling is that way, too. The pollster never asks, "Who do you think is a really good candidate in terms of the social and public values you most cherish as a citizen?" He asks, "Who do you like? Who are going to vote for? What's your party preference?" He might as well be asking, "What kind of soap do you like? What brand of car? What's your favorite color?"

Polls ask us, demand that we express private preferences, show our unalloyed, undeliberated prejudices. There are never qualifications. A pollster who said "Please look at this information and reconsider who you thought was the best candidate in light of these questions. Now what do you think?" This would be "contaminating" the sample. Influencing the outcome! The rule is: "Don't think about it, don't reflect, just tell me quick, who do you like?" Impulsive, un-reflective responses—childlike in their simplicity—are not what they want to avoid, they are want they want to tap. To be sure, there are some social scientists who have tried to develop "deliberative polling" techniques (see the important work of James Fishkin, for example), but such efforts are marginal to the commercial polling industry.

The polling of undeliberated impulses is just a feature of a society of consumers who are constantly subjected to infantilization. We not only rely on consumers as citizens, we increasingly try to infantilize consumers and make them more like children. We're looking for impetuous, unreflective, undeliberative reactions and we when we get it, we call it the new citizenship.[2]

We live in a society that produces more goods than we need. Capitalism needs to sell goods in order to survive so it's got to figure out how to get us to buy them. It wants people to buy stuff they don't need because most of the middle class at least in the developed world has most of what it needs. "I thought I had all I needed until I found out about the new iPod, now I need that. I thought I had the car I wanted until I saw that cool Hummer, now I need that." American capitalism today is engaged not in the manufacture of goods to meet needs but the manufacture of needs to sell all the goods it has to produce to stay in business. It's a serious problem because if capitalism requires that kids become consumers and consumers become kids, the consequence is a nation of child-like consumers who not only buy all the goods the market needs to sell them, but who also become child-like in their political choices and in their public judgments. If the only relevant political question is "Do you want to pay taxes?" the obvious answer is "No, I don't!" If the question is "Do we as citizens need to pay taxes to create the kind of common goods and social justice and national security we want?" the answer becomes "I don't like taxes, but we need to pay them in order to live in the kind of free, just and secure country we all wish to live in as deliberative citizens." We have a political system, however, that asks the first kind of question but rarely the second.

---

2 For an extensive critique of the consumerization of politics, see my *Consumed: How Markets Corrupt Children, Infantilize Adults And Swallow Citizens Whole* (New York: W. W. Norton & Co., 2007).

This makes for some perverse ironies: Americans often go to Paris and are profoundly impressed: "God I do love Paris, look at this beautiful city, why can't New York and Pittsburgh and Los Angeles look like this?" Why? Because Parisians pay something like 60% of their income in taxes to secure a safe, beautiful public sector, while Americans won't pay taxes but want all the benefits that come from paying them for free. Europeans don't like taxes either, but once they deliberate about it, they understand that taxes are the price of admission to the city of justice, the city of art, the city of rapid transit, the city of beauty. Encouraged not to deliberate but to be "selfish" and "impulsive," Americans are led to choices that benefit individuals (especially those who can *buy* education, health and security privately) but is devastating to those without their own wealth, and destructive to the public realm in which all must live. Even the private choices of the wealthy, which seem to benefit them, can boomerang back and hurt them. Gas-guzzling SUVs and trucks are affordable even when prices are high for the rich, but they make America import-dependent in the energy realm and that leads to foreign wars (Iraq?) that impact us all; they increase global warming, and that impacts us. There is no way to comprehend all this, however, in the absence of civic deliberation, or when we regard ourselves as political consumers rather than as political citizens.

Even in the sectors where civic communication might be expected, commercialization has deprived Americans of a useful medium. Twenty years ago, impressed by its democratic architecture and educational potential, people talked about the internet as a great civic and democratic medium. Today it's become one large virtual shopping mall and gamester venue, a place for me not us—and MySpace not OurSpace; YouTube, not OurTube, FaceBook not CitizenBook. Kids are drawn in, but primarily in order to sell to them as consumers-to-be. The notion that the kids might together create a space where they can talk about issues that affect them all and maybe begin to understand the power they can have when they reflect and act in common scarcely exists. Commerce and consumerism have other objectives in mind.

So where does this leave us? Deliberation today, the essence of democracy, remains what is has always been: the ability to think like a citizen not a consumer, to think in public and in common rather than in private terms, to think in terms of "we" not "me." But its practices are in deep trouble, because capitalism today is mandating in a manner that is both counter-productive and anti-democratic the producing, marketing and selling of products we don't need or even (until the marketers get through with us) want. Deliberation is in trouble because we've moved from the small polis and the modest republic to a global society; from the parochial "we" of the township through the society-wide "us" of large multi-cultural, nation-states, to the anonymous billions of an interdependent, omni-cultural world seemingly beyond not just democracy but governance itself. If it's daunting to fashion an American or a Chinese citizen, it seems impossible to create a world citizen.

Citizenship starts locally. It's easy to create citizens of, say, a fraternity or sorority, not so difficult to integrate members into a local civic association, harder still to make real citizens out of a varied population living in a national territory. But a global citizen? What is that? One can love Pittsburgh, perhaps feel at home in Pennsylvania, maybe even, with equal doses of patriotism, civic faith and political imagination come to think of oneself as an American, a Frenchman, a Mexican. But to conceive oneself as Barack Obama did in Berlin as a citizen of the world? That's an abstraction that doesn't seem to mean anything. Many Americans and not a few pundits rolled their eyes at Obama's turn of phrase. How to put flesh on the bones of such a vague idea? How to conceive of deliberation—prudent debate among a community of concerned citizens—on the planetary scale? How to think across the boundaries not just of white and black, rich and poor, this nationality and that nationality, but across the interests and cultures and religions and ideologies that separate us around the globe? That is the challenge of democracy facing a new world of interdependence.

Rousseau would say "democratic deliberation didn't even work in the 18th century with the then quite modestly-sized nation-state, how can it possibly function on a global level in a commercialized, privatized world?" Nonetheless, I'm an American. Which means I'm an irredeemable optimist.

My current work at Demos focuses on a project aimed at producing a global governance paradigm appropriate to the new world of interdependence. (See www.civworld.org for details.) It asks the question as to how we might extend citizenship and the civil society on which it rests to a global plane where it can undergird some soft forms of global governance suitable to global deliberation and counteract the effects of consumerism and privatization. Among the ideas we explore are these ten—summarized here to demonstrate that the quest for global forms of deliberative democracy is not only a necessary but a realistic one:

1. Civic Education transformed into a tool of teaching civic interdependence, including service education in the international arena as a means of generating activities that build "bridging capital."

2. The "Art of Common Space" as a strategy aimed at engaging architects and artists in conceiving public places and spaces in a world of increasingly privatized space, and global places and spaces in a world still territorially defined by nation-states.

3. New Technology and the Internet, recalling their original aims, as instruments of building democratic communication globally, and establishing 'virtual democratic spaces' that nurture global citizenship.

4. Non-governmental Organization Networks that use the civic propensities of national NGOs as building bricks for a global civil society.

5. Foundation Networks that use the resources and visions of the philanthropic sector as assets in building a global civil society.

6. Multinational Corporation Networks that use the already globally engaged business and market assets of the economic sector as another way to foster global civic cooperation.

7. International Financial Institutions (IMF, WTO, World Bank) as already existing transnational organizations which, though currently representing the interests of investors, bankers and traders, can become agents of global civil society and justice.

8. Multicultural Global Cities as building blocks (alternative to nation-states) of global cities on the basis of their cosmopolitan demographics and rootedness in communication, trade, finance and the arts.

9. The United Nations system which, despite its baggage and its history as an assembly of sovereign nation states, can through

the Secretary General's Office and its system of Commissions and special organizations (UNESCO, WHO) help craft and support new global civic and political institutions.

10. Confederalism as an architecture of devolved powers and the layering of authority especially suitable to the first stages of a global structure based on soft governance rather than hard "government."

These ideas might in turn facilitate the founding of a global *non-voting* civic parliament (a kind of global *loya jirga* representing the "tribes" that are today our NGOs, corporations, foundations and state institutions). This entity, even as a normative ideal, suggests what the first stage of a global governance institution not only rooted in but emanating out of civil society might look like. It would be the world's first deliberative assembly—not yet empowered to make decisions, but by including citizens everywhere in a virtual version of the global assembly, inaugurate and model deliberation at the global level.

Of course there is a great deal of work to be done prior to moving across national boundaries. Many people have a hard time making out the difference between "me" and "we." Most think the consumer *is* the citizen and it is enough be a consumer and shop to exercise democratic choice. The more enlightened understand that voting is also necessary, but often cannot think beyond voting. When following the trauma of September 11th, President Bush looked to reassure Americans who were actually begging to be citizens, what he said was: "Don't worry we'll take care of security and reconstruction; you all, you go shopping." What a terrible thing to say! For the silver lining of the tragedy on 9/11 is that it did pull Americans together; it even pulled the world together. For a moment, the world, including our adversaries in Indonesia, Sudan, and Libya agreed: "What was done in New York was vicious, unacceptable—bad for the globe, bad for the human race." It was a moment where there was a hint of global thinking, of Americans thinking as global citizens and others responding in kind. Yet the President's response was to call on us to get back to the mall, back to being consumers, back to being privatized, selfish, shoppers.

With this, it was easy for the Sudanese to go back to being Sudanese and the Afghans back to being Afghans and now we are all back in a divided world where the very thought of what might bring us together is elusive. In the summer of 2008, seven years of trying to make global trade more just and fair to developing nations (the so-called Doha Round) ended in failure. Inequality has grown rather than diminished. Yet accommodating the brute realities of interdependence remains the challenge of democracy if it is to survive. Because for deliberation to survive interdependence, we will have to find ways to create a meaningful and salient form of global citizenship. We require instruments to deal with our problems as large and encompassing and as interdependent as the challenges we face.

Democracy has always faced challenges, however. In the 18th century, it seemed to Rousseau that it might not survive the coming of the nation state, yet with ideas like federalism, representation and the separation of powers, it did. Today we are moving towards supra-sovereign forms of civic community and identity, and as the menu of suggestions offered above demonstrate, there are viable ways forward for democracy into the era of interdependence.

How far we have come may be indicated by the new civic identity many young Europeans have assumed. Ask a young Italian or a young German, "Who are you, what's your identity?" and she is as likely to say "I am a European" as "I am an Italian" or "I am a German." How amazing this is, given the context of Europe's history of war, enmity and reciprocal slaughter. What this shows is that despite their powerful national divisions, they have found a way to begin to think civically about their common membership in a larger Europe. If the Germans and French and Italians can do it, Americans, Japanese, and Brazilians should also be able to do it.

To do so, however, does mean that we have to come back to an understanding of the fundamental distinction between deliberative public judgment in a genuine political democracy concerned with common goods and common ground, and the kind of "consumers republic" that treats selfish individuals—rights-bearing, narcissistic shoppers—as surrogates for citizens. That is a sure recipe for failure. The recipe for success is more challenging, and its ingredients remain indeterminate. But we know this much: it is not the recipe yielded by either terrorism and anarchy, or the war on terrorism and the old-fashioned kinds of hegemonic sovereignty that once contained anarchy. It is neither the continuing sovereignty of the antiquated nation-state, nor the malicious interdependence of predatory markets. It is a recipe that takes the democratic ideals of self-government and prudent deliberation by citizens, and extends them to a global civil society and a global citizenry. Hard? To be sure. Impossible? No more so than democracy was in the absolute monarchies of sixteenth century Europe. Nor more so than racial justice was in early nineteenth century slave plantation America. Democracy has always been hard at each critical juncture in its history. This is but one more challenge.

BIBLIOGRAPHY

Barber, Benjamin. *Consumed: How Markets Corrupt Children, Infantilize Adults And Swallow Citizens Whole.* New York: W. W. Norton & Co., 2007.

—. Keynote Address: "The Decline of Capitalism and the Infantilist Ethos." Carnegie Mellon University, September 21, 2006.

CHAPTER 3

Deliberation, but Voting Too

Gerry Mackie

Introduction

The deliberative conception of democracy, by many accounts, arose in reaction to the aggregative conception of democracy. Two major and two minor tributaries joined to form the now mighty river of deliberationism, I suggest. The first, minor, current was the participatory ethos of the New Left. In the United States after World War II, the new science of politics described and prescribed an apathetic citizenry governed by the power equilibrium bargains of a plurality of self-seeking interest groups. The great civil rights movement, however, was neither apathetic, nor essentially self-seeking, nor in equilibrium. The Port Huron Statement of the Students for a Democratic Society (1962) found the American democracy to be apathetic and manipulated, and called for a participatory democracy in the political, economic, and social arenas. The statement reflected, rather than directed, the emergence of thousands of participatory experiments (for example, enabling legislation for the War on Poverty called for maximum feasible participation of the poor). The whole world seemed to change in 1968, with the movement against the Vietnam war, the Paris student revolt, the Prague Spring, and the Chinese Cultural Revolution. This spirit manifested in political theory proper with Carole Pateman's *Participation and Democratic Theory* (1970). The personal was the political. From the civil rights to the antiwar to the feminist movement, in rebellion against the Old Right and the Old Left, the main political action was decentralized, face-to-face, and often organized by consensus rule. Although momentarily liberating, these many unitary democracies proved limited in scope and otherwise unsustainable, as hinted in Jane Mansbridge's

Beyond Adversary Democracy (1980). Whatever was the failing of liberal representative democracy, participation was a palliative, not a cure.

In political science, interest-group pluralism was overtaken, not by participation, but by the economic theory of democracy. The rational-choice school replaced the self-seeking group with the self-seeking individual of economics. Just as consumers purchase commodities in the market, so do citizens cast their vote in the democracy. Just as the formal and numerical qualities of the price system opened academic careers to mathematical talent, so did the formal and numerical qualities of the voting system. William Riker, leader of the rational-choice school, declared that voting is the central act of democracy:

> All the elements of the democratic method are means to render voting practically effective and politically significant, and all the elements of the democratic ideal are moral extensions and elaborations of the features of the method that make voting work.[1]

Although discussion has as much to do with democracy as voting, it is much harder to mathematize, and thus there were few career rewards in political science for theorizing discussion. The emigration of *homo economicus* to politics displaced several earlier ideals of democracy. If in the free market the many self-interests of individuals sum to a common good, and perhaps the same would be true of the democratic forum? Riker knocked out such frail hope with his *Liberalism against Populism* (1982): not only are voters self-interested, but voting is in principle arbitrary and meaningless, there is no common good. Voting was siphoned dry of normative content. Good is revealed only by free market exchange. Thus, according to mathematics, democracy should be minimized and the market maximized. The dead-ending of the aggregative conception of democracy was the first major current in the rise of deliberationism.

Meanwhile, amidst radical democratic ferment, the German social theorist Jürgen Habermas fought for an escape from the pessimistic dead end of Frankfurt critical theory. His *Theory of Communica-*

---

[1] William Riker, *Liberalism Against Populism: A Confrontation Between the Theory of Democracy and the Theory of Social Choice* (Prospect Heights: Waveland Press, 1982), 5.

tive Action[2] sought to restore emancipatory reason by theorization of communicative action, an indispensable supplement to the impoverished strategic account of action. Communicative action brings about an understanding, strategic action a response. Normative validity is redeemable in an *ideal speech situation*, where no one is excluded, anyone can introduce a question, and no one is prevented by internal or external coercion from exercising his or her rights. The force of the better argument would lead to consensus in this hypothetical, frankly counterfactual, situation, and such consensus would define the true and the right. If the ideal situation would define *justice*, some approximation of the ideal situation in real political institutions would establish democratic *legitimacy*.

In the English-speaking world John Rawls's *Theory of Justice* (1971) restored the prestige of normative political theory, after fifty years of disdain and decay. Rawls admirably defended social liberalism, but democracy was secondary in his scheme. The Habermasian fountain revived arid American democratic theory, thanks to Seyla Benhabib, John Bohman, Simone Chambers, John Dryzek, amongst other interlocutors. Europeans Bernard Manin and Jon Elster added innovative responses to Habermas on democracy. Political philosophers in the orbit of Rawls (Cohen 2002, Gutmann and Thompson 1996, Freeman 2000), perhaps repelled by Riker (Cohen 1986) and attracted by Habermas (Cohen 1999), erected more direct justifications of democracy on Rawlsian and deliberative foundations. Rawls and Habermas went face-to-face intellectually in a 1995 issue of the *Journal of Philosophy*, and the circle seemed to be complete when Rawls declared himself a deliberative democrat.[3] The Rawlsian contribution is the second minor current in the rise of deliberationism.

Voting and discussion are each essential to democracy. In the 1980s the aspiring democratic theorist encountered a theory of voting populated by self-interested citizens and an absence of the common good except in the case of unanimity, and a theory of discussion populated by impartial citizens and pursuit of a common good defined by rational consensus. Is it any wonder that there was a stampede away from voting and to discussion? Philosopher Samuel Freeman, in "A Sympathetic Comment" on deliberationism,

---

[2] In German, both volumes (1981); in English, vol. 1 (1984), vol. 2 (1987).

[3] John Rawls, *Law of Peoples* (Cambridge: Harvard University Press, 1999), 139.

observed that, "For many normative political theorists, the revival of interest in democratic deliberation can bring welcome relief from the seeming predominance of rational choice theory in normative discussions."[4]

In the remainder of the essay, I first relate my extensive practical experience with democratic discussion and voting, and how that led me to challenge pessimistic interpretations of democracy taught in graduate schools of political science. I compare the deliberative and aggregative conceptions of democracy, and conclude that the distinctive feature of deliberation is the giving of reasons, not its other hypothesized benefits. Then I contend that deliberative democrats uncritically accept the political science discipline's cynical account of democratic voting. I argue that voting beneficially transforms citizen's preferences from self-interested to public-interested, and recite the overwhelming evidence that voters are in fact public-spirited. I claim that the beneficially transformative effects of deliberation are due as much to voting as to discussion. I conclude with a call for more normative attention to democratic voting.

A Personal Aside

I have an offbeat history for an academic, and for that reason the editor asked me to tell some of that story as it relates to democratic theory. It is somewhat embarrassing to depart from the austere norms of academic writing, but here goes. I come from a quite modest background in Oregon, from among people who worked the woods and the sea. I could not afford to finish college, but by some fluke I was a keen autodidact. I came of age at the peak of participatory enthusiasms, and unthinkingly absorbed those values and put them into effect in my own life. I started to work in the woods, doing forestry, because the money for that was good back then. I helped organize a forestry workers' cooperative that became large, held elected executive positions in that cooperative; helped organize a league of such cooperatives in the Northwest, and was its elected head; was a local, state, and federal lobbyist for forestry workers; worked in issue and candidate politics at the local and state levels,

---

[4] Samuel Freeman, "Deliberative Democracy: A Sympathetic Comment," *Philosophy and Public Affairs* 29, no. 4 (2000): 416.

organized political campaigns and helped elect local officials, served as the policy aide to a county commissioner for three years; worked as a radio and weekly journalist covering the state legislature; among other political activities. Our large workers' cooperative bridged to a great many other participatory activities, from neighborhood groups to gubernatorial campaigns, and was a forum in which many people learned skills of democracy and leadership. At times, I attended a dozen meetings a week. It was our Athens.[5]

I won't pretend that our affairs were wholly idyllic. We experienced the hopes, the tragedies, the compromises, and the blunders common to all human pursuits. To deliberate in the democratic workplace was more satisfying than being bossed around by an arbitrary autocrat, and we had deliberation aplenty. It was our strength, although one of the first things we learned was to economize severely on deliberation. We were not a debating society but an economic enterprise on which people relied for their livelihood, and against the instincts of the times we quickly evolved from chaotic unstructured consensus to formal organization, specialized officers and committees, rules of order, majority rule voting, and increasingly disciplined limits on debate. I loved deliberation, but, I have to say, I came to love majority voting even more. Voting settles the issue and results in a binding obligation. The point of the process is to obtain a decision in order to get things done, things that urgently need to be done for the general benefit of all. No matter how clever or rhetorical are debaters, every voter, including those inevitably quiet or shy, has equal influence on the decision. As time passes, one can reflect on who was right and who was wrong in predicting the prudential and moral consequences of decisions. Beginning from a moralistic expectation that everyone should participate in all decisions, I slowly learned the liberal lesson that people have a plurality of aims in life: to raise their children, to build their homes, to follow their art, to enjoy spontaneity.

Thus, when I entered graduate study of political science in middle age I had far more experience and confidence than the typical student. If a swank formal model was contrary to my experience, I wasn't afraid to reject it. Game theory provided many great

---

[5] Gerry Mackie, "Success and Failure in an American Workers' Cooperative Movement," *Politics and Society* 22 (1994): 215-35.

insights into the puzzles of collective action I had encountered, and social choice theory many insights into the nature of various voting rules, but each was also empirically flawed. The rational choice literature rather credulously idealized the market, and its most popular version in political science mockingly and even bitterly intoned against the value of democracy. Here are some examples. All political communication, including public deliberation, is nothing but cheap talk, not credible because not backed by incentives to be truthful. Or: look at any actual democratic arena: people debate, but nobody changes their minds, hence discussion is an irrational waste of effort. The logical vagaries of voting rules, including the famous paradox of voting, are such that democratic outcomes are inevitably arbitrary and meaningless. Hence democracy should be minimized and the market maximized. And it's irrational to vote, we were told, and even more irrational to be knowledgeable about public issues. Although most citizens vote in the advanced democracies (the U.S. has unusually low turnout), the fact that they do was dubbed the paradox of nonvoting.

I too was tempted by these pessimistic results to turn to the study of democratic deliberation, and having had the good fortune to study with John Dryzek, Bernard Manin, and Jon Elster, each a pioneer of deliberative democracy, I planned a dissertation on the topic. Chapter two of the original outline was supposed to be a brief challenge to the mainstream view in political science that democratic voting is arbitrary and meaningless, but that chapter gradually expanded to 600 pages, and I renamed the project "A Preface to Deliberative Democracy." A revision was published as *Democracy Defended* (2003). I argued that problems of cycling, agenda control, strategic voting and multidimensional manipulation are not sufficiently harmful, frequent, or irremediable to be of normative concern. I also examined every serious empirical illustration of cycling and instability, and found that almost every empirical claim was erroneous, and none is normatively troubling. In another essay I argued against the influential idea that political communication is noncredible cheap talk.[6] I said that speakers are constrained by recurrent interaction about knowable information among multiple senders and multiple

---

[6] "All Men are Liars: Is Democracy Meaningless?" in *Deliberative Democracy*, ed. Jon Elster (Cambridge: Cambridge University Press, 1998).

receivers. I also examined the question of whether democratic deliberation changes minds.[7] We witness much persuasion, but apparently
little attitude change. I suggest that attitude change is real, but hard to
notice, because typically it is latent, indirect, delayed, and disguised.
Recently I have challenged the idea that it is irrational to vote,[8] and
irrational to be knowledgeable about public affairs.[9] I consider both
voting and discussion to be essential features of democracy.

Aggregation versus Deliberation

What is the distinction between aggregative and deliberative democracy? Is it that deliberation transforms preferences and aggregation does not? Is it that deliberation involves discussion (or no
voting) and aggregation involves voting (or no discussion)? Is it
that public deliberation allows the reciprocal exchange of reasons
acceptable to all?

Sometimes the contrast between the two conceptions of democracy is said to be that deliberation transforms preferences, but
that aggregation accepts them as fixed and unchanging: "Most
proponents of deliberative democracy emphasize that this model
conceptualizes the process of democratic discussion as not merely
expressing and registering, but as *transforming* the preferences, interests, beliefs, and judgments of participants."[10] The contrast is first
developed in Elster,[11] who does not mistake it as essential. The social
choice theory following from Arrow takes preferences as given and
fixed, but only as a modeling convenience, not as a fundamental.
One reason for this is that the question of preference formation
and revision can be left to other disciplines. Another reason is that

---

[7] Gerry Mackie, "Does Democratic Deliberation Change Minds?" *Philosophy, Politics
and Economics* 5, no. 3 (2006): 279-304.

[8] "Why It's Rational to Vote" (paper presented at the Victoria Colloquium in
Political, Social, and Legal Theory, University of Victoria, Victoria, BC, October
5, 2007).

[9] "Rational Ignorance and Beyond" (paper presented at "Collective Wisdom:
Principles and Mechanisms," College de France, May 22-23, 2008).

[10] Iris Young, *Inclusion and Democracy* (Oxford: Oxford University Press, 2000), 26.

[11] Jon Elster, "The Market and the Forum: Three Varieties of Political Theory," in
Foundations of Social Choice Theory, ed. Jon Elster and Aanund Hyland (Cambridge:
Cambridge University Press, 1986).

the standard choice model can't deal with more than one chang-ing parameter at a time. Change in a single belief is easily modeled. Suppose I have been led to believe that we should invade a coun-try because it possesses nuclear weapons: $Invade_{Nuke}$ > Not Invade. Through public deliberation I am persuaded that the country has no nukes, and my preference is: Not Invade > $Invade_{NoNuke}$. My overall preferences are consistent: $Invade_{Nuke}$ > Not Invade > $Invade_{NoNuke}$. Change in many individual desires and beliefs could be modeled these days with parallel-constraint-satisfaction networks of coher-ence, of which the standard model is, controversially, a special case ("preferences used in decision making are not fixed, as assumed by classical theories of rational choice, but rather are reconstructed in the course of decision making," say Simon, Krawczyk, and Holyoak about the constraint-satisfaction model of choice[12]).

Further, usually social choice results are true for any logically possible arrangement of individual preferences. Thus, in the ab-stract, the pathologies of democratic voting which Riker claims are shown by social choice theory would apply to public-spirited pref-erences as well as to narrowly selfish preferences, to postdelibera-tive preferences as well as to predeliberative preferences. There are no such pathologies when the vote is unanimous, and ideal delib-eration promises rationally agreed consensus (and practical delib-eration probably the reduction of disagreement). Deliberationists have hoped that reduction of disagreement would ease the alleged pathologies of voting.[13] Some might bite if voters were only self-interested, but, empirically, they are not; and I suggest that *predelibera-tive* preferences are probably sufficiently public-spirited to avoid the pathologies. And the electoral system of a polity can be designed to further discourage pursuit of partial interests over the general interest, without reference to deliberation, as we shall see. Moreover,

---

[12] Dan Simon, Daniel C. Krawczyk and Keith C. Holyoak, "Construction of Preferences by Constraint Satisfaction," *Psychological Science* 15, no. 5 (2004): 335. See also Paul Thagard, *Coherence in Thought and Action* (Cambridge: Bradford Books, 2000).

[13] For a further account of these possibilities, see John S. Dryzek and Christian List, "Social Choice Theory and Deliberative Democracy: A Reconciliation," *British Journal of Political Science* 33 (2003): 1-28. For empirical evidence of the same, see Cynthia Farrar et al., "Disaggregating Deliberation's Effects: An Experiment within a Deliberative Poll," *British Journal of Political Science*, forthcoming.

the transformation of preferences is not essential to deliberation: suppose that the citizens already have complete, transitive, well-informed preferences, oriented to the common good, and backed by reasons acceptable to all. Adding public deliberation would manifest those reasons, perhaps with process-benefits for the participants, but would not change individual preferences or the social outcome. Finally, no one claims that discussion necessarily reduces disagreement, only that it does so more often than not. Discussion *can* make for fairer and better decisions. According to Mendelberg's literature review, "If it is appropriately empathetic, egalitarian, open-minded, and reason-centered," then,

> Deliberation is expected to lead to empathy with the other and a broadened sense of people's own interests through an egalitarian, open-minded and reciprocal process of argumentation. Following from this result are other benefits: citizens are more enlightened about their own and others' needs and experiences, can better resolve deep conflict, are more engaged in politics, place their faith in the basic tenets of democracy, perceive their political system as legitimate, and lead a healthier civic life.[14]

Or,

> How does or might deliberation shape preferences, moderate self-interest, empower the marginalized, mediate difference, further integration and solidarity, enhance recognition, produce reasonable opinion and policy, and possibly lead to consensus?[15]

The problem is that theorists of deliberative democracy tend to define *deliberation* in a question-begging manner: discussion which tends to make for fairer and better decisions is deliberation, and discussion which tends not to is *not* deliberation:

---

[14] Tali Mendelberg, "The Deliberative Citizen: Theory and Evidence," in *Political Decision Making, Deliberation and Participation: Research in Micropolitics*, vol. 6, ed. Michael X. Delli Carpini, Leonie Huddy, and Robert Y. Shapiro (Greenwich: JAI Press, 2002), 154.

[15] Simone Chambers, "Deliberative Democratic Theory," *Annual Review of Political Science* 6 (2003): 309.

Deliberation is debate and discussion aimed at producing reasonable, well-informed opinions in which participants are willing to revise preferences in light of discussion, new information, and claims made by fellow participants.[16]

My impression is that discussion often ameliorates problems between people, but that sometimes it make things worse. Even the exchange of reasons acceptable to all could be dispiriting. The false consensus effect describes a propensity to assume that others are like us in their beliefs and desires. Speaking from experience, suppose that deep discussion among putative allies in a political coalition shatters illusions of solidarity by disclosing that the factions have mutually detestable reasons for their unity on political action.

Which institutional arrangements promote good discussion, which discourage bad discussion, and how? Other than common sense (which I don't dismiss), we can't say. There are many studies, and a batch of review articles summarizing the empirical research on collective deliberation. Those review articles are themselves summarized by Dennis Thompson, a leading theorist of deliberative democracy: "taken together the results are mixed or inconclusive."[17] It's fair to say that there is a crisis of empirical discontent among deliberative democrats.[18]

The beneficial transformation of preferences through public discussion is associated with, but is not identical to the central distinguishing feature of the deliberative conception: public discussion involving the reciprocal exchange of reasons that all can accept as democratic citizens.[19] This moral value is intrinsic to the deliberative

---

[16] Ibid.

[17] Dennis Thompson, "Deliberative Democratic Theory and Empirical Political Science," *Annual Review of Political Science* 11 (2008): 497-520.

[18] Jürgen Habermas, "Political Communication in Media Society," *Communication Theory* 16 (2006): 412-26. Diane C. Mutz, "Is Deliberative Democracy a Falsifiable Theory?" *Annual Review of Political Science* 11 (2008): 521-38. Michael Neblo, "Family Disputes: Diversity in Defining and Measuring Deliberation," *Swiss Political Science Journal* 13, no. 4 (2007): 527-57. Shawn W. Rosenberg, ed., *Can the People Govern? Deliberation, Participation, and Democracy* (Basingstoke: Palgrave Macmillan, 2007). Dennis Thompson, "Deliberative Democratic Theory and Empirical Political Science," *Annual Review of Political Science* 11 (2008): 497-520.

[19] Among others, Amy Gutmann and Dennis Thompson, *Democracy and Disagreement*

process, and its value is independent from any change for the better or worse in the correctness of collective decisions. In the ideal marketplace the consumer is sovereign. So long as there is free exchange and no negative externalities, the consumer is free to choose without having to justify her choices to the polity, according to the liberal view. But in political choice the voter is asked to express preferences over states of affairs that differ in the way they affect other people, and it is here that the economic theory of democracy's analogy of consumer to voter fundamentally fails.[20] We have a right to ask that such other-affecting preferences be justified. We should be given reasons for binding collective actions, and we should be able to offer reasons, and these reasons should be of the type acceptable to all.

For Freeman the distinction between the deliberative and the aggregative conception is not that one involves voting and the other does not, nor is it that one involves discussion and the other does not:

> The relevant distinction . . . concerns the object about which citizens deliberate and vote and the kinds of *reasons* that they take into account in coming to their collective decision. Whereas an aggregative view counsels voting one's informed preferences regarding one's own good or partial group interests . . . deliberative democracy counsels voting one's deliberated judgments (or informed preferences) for the common good.[21]

Freeman continues that such judgments are made for reasons that all can accept as democratic citizens, along the lines of Rawlsian public reason. Freeman, I believe, correctly recognizes the giving of reasons as distinctive of deliberation. Unlike a number of deliberative theorists, he also properly mentions voting in all of his descriptions and prescriptions concerning democracy. In the next section I'll argue that the object of voting is the common good. If so, that leaves the giving of reasons as the one distinctive feature of deliberation. Discussion, when it tends to the good, is deliberation. Thus,

---

(Cambridge: Harvard University Press, 1996).

[20] Jon Elster, "The Market and the Forum: Three Varieties of Political Theory," in *Foundations of Social Choice Theory*, ed. Jon Elster and Aanund Hyland (Cambridge: Cambridge University Press, 1986).

[21] Samuel Freeman, "Deliberative Democracy: A Sympathetic Comment," *Philosophy and Public Affairs* 29, no. 4 (2000): 337.

deliberation tends to the good. Voting, in comparison, is usually bad, certainly sans deliberation. Or is it?

Wrong Theory of Voting

Voting has the same relationship to deliberation in much deliberationist theory as sex has to love in the Victorian marriage: it is necessary, frequent, of profound result, but is suspect and mentioned only in fleeting allusion.

> Talk-centric democratic theory replaces voting-centric democratic theory. Voting-centric views see democracy as the arena in which fixed preferences and interests compete via fair mechanisms of aggregation. In contrast, deliberative democracy focuses on the communicative processes of opinion and will-formation that precede voting.[22]

> The essence of democracy itself is now widely taken to be deliberation, as opposed to voting, interest aggregation, constitutional rights, or even self-government.[23]

Deliberative theorists correctly reject the aggregative conception of *democracy*, but many mistakenly accept the aggregative conception of *voting* as merely the expression of untransformed self-interest. They rarely consider the possibility that voting, in its own right, could be morally noble and could tend to beneficial transformation of preferences. What is the aggregative conception of democracy?

> Voters pursue their individual interest by making demands on the political system. . . . From the interchange between self-interested voters and self-interested brokers emerge decisions that come as close as possible to a balanced aggregation of individual interests.[24]

---

[22] Chambers, 308.

[23] John S. Dryzek and Christian List, "Social Choice Theory and Deliberative Democracy: A Reconciliation," *British Journal of Political Science* 33 (2003): 1.

[24] Mansbridge, qtd. in Young, 19.

Individuals vote their private preferences and group interests . . .
in effect they act like economic agents removed to a different
forum. What point could there be in public discussion of their
self-seeking and competing group purposes with others who
have opposing interests?[25]

Voting is sometimes omitted altogether from deliberative definitions
of democracy:

Democracy, in my view, is best understood as a model for organizing the collective and public exercise of power in the major
institutions of a society on the basis of the principle that decisions affecting the well-being of a collectivity can be viewed as
the outcome of a procedure of free and reasoned deliberation
among individuals considered as moral and political equals.[26]

Deliberation oriented to the common good *replaces* voting oriented to one's selfish interest, or, in more careful formulations such
as Elster's or Freeman's, public deliberation *remedies* selfish voting.

Ideal voting, however, partakes of freedom, equality, and justice almost as much as does ideal discussion. In the ideal speech
situation, no one is excluded, anyone can introduce a question, no
one is prevented by internal or external coercion from exercising
their rights, there is equal respect, and an orientation to impartiality.[27] The very same could be said about the *ideal voting situation*.
Voting requires that all citizens should have the right to vote, and
urges that all should vote. The agenda is open, any one citizen
can introduce a question or stand for office. Citizens should enjoy all those basic rights necessary to their freedom and equality,
not just political rights; these basic rights should be specially protected against majoritarian errors, and this minimizes deception
and coercion of voters. Voting requires that each citizen should
have equal influence, one vote, whatever are the inequalities in the

---

[25] Freeman, 373.

[26] Seyla Benhabib, "Toward a Deliberative Model of Democratic Legitimacy,"
in Benhabib, ed., *Democracy and Difference: Contesting the Boundaries of the Political*
(Princeton: Princeton University Press, 1996): 68.

[27] Chambers, 238-9.

economic, social, or argumentation arenas. In voting, each citizen should render her judgment on the common good; and those judgments should be aggregated by procedures which are both fair in preserving equal influence, and accurate in combining judgments. A voter should be adequately informed and should adequately consider reasons for and against an alternative. The Condorcet Jury Theorem suggests that if the judgments of voters are independent and are on average better than random, then the aggregation of such judgments rapidly approaches correctness as the number of voters increases. Ideal voting perhaps falls short in obliging individual deliberation over alternatives but not public deliberation. But one could amend the account of ideal voting to oblige public deliberation for the sake of properly reasoned voting (deriving public deliberation from voting, rather than bringing in voting as an untheorized afterthought to nonexistent rational consensus).

Just as there is good discussion and bad discussion, so is there good voting and bad voting. Voting would be bad to the extent it did not conform to the ideal of voting. A voting rule could be fair but inaccurate, for example, add up equal votes (fair), but then do the opposite of what the majority wants (inaccurate). A voting rule could be more accurate, in that the social outcome is more responsive to the votes cast, but less fair, say, in allocating votes proportional to income. Voting would be bad if citizens vote their private interest rather than the public interest, or if citizens vote on the basis of negligently erroneous information, or if citizens are deceived or coerced. And when we praise voting we mean to praise voting in its ideal aspect, good voting, not bad voting.

The moral account of voting is nothing new. Something distantly resembling it can be found in Rousseau, who opposed public deliberation. Perhaps he intuited that voting itself has a transformative force: each citizen is to vote his opinion about the content of the general will, not his private will and his unfair advantage. Utilitarian, elitist, pluralist, and economic conceptions of democracy have submerged the moral account. The rational-choice model, in the hands of tough-minded men, finally drowned the moral illusion, or so it was believed. Whether or not desirable, the moral account was infeasible. The tough-minded view won by *assumption*, however, not by reason, not by evidence. There is a great deal of confusion about rational-choice theory, among both its proponents and opponents.

In its general form, it assumes that humans are purposive, possessing consistent desires and beliefs, and is a hermeneutic method as much as an explanatory one. It is a method I find useful in understanding politics. A special form of rational-choice theory assumes *additionally* that humans are exclusively motivated by material self-interest, and this form has explanatory (and, often, ideological) ambitions. In studying purely economic transactions, with no negative externalities, and no other-affecting preferences involved, it can be quite useful to assume that people want more rather than less money, although the assumption is not entirely accurate even in that realm. The material self-interest assumption fails in explanatory power the further we depart from the ideal market, however. Honor, for example, can't be bought.

Voting Morally Transforms Preferences

It was a mistake for political scientists to concoct a market model of voting and democracy, assuming individuals exclusively motivated by material self-interest. The vessel soon struck two puzzling shoals, foundered, and will never be resuscitated. The first puzzle arises from Arrow's Impossibility Theorem and associated social choice results. Those results predict that given a purely redistributive task, purely self-interested voters, and a pairwise voting rule, winning coalitions will never be larger than the barest majority, and will be hopelessly unstable as one after another coalition forms. Problem: in actual legislatures it is observed that redistributive tasks tend to be passed by universal and thereby stable coalitions. One way this could come about is if legislators, although primarily self-interested (rather, interested for their constituency), are secondarily interested directly in fairness.[28] The second puzzle is that rational *and self-interested* individuals would not bother to vote in mass elections, since the expected value of voting (the probability of being decisive times the benefit that would ensue) would never exceed the effort and opportunity costs of voting. Problem: in real democracies many people vote.

An economist would be "embarrassed to be seen at the voting booth."[29] It's extremely unlikely that any one vote would break a tie,

---

[28] Gerry Mackie, *Democracy Defended* (Cambridge: Cambridge University Press, 2003), 99-108.

and when a single vote does not break a tie it has nothing to do with the outcome. Since voting is costly, almost any single vote would be irrational. The paradox of nonvoting was first stated by Downs,[30] and is often formulated as follows. B is the individual's Benefit from a winning election outcome, C is the Cost of the individual voting, and p is the Probability that an individual's vote is pivotal in causing the winning election outcome. An individual would vote then, when $pB - C > 0$. The probability of being pivotal, however, is minuscule, effectively zero; for any individual, the act of voting is all cost and almost no benefit, and hence no one should vote.

Elsewhere, I develop a contributory theory of voting.[31] Its argument can be summarized with a simple example. Suppose, reasonably, that one likes playing basketball for the sake of winning, winning by the largest margin, and losing by the smallest margin. The paradox, however, insists that only winning counts, and thus it would be irrational to play on the team if one expected to lose or if to win by more than one point. Past responses to the paradox say: Who cares about the score? It's stupid to play, or one is paid to play, or it's one's duty to play. Or one expresses a desire for victory in play.

The paradox of nonvoting assumes that voters value only the winning of an election. Their utility function would look like the one in Figure 3.1.

From the diagram, it can be seen that unless one's additional vote pivotally causes the outcome, it is of no marginal value. It would be futile or redundant. If 39 voters out of 100 vote for a cause, a 40th vote for the cause changes nothing. If 51 out of 100 vote for a cause, a 52nd vote for the cause changes nothing. The claim that voting is irrational often confounds two logically independent claims: redundancy and imperceptibility.

It's likely that many voters value both winning, and how much their cause wins or loses by, the latter termed the mandate value of voting. Their utility functions would look like the one in Figure 3.2.

Each voter's contribution is pivotal to the mandate value. None is futile or redundant. If 39 out of 100 votes for a cause, a 40th ad-

---

[29] Stephen J. Dubner and Steven D. Levitt, "Why Vote?" *New York Times Magazine*, November 6, 2005.

[30] Antony Downs, *An Economic Theory of Democracy* (New York: Harper and Row, 1957), 244-6.

[31] Mackie (2008b).

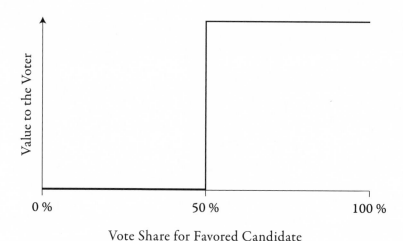

Vote Share for Favored Candidate

Figure 3.1: Voter values winning only

vances its mandate value. If 52 out of a 100 vote for a cause, a 53rd advances the mandate value. In a mass democratic election between two major parties, for example, a large mandate for the left party in the last election would in the present term of office shift their governing policies left and assumin no change among voters shift the policies of both parties left in the next election.[32]

Voters are mostly oriented to the public interest rather than to simple self-interest. In older studies, aggregate data showed that voters turned against incumbents when the economy was bad, apparently supporting the pocketbook model of voting. Kinder and Kiewiet (1981) were able to look at individual rather than aggregate data. Analysis of individual data showed little relationship between an individual's personal economic grievances, the pocketbook variable, and her assessment of the nation's economic health, the prosocial variable. Moreover, it showed that personal economic grievances had little or nothing to do with preferences for congressional or presidential candidates, but that assessment of national conditions is correlated with political preferences. Sears and Funk (1990) carried out some of their own studies and summarized the literature in an influential review. They say that in their work self-interest variables

---

[32] James H. Fowler and Oleg Smirnov, *Mandates, Parties, and Voters* (Philadelphia: Temple University Press, 2007).

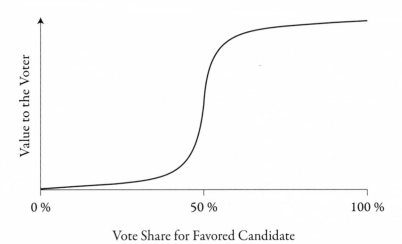

Vote Share for Favored Candidate

Figure 3.2: Voter value winning & mandate

account for on average four percent of variation in regressions, a minor explanatory contribution. See Citrin and Green (1990), and Lewin (1991) for similar summaries.

With respect to the prosocial voting identified by Kinder and Kiewiet, Funk and Garcia-Monet (1997) investigated through analysis of the American National Election Study the objection that self-interest could operate indirectly through perceptions of national economic conditions to influence political preferences. They find quite a modest contribution from an indirect effect, and that the total direct and indirect effect of self-interest is low. In further work, Funk (2000) finds a dual influence of self-interest and societal interest in public opinion. Chong, Citrin, and Conley (2001) find that prosocial priming weakens but does not eliminate self-interest when personal stakes are clear, and that people with low stakes in an issue respond strongly to prosocial priming. See also Brodsky and Thompson (1993) and Shabman and Stephenson (1994) for studies of one-issue local elections where it is shown that many citizens voted for a public good contrary to their objective material self-interest. From five observations about American voting behavior Jankowski (2002) infers that the best explanation is some altruism on the part of voters. In an analysis of the 1995 National Election Survey Pilot Study, Jankowski (2007) finds that agreement with a statement that these days people are not kind enough to others is significantly related to voter turnout. Fowler (2006) shows that people who care for others are more likely to vote. In addition, voters are most strongly motivated by duty and by desire to influence the social outcome.[33]

The American Citizen Participation Study, for example, asked an instructive series of questions about citizens' motivations to vote (see Table 1).

Table 1. Self-Reported Reasons to Vote

Reasons People Give Us for Voting	% Not Very Important	% Somewhat Important	% Very Important
Direct Instrumental			
Chance to Make Community or Nation a Better Place to Live	3	14	83
Chance to Influence Public Policy	10	26	65
Further Party Goals	35	30	35
Get Help from Official on Family Problem	79	14	8
Moral			
My Duty as a Citizen	4	18	78
Do My Share	14	41	45
Indirect Instrumental			
Recognition from People I Respect	71	18	11
Didn't Want to Say No to Someone Who Asked	88	9	3
Intrinsic			
Exciting to vote	63	23	14

Source: Compiled by author from American Citizen Participation Study (ICPSR Study No. 6635, 1990)

---

[33] See Gerry Mackie "Why It's Rational to Vote." (paper presented at the Victoria Colloquium in Political, Social, and Legal Theory, University of Victoria, Victoria, BC, October 5, 2008) and references therein.

Prosocial motivation dominates: half the respondents said at least one particular problem motivated them to vote, and for 9% of them myself, family, or others were affected by the problem, for 46% all the community was affected, and for 45% all the nation was affected. Most intend to influence the outcome: 97% say the chance to make the community or nation a better place to live is somewhat or very important, 91% say the chance to influence public policy is somewhat or very important, 65% say that furtherance of party goals is somewhat or very important, 22% say that getting help from an official on a family problem is somewhat or very important. Most are morally motivated to vote: 96% say that my duty as a citizen is somewhat or very important, 86% that to do my share is somewhat or very important.

Given that so many voters name both influence and duty, someone who says that she has a duty to vote likely means that she has the consequentialist duty to advance the public good, that is, she is instrumentally motivated. Side payments for voting are not very important: 71% say so about obtaining recognition from people I respect, 88% about not wanting to say no to someone who asked. Finally, few vote because they find it exciting to do so.

These responses are consistent with the contributory theory. Label the number of citizens N, the number of voters for one of the causes n, a voters' contribution to that cause roughly $1/n$, and her discounting of benefit to any other individual $æ$ $(0 < æ < 1)$, and a citizen will vote when $1/n\ (B_{self} + æNB_{society}) - C > 0$.[34] The term for benefit to self, B_{self}, is small compared to the term for benefit to society, $B_{society}$, and, when each is multiplied by $1/n$ contribution, benefit to self usually goes to almost nothing, leaving benefit to society as the principal motivation for voting. If so, then, just as deliberation may operate as a filter to exclude unjustifiable preferences, voting may operate as a filter to exclude self interest and include public interest as input to collective decisions.

---

[34] Adapted from Aaron Edlin, Andrew Gelman, and Noah Kaplan, "Voting as a Rational Choice: The Effect of Preferences Regarding the Well-Being of Others," *Rationality and Society* 19 (2007): 293-309.

Voting Structures Discussion

Although it is possible to imagine talk without voting, the tendency of the deliberationists, and it is possible to imagine voting without talk, the tendency of the aggregationists, the two in combination are greater than the sum of the parts, and *together* are essential to democracy. Deliberative theory develops well the advantages of talk leading up to voting. Deliberation has the moral advantage of offering reasons for and against alternatives, reasons acceptable to all, and this is its greatest contribution. Maybe it also tends to orient preferences towards the common good, and to yield other good benefits. Might voting, though, improve deliberation? Most assuredly. That every citizen has the right to an equal vote means that generally arguments must appeal to all citizens, or to a majority of citizens on a specific issue. The act of voting tends to screen out private preferences and screen in public preferences. A common objection to deliberation in practice is that it would privilege those most skilled in argument, and those most skilled in argument could be rich, white, male and use their skill to defend unfair advantages. Whether advantaged or disadvantaged in this world, many of us have experienced some bullying sophist, whose arguments we momentarily cannot answer, but whom we know nevertheless to be wrong. Voting levels the deliberative playing field. Not only must the deliberator address the whole audience, each individual voter reserves her own judgment, not alienating it to any expert. Ideally, the democratic association benefits from the information and argument of contesting experts but preserves its individual and collective judgments. Speakers do not each have the same weight in the judgments of the listeners, and this is as it should be. The individuals who would be bound by decision vote for the alternative each sees as supported by the best arguments, and each has an equal vote, and this is as it should be.

Thompson tells us that the defining elements of deliberation are a state of disagreement, a collective decision, and the legitimacy of the decision.[35] Disagreement about what to do and the need for jointly binding decision on actions compose the circumstances of deliberative democracy, he says. I say, however, that deliberation is *not* a method of collective decision. Discussion, helpful or harmful,

---

[35] Dennis Thompson, "Deliberative Democratic Theory and Empirical Political Science," *Annual Review of Political Science* 11 (2008): 497-520.

is often not even associated with decision. By prior convention, voting is the usual method of decision in a democracy. And voting is at least as important as discussion in bringing about the right process and outcome. In the most highly idealized deliberative process the decision is agreed to by all, and it is the unanimity voting rule, not discussion itself, that motivates each deliberator to address herself to the concerns of all. In the absence of the unanimity constraint, the deliberator would have little motivation to get beyond her own point of view. Ideal consensus is a situation of the highest abstraction where there is no social and political status quo. In any world like ours, with a status quo, majority rule is the best approximation of unanimity rule.[36] Otherwise the consensus requirement would allow any one person to veto change from an unjustified status quo. In a world with a status quo, and ongoing majority rule over a series of provisional decisions, again it is the voting rule that properly motivates the deliberators.

The legitimacy of the decision, says Thompson, requires mutual justification, a process characterized by public-spiritedness, equal respect, accommodation, and equal participation.[37] Again, I say that ideal voting is characterized by the same features. Voting is public-spirited, and the egoistic have no incentive to vote. It expresses equal respect in that all have the right to vote. It is accommodating in that the winner on one issue can be the loser on the next. It allows for equal participation: almost all are capable of casting a vote, but not many can offer explicit justifications. The point though is not to stage a contest between discussion and voting, but to stress the neglect in the literature of their essential connection.

Papua New Guinea (PNG) is a liberal democracy. Due to its geography it contains several thousand separate and competing clans, and is the most ethnically fragmented country on earth. Electoral violence is not rare, and communal violence is a problem. Deliberative democracy, as it stands today, would likely recommend to PNG involving more people in more public discussion about more public issues. If Reilly's analysis is correct,[38] a change in voting rule would

---

[36] Gerry Mackie, "Astroturfing Infotopia," *Theoria*, forthcoming.

[37] Thompson, 504.

[38] Benjamin Reilly, *Democracy in Divided Societies: Electoral Engineering for Conflict Management* (Cambridge: Cambridge University Press, 2001).

probably reduce violence, and, I add, would beneficially restructure public discussion in PNG. PNG now uses plurality rule: voters cast one vote, and the candidate with the most votes wins, even if he does not attain a majority. In the U.S. and the U.K. plurality rule induces a reduction in the number of candidates and parties because voters tend not to vote for their most-favored candidate but for one of the front-running candidates with a chance of winning. This is not observed in PNG, where voters cast a single vote for their own ethnic candidate. As a result, half the members of parliament are elected with less than 30% of the vote. By 1997, the average number of candidates per electorate was 22. One candidate won with as little as 6.3% of the vote. Such narrowly elected candidates respond to the demands of the narrow base that elects them, exacerbating electoral violence and communal violence.

Before independence, PNG used the alternative vote, the voting rule of its colonial power, Australia. Under the alternative vote, the voter rank-orders all the candidates, or the first few anyway. In those circumstances voters would cast their first preference for their local coethnic, but the voting rule elicited cross-group candidates who solicited second and third preferences from voters in many groups. The way the alternative vote works, candidates with fewer first-preferences tend to be eliminated, and candidates winning more second and third preferences across several groups tend to be selected. The discourse of the cross-group candidates was more oriented to the general interest. And the discourse, and decisions, of a parliament of such officials is likely to differ systematically from the discourse and decisions of officials elected by plurality rule. Electoral and parliamentary discourse in turn influences the remainder of political discourse in the country (the horse-race nature of American election coverage has a lot to do with candidate incentives under the plurality rule: vote for me because I'm one of the front-runners). Changing the voting rule from plurality to the alternative vote would probably improve public deliberation in PNG more than would any directly deliberative remedy. Similarly, the media system in a country—its ownership structure, its regulatory constraints, its technology, its professional norms—probably has more to do with the quality of public deliberation than, say, experiments in municipal participation. In the United States, easing labor union organization, and thereby creating a countervailing power to business interests in the public sphere, could do more for deliberation and the justice of outcomes than would a large number of deliberative opinion polls.

Bächtiger et al. are among the few to study deliberation across different political institutions.[39] They construct a discourse quality index (analogous to early comparative regime research which for simplicity relied on a procedural definition of democracy) with four elements: participation, justification, respect, and constructive politics. They found that discourse quality is higher in consensus systems than in competitive systems, in presidential competitive systems than in parliamentary competitive, in nonpublic meetings than in public meetings, and on topics of elite agreement rather than disagreement. Each of these institutions has its advantages and disadvantages, aside from its effect on discourse quality. We would want to weigh all those considerations in choosing among institutions. It is worrisome that each of the discourse-improving institutions is also one that reduces accountability of representatives to the citizenry (it's harder to know who to blame in a consensus coalition, in a presidential regime, and in a system of closed meetings, and the political elite can collude against the population). Bächtiger et al. also find no relationship between discourse quality and the justice of outcomes.[40]

Conclusion

Dryzek writes that, "Deliberative democracy now constitutes the most active area of political theory in its entirety (not just democratic theory)."[41] The debut of a research community devoted to the empirical investigation of democratic discussion is welcome. It will be decades before discussion receives as much empirical attention as voting has in political science. Political science treatments of voting are often conceptually confused, and sometimes are ideologically hostile to democratic governance. Voting, oddly

---

[39] André Bächtiger et al. "Deliberation in Legislatures: Antecedents and Outcomes," in *Can the People Govern? Deliberation, Participation, and Democracy*, ed. Shawn W. Rosenberg (Basingstoke: Palgrave Macmillan, 2007).

[40] Ibid.

[41] John Dryzek, "Theory, Evidence, and the Tasks of Deliberation," in *Can the People Govern? Deliberation, Participation, and Democracy*, ed. Shawn W. Rosenberg (Basingstoke: Palgrave Macmillan, 2007), 237.

enough, is one of the least active areas in political theory, and I propose to remedy that neglect.

ACKNOWLEDGMENTS

I thank Nuffield College for hospitality when some of these thoughts were first worked out; and Professor Robert Cavalier, CAEEPP, and Social and Decision Sciences, at Carnegie-Mellon University, for the opportunity to present in its Humanities Lecture Series, 20 February 2007.

BIBLIOGRAPHY

Bächtiger, André, Markus Spörndli, Marco R. Steinberger, and Jürg Steiner. "Deliberation in Legislatures: Antecedents and Outcomes." In *Can the People Govern? Deliberation, Participation, and Democracy*, edited by Shawn W. Rosenberg. Basingstoke: Palgrave Macmillan, 2007.

Benhabib, Seyla. "Toward a Deliberative Model of Democratic Legitimacy," in *Democracy and Difference: Contesting the Boundaries of the Political*, edited by Seyla Benhabib. Princeton: Princeton University Press, 1996.

Brodsky, David M., and Edward Thompson III. "Ethos, Public Choice, and Referendum Voting." *Social Science Quarterly* 74 (1993): 286-99.

Chambers, Simone. *Reasonable Democracy: Jürgen Habermas and the Politics of Discourse*. Ithaca: Cornell University Press, 1996.

——. "Deliberative Democratic Theory." *Annual Review of Political Science* 6 (2003): 307-26.

Chong, Dennis, Jack Citrin, and Patricia Conley. "When Self-Interest Matters." *Political Psychology* 22 (2001): 541-70.

Citrin, Jack, and Donald Green. "The Self-Interest Motive in American Public Opinion." *Research in Micropolitics* 3 (1990): 1-28.

Cohen, Joshua. "An Epistemic Conception of Democracy." *Ethics* 97, no. 1 (1996): 26-38.

——. "Reflections on Habermas on Democracy." *Ratio Juris* 12, no. 4 (1999): 385-416.

——. "For a Democratic Society." In *The Cambridge Companion to Rawls*, edited by Samuel Freedman, 86-138. Cambridge: Cambridge University Press, 2002.

Dahl, Robert A. *How Democratic is the American Constitution?* New Haven: Yale University Press, 2002.

Downs, Antony. *An Economic Theory of Democracy*. New York: Harper and Row, 1957.

Dryzek, John S., and Christian List. "Social Choice Theory and Deliberative Democracy: A Reconciliation." *British Journal of Political Science* 33 (2003): 1-28.

Dryzek, John S., and Christian List. "Theory, Evidence, and the Tasks of Deliberation." In *Can the People Govern? Deliberation, Participation, and Democracy*, edited by Shawn W. Rosenberg. Basingstoke: Palgrave Macmillan, 2007.

Dubner, Stephen J. and Steven D. Levitt. "Why Vote?" *The New York Times Magazine*, November 6, 2005.

Edlin, Aaron, Andrew Gelman, and Noah Kaplan. "Voting as a Rational Choice: The Effect of Preferences Regarding the Well-Being of Others." *Rationality and Society* 19 (2007): 293-309.

Elster, Jon. "The Market and the Forum: Three Varieties of Political Theory." In *Foundations of Social Choice Theory*, edited by Jon Elster and Aanund Hyland. Cambridge: Cambridge University Press, 1986.

Farrar, Cynthia, James S. Fishkin, Donald P. Green, Christian List, Robert P. Luskin, and Elizabeth Levy Paluck. "Disaggregating Deliberation's Effects: An Experiment within a Deliberative Poll." *British Journal of Political Science*. Forthcoming.

Fowler, James H. "Altruism and Turnout." *The Journal of Politics* 68 (2006): 674-83.

— and Oleg Smirnov. *Mandates, Parties, and Voters*. Philadelphia: Temple University Press, 2007.

Freeman, Samuel. "Deliberative Democracy: A Sympathetic Comment." *Philosophy and Public Affairs* 29, no. 4 (2000): 371-418.

Funk, Carolyn L. "The Dual Interest of Self-Interest and Societal Interest in Public Opinion." *Political Research Quarterly* 53 (2000): 37-62.

— and Patricia A. Garcia-Monet. "The Relationship Between Personal and National Concerns in Public Perceptions About the Economy." *Political Research Quarterly* 50 (1997): 317-42.

Gutmann, Amy and Dennis Thompson. *Democracy and Disagreement*. Cambridge: Harvard University Press, 1996.

Habermas, Jürgen. *Theory of Communicative Action*. 2 vols. Boston: Beacon Press, 1987. Original work published 1984.

—. "Political Communication in Media Society." *Communication Theory* 16 (2006): 412-26.

Jankowski, Richard. "Buying a Lottery Ticket to Help the Poor." *Rationality and Society* 14 (2002): 55-77.

—. "Altruism and the Decision to Vote." *Rationality and Society* 19 (2007): 5-34.

Kinder, Donald M., and Roderick Kiewiet. "Sociotropic Politics: The American Case." *British Journal of Political Science* 11 (1981): 129-61.

Levinson, Sanford. *Our Undemocratic Constitution.* Oxford: Oxford University Press, 2006.

Mackie, Gerry. "Success and Failure in an American Workers' Cooperative Movement." *Politics and Society* 22 (1994): 215-35.

—. "All Men are Liars: Is Democracy Meaningless?" In *Deliberative Democracy*, edited by Jon Elster. Cambridge: Cambridge University Press, 1998.

—. *Democracy Defended.* Cambridge: Cambridge University Press, 2003.

—. "Does Democratic Deliberation Change Minds?" *Philosophy, Politics and Economics* 5, no. 3 (2006): 279-304.

—. "Rational Ignorance and Beyond." Paper presented at "Collective Wisdom: Principles and Mechanisms," College de France, May 22-23, 2008a.

—. "Why It's Rational to Vote." Paper presented at the Victoria Colloquium in Political, Social, and Legal Theory, University of Victoria, Victoria, BC, October 5, 2008b.

—. "Astroturfing Infotopia." *Theoria.* Forthcoming.

Mansbridge, Jane. *Beyond Adversary Democracy.* New York: Basic Books, 1980.

Mendelberg, Tali. "The Deliberative Citizen: Theory and Evidence." In *Political Decision Making, Deliberation and Participation: Research in Micropolitics*, vol. 6, edited by Michael X. Delli Carpini, Leonie Huddy, and Robert Y. Shapiro. Greenwich: JAI Press, 2002.

Mutz, Diane C. "Is Deliberative Democracy a Falsifiable Theory?" *Annual Review of Political Science* 11 (2008): 521-38.

Neblo, Michael. "Family Disputes: Diversity in Defining and Measuring Deliberation." *Swiss Political Science Journal* 13, no. 4 (2007): 527-57.

Pateman, Carole. *Participation and Democratic Theory.* Cambridge: Cambridge University Press, 1970.

Rawls, John. *A Theory of Justice.* Cambridge: Harvard University Press, 1971.

—. *Law of Peoples.* Cambridge: Harvard University Press, 1999.

Reilly, Benjamin. *Democracy in Divided Societies: Electoral Engineering for Conflict Management.* Cambridge: Cambridge University Press, 2001.

Riker, William. *Liberalism Against Populism: A Confrontation Between the Theory of Democracy and the Theory of Social Choice.* Prospect Heights: Waveland Press, 1982.

Rosenberg, Shawn W., editor. *Can the People Govern? Deliberation, Participation, and Democracy*. Basingstoke: Palgrave Macmillan, 2007.

Sears, David O. and Carolyn L. Funk. "The Limited Effect of Self-Interest on the Political Attitudes of the Mass Public." *The Journal of Behavioral Economics* 19 (1990): 247-71.

Shabman, Leonard, and Kurt Stephenson. "A Critique of the Self-Interested Voter Model: The Case of a Local Single Issue Referendum." *Journal of Economic Issues* 4 (1994): 1173-86.

Simon, Dan, Daniel C. Krawczyk, and Keith C. Holyoak. "Construction of Preferences by Constraint Satisfaction." *Psychological Science* 15, no. 5 (2004): 331.

Thagard, Paul. *Coherence in Thought and Action*. Cambridge: Bradford Books, 2000.

Thompson, Dennis. "Deliberative Democratic Theory and Empirical Political Science." *Annual Review of Political Science* 11 (2008): 497-520.

Warren, Mark and Hilary Pearse, editors. *Designing Deliberative Democracy: The British Columbia Citizen's Assembly*. Cambridge: Cambridge University Press, 2008.

Young, Iris M. *Inclusion and Democracy*. Oxford: Oxford University Press, 2000.

CHAPTER 4

Learning Democratic Communication through "Deliberative Polling"

Christian List and Anne Sliwka[1]
Translated by Klaus Jürgen List

Introduction

One fundamental thesis within the rapidly-growing literature on deliberative democracy is that the stability and quality of a democracy depend not only on formal institutions such as the electoral system or the structure of parliamentary representation. They depend also on certain democratic competences of the citizens, especially their capacity for democratic communication. According to this thesis, above all the capacity for democratic deliberation, i.e., for argumentation, evaluation and for a balanced decision between policy alternatives, belongs to the central competences relevant to maintaining and developing a democracy.[2]

From this point of view, even the breakdown of a democracy cannot be reduced to the failure of democratic institutions alone but

---

[1] Christian List, London School of Economics, Department of Government, London WC2A 2AE, UK. Anna Sliwka, Universität Trier, Abteilung Bildungswissenschaften; 54296 Trier, Germany. This paper was originally published in German under the title "'Deliberative Polling' als Methode zum Erlernen des demokratischen Sprechens," *Zeitschrift für Politik* 51, no. 1 (2003): 87-105.

[2] On the theory of deliberative democracy, see among many others: John Bohman and William Rehg, eds., *Deliberative Democracy: Essays on Reason and Politics* (Cambridge: MIT Press, 1977); Joshua Cohen, "Deliberation and Democratic Legitimacy," in *The Good Polity: Normative Analysis of the State*, ed. Alan Hamlin and Philip Pettit (Oxford: Basil Blackwell, 1989), 17-34; J.S. Dryzek, *Discursive Democracy: Politics, Policy and Political Science* (New York: Cambridge University Press, 1990); John S. Dryzek, *Deliberative Democracy and Beyond* (Oxford: Oxford University Press, 2000); Jon Elster, introduction to *Deliberative Democracy*, ed. Jon Elster (New York: Cambridge University Press, 1998), 1-18; Amy Gutmann and Dennis Thompson, *Democracy and Disagreement* (Cambridge: Harvard University Press, 1996); Michael Becker, "Politik als Verständigungsprozess—Modelle deliberativer Demokratie," *Zeitschrift für Politik* 47, no. 2 (2000).

may also result from the absence of the right kinds of democratic attitudes or democratic habits of communication among the citizens. Thus it is sometimes said that the collapsing Weimar Republic of the 1920s and 1930s was a "democracy without democrats."

If one holds this fundamental thesis and considers the promotion of democratic competences to be normatively desirable, one has to ask the empirical and pragmatic question as to which means would best promote these competences in society. This question is at the centre of the debate on civic education: What part can and should educational contexts, such as schools and universities, play in the promotion of democratic competences?

In this paper, we suggest that the method of Deliberative Polling as developed by James Fishkin and his colleagues can be successfully applied to promote democratic competences in educational contexts.[3] We report on a project modeled on Deliberative Polling that we carried out within an educational context, a so-called "Schülerakademie," or students' academy, in Germany, as described below, and we discuss its results from the perspective of various theoretical criteria. It turns out that Deliberative Polling—apart from its qualitative importance in the learning of democratic communication—may have positive effects on two important quantitative criteria: first, on the state of informedness of the participants and second, on the collective cohesion of their preferences. Both criteria will be discussed in more detail below.

The paper is structured as follows. In section 2, we briefly discuss the theoretical background, namely the controversy between so-called aggregative and deliberative models of democracy. In section 3, we outline several existing proposals on how democratic communication can be taught in educational contexts. In section 4, we explain the method of Deliberative Polling. In section 5, we report on our own deliberation project and evaluate its results. In section 6, we draw some conclusions.

---

[3] For introductory overviews, see James S. Fishkin, *Democracy and Deliberation* (New Haven and London: Yale University Press, 1991); Fishkin, *The Voice of the People* (New Haven and London: Yale University Press, 1995). As noted above, "Deliberative Polling" and "Deliberative Poll" have been registered as trademarks by James Fishkin and his colleagues.

Aggregative and Deliberative Models of Democracy

The contemporary debate in the theory of democracy is character-ized by the prominence of two diametrically opposed models of democracy: *aggregative democracy* and *deliberative democracy*.

According to the *aggregative model*, democratic decision-making consists primarily in the aggregation of conflicting individual pref-erences, particularly through voting. Democracy is conceived of as an "input-output system": Certain individual inputs, such as indi-vidual preferences or votes, are aggregated into resulting collective outputs, such as collective preferences or decisions. Crucially, the individual inputs are taken to be exogenously given and fixed; they do not change in the process. On this model, the central democratic institution is the electoral system or method of aggregation used. The method of aggregation can be described as a mechanism trans-forming any given combination of individual preference orderings on the relevant political alternatives into a single collective prefer-ence ordering on them.[4] From the perspective of the aggregative model of democracy, the quality of a democracy depends, to a great extent, on the quality of its aggregation method.

The deliberative model, by contrast, does not focus on the me-chanical aggregation of individual preferences into collective ones but on the importance of deliberating about these preferences. Accordingly, democracy is seen as a communicative system, as the entirety of those social processes (involved in the formation of opinions as well as in the development of strategies of learning and acting) which lead to collective decisions. Thus, the quality of a de-mocracy depends on the quality of those processes, and not only on the quality of the underlying formal institutions.

The Problem of Aggregation: Condorcet's Paradox and Arrow's Impos-sibility Theorem

Condorcet's Paradox is a classic 18th-century result from the theory of social choice showing that the aggregation of pluralistic individu-

---

[4] In the mathematical model, the individuals are represented by the numbers 1, 2, .. ., *n*. Each individual, *i*, holds a preference ordering, P_i, on a set of alternatives, *x, y, z, . . .* An *aggregation method* is a function, *F*, which assigns to each vector of individual preference orderings, $<P_1, P_2, . . ., P_n>$ (consisting of one preference ordering for each individual), a single collective preference ordering, *P*.

al preferences into collective decisions is a non-trivial problem.[5] The Paradox demonstrates that majority voting, arguably the most familiar and established method of aggregation, may lead to inconsistent collective preferences. Consider a situation in which three individuals (voters 1, 2, 3) have to make a collective decision on three alternatives (candidates x, y, z). The individuals (voters) have the following preferences (the symbol ">" means "is preferred to"):

Individual 1: $x > y > z$
Individual 2: $y > z > x$
Individual 3: $z > x > y$

The collective preference is now to be determined by majority comparisons between pairs of alternatives: a majority of two out of three (consisting of individuals 1 and 3) prefers x to y, another majority of two out of three (consisting of individuals 1 and 2) prefers y to z, and a third majority of two out of three (consisting of individuals 2 and 3) prefers z to x. The collective preference is therefore $x > y > z > x$, a "cyclical" and thus inconsistent preference relation. In particular, there does not exist a *Condorcet Winner*. A *Condorcet Winner* is defined as an alternative which is preferred to any other alternative by a majority (or at least one half) of the individuals. The Condorcet Winner criterion is seen, by many democratic theorists, as a plausible formalization of the criterion of the "general will."[6]

Is Condorcet's Paradox just the result of an artificial thought experiment or is it an indicator of a more fundamental problem which may arise in the aggregation of diverse individual preferences? The Paradox itself shows only that one particular, plausible method of aggregation—namely pairwise majority voting—may lead to inconsistent collective preferences. It does not say anything about whether this problem could be solved by means of a different, equally plausible method of aggregation. Arrow's Impossibility Theorem addresses this further question.[7] If we introduce five seemingly compelling minimal conditions which an aggregation method should fulfill,

---

[5] See Iain McLean and Fiona Hewitt, eds., *Condorcet: Foundations of Social Choice and Political Theory* (Cheltenham: Edward Elgar, 1994).

[6] See, e.g., David M. Estlund et al., "Democratic Theory and the Public Interest: Condorcet and Rousseau Revisited," *American Political Science Review* 83 (1989): 1317-40.

[7] See Kenneth W. Arrow, *Social Choice and Individual Values* (New York: Wiley, 1951).

Arrow's Theorem shows that there does not exist any aggregation method which fulfils those conditions simultaneously. The conditions to be fulfilled are the following:

Unrestricted domain (U): Every logically possible combination of individual preference orderings on the relevant political alternatives is admissible as an input to the aggregation.

Transitivity (T): The collective preference relation generated by the aggregation method constitutes a consistent ordering. In particular, if x is collectively preferred to y and y is collectively preferred to z, then x is also collectively preferred to z.

The weak Pareto principle (P): If *all* individuals prefer x to y, then x is also collectively preferred to y.

Non-dictatorship (D): There exists no antecedently fixed individual (a "dictator") whose individual preference always determines the collective one, in the sense that whenever this individual prefers x to y, then x is also collectively preferred to y.

Independence of irrelevant alternatives (IIA): The collective preference between any two alternatives x and y depends only on individual preferences between x and y, not on individual preferences involving other alternatives.

These conditions are taken to be *minimal*, in so far as one would ideally expect an aggregation method to satisfy further, more demanding conditions.[8]

Theorem (*Arrow's Impossibility Theorem*): There exists no aggregation method which simultaneously satisfies conditions (U), (T), (P), (D) and (IIA).

---

[8] Examples of such conditions include *anonymity (A)*, which requires (informally speaking) that all individuals have equal weight in the aggregation, as well as *the strong Pareto principle (StP)*, which requires that x be collectively preferred to y if *no* individual prefers y to x and *at least one* individual prefers x to y. These conditions are logically more demanding than Arrow's conditions in the following sense: condition (A) implies condition (D), but not the other way round; and condition (StP) implies condition (P), but not *vice versa*.

Arrow's theorem implies that any method of aggregation must necessarily violate at least one of Arrow's conditions. A lot could be said about which of these conditions may need to be given up, but this is not the topic of the present paper.

Deliberation and Consensus

The solvability of aggregation problems depends, above all, on how different the preferences across different individuals are. It is obvious that, in the case of complete unanimity among all individuals' preferences, the aggregation of these preferences does not present any difficulties.

One hypothesis supported by early advocates of the deliberative model of democracy is that an appropriate phase of deliberation prior to making a decision may change individual preferences to such an extent that a complete consensus (i.e., unanimity of preferences) is achieved. If this is the case, Condorcet's Paradox will be avoided and Arrow's aggregation problem will be bypassed.

Jon Elster, for example, summarizes this hypothesis as follows: "The core of the theory (of deliberative democracy) [. . .] is that rather than aggregating or filtering preferences, the political system should be set up with a view to changing them by public debate and confrontation. The input to the social choice mechanism would then not be the raw, quite possibly selfish or irrational preferences [. . .], but informed and other-regarding preferences. Or rather, there would not be any need for an aggregation mechanism, since a rational discussion would tend to produce unanimous preferences."[9]

Independently of whether a complete consensus is desirable or not, however, there is no empirical evidence that, under normal circumstances, deliberation can reliably bring about such a consensus. Accordingly, the hypothesis that deliberation could solve the problem of democratic aggregation by producing a complete consensus seems empirically and pragmatically questionable.

Deliberation and Meta-consensus

A less demanding but nevertheless interesting hypothesis says that, under normal circumstances, deliberation cannot bring about

---

[9] See Jon Elster, "The Market and the Forum," in *Foundations of Social Choice Theory*, ed. Jon Elster and Aanund Hylland (Cambridge: Cambridge University Press, 1986), 103-32.

a complete consensus but a meta-consensus.[10] A *meta-consensus*, as understood for the present purposes, requires that the individuals agree upon the ideological dimension underlying the given decision problem and that the individual preferences of all the individuals can be systematically arranged on the same right-left axis. This does not require a complete consensus in the form of unanimity of preferences. To give an example from politics, a meta-consensus could consist in the fact that all individuals agree on the ideological left-right alignment of the political parties (in Germany, for instance, in the order PDS, Green Party, SPD, FDP, CDU, CSU) without reaching an agreement as to which party is to be preferred most. The individuals agree on the *structuring* of the decision problem but not necessarily on the preferred *solution*.

A combination (in the mathematical model, a vector) of individual preference orderings is called *single-peaked*, if (roughly speaking) there exists at least one left-right alignment of the alternatives (candidates) so that each individual (voter) has a most preferred position on that left-right axis and prefers alternatives (candidates) the less, the further they are away from his or her most preferred position on the axis.

Figure 4.1 shows an example of two preference orderings which are single-peaked with regard to the same left-right axis (i.e., the axis x-z-v-y-w). If the preference orderings of all the individuals fulfill the criterion of single-peakedness with respect to the same left-right alignment of alternatives (candidates), this can be an observable implication of a meta-consensus.[11] The importance of the notion of single-peakedness—and more generally, of the idea of a meta-consensus—lies in the fact that single-peakedness is sufficient for avoiding Condorcet's paradox and thereby circumventing the problem posed by Arrow's Impossibility Theorem.[12]

---

[10] Different versions of this hypothesis can be found in David Miller, "Deliberation and Social Choice," *Political Studies* (special issue) 40 (1991): 54-67; Jack Knight and James Johnson, "Aggregation and Deliberation: On the Possibility of Democratic Legitimacy," *Political Theory* 22 (1994): 277-96; Christian List, "Two Concepts of Agreement," *The Good Society* 11 (2002): 72-9; and John S. Dryzek and Christian List, "Social Choice Theory and Deliberative Democracy: A Reconciliation," *British Journal of Political Science* 33 (2003): 1-28. The idea of "meta-consensus" was made explicit in this particular literature in Christian List, "Two Concepts of Agreement" *The Good Society* 11, no 1 (2002), 72-79.

[11] See List, "Two Concepts of Agreement," as cited above.

[12] For simplicity (to avoid the possibility of harmless majority ties), we can assume in the mathematical model that the number of individuals, n, is odd.

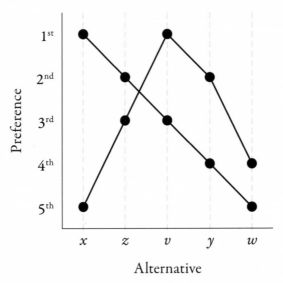

Figure 4.1: Single-peaked preferences, same left-right axis

Theorem (*Black's median voter theorem*): If all individuals' preference orderings are single-peaked with respect to the same left-right alignment of the alternatives, then there exists a Condorcet winner (as defined above), namely the most preferred alternative of the median individual relative to the given left-right alignment.[13]

In particular, as a corollary, one can show that, if we replace Arrow's condition of *unrestricted domain (U)* by the weaker condition of *single-peaked domain (SP)*, then we get a *possibility result* in contrast to Arrow's original *impossibility result*:

Single-peaked domain (SP): Every combination of individual preference orderings which are single-peaked with respect to the same left-right alignment of the alternatives is admissible as input to the aggregation.

Theorem (*Possibility Result of Black and Arrow*): There exists an

---

[13] See Duncan Black, "On the Rationale of Group Decision-Making," *Journal of Political Economy* 56 (1948): 23-34.

aggregation method which simultaneously satisfies conditions (SP), (T), (P), (D) and (IIA), namely pairwise majority voting.[14]

Over and above the possibility result of Black and Arrow, one can show that even a high degree of *partial* single-peakedness is likely to ensure the avoidance of aggregation paradoxes.[15] We have a situation of *partial* single-peakedness (sometimes also called *proximity to single-peakedness*), if the preference orderings of a *subset* of the individuals, but not necessarily of all of them, satisfy the criterion of single-peakedness with respect to the same left-right alignment of the alternatives.

In our discussion of Deliberative Polling below, we look at the question of whether there is any empirical support for the hypothesis that deliberation can bring about a meta-consensus. The present theoretical considerations already give us some initial reasons to think that deliberative processes might be of relevance for the solution of aggregation problems. However, the key to a deliberative solution to aggregation problems is likely to lie not in a deliberation-induced consensus, as hypothesized by early proponents of deliberative democracy, but in a deliberation-induced meta-consensus.

Existing Proposals on Learning Democratic Communication in Educational Contexts

Deliberation means free speech governed by reason, often (but not always) aimed at obtaining a gradual agreement on the preferences of the individuals involved. As explained above, deliberation is frequently advocated, because carefully considered discussion would facilitate the search for a solution acceptable to everybody involved and thus for a consensus, or at least a common structuring of problems: a meta-consensus.

---

[14] See Black; Arrow.

[15] See, for example, R. G. Niemi, "Majority Decision-Making with Partial Unidimensionality," *American Political Science Review* 63 (1969): 488-97. For further discussion, see Christian List et al., "Can Deliberation Increase Preference Structuration? Evidence from Deliberative Polls," (paper presented at the Conference of the American Political Science Association, Washington, DC, 2000), revised in 2006 under the title "Deliberation, Single-Peakedness, and the Possibility of Meaningful Democracy: Evidence from Deliberative Polls," http://personal.lse.ac.uk/list/PDF-files/DeliberationPaper.pdf.

At present, educational contexts, such as schools and universities, offer only limited opportunities for learning the technique of democratic deliberation. Simple didactic forms, such as cooperative learning and mediation, contain certain elements of deliberation. In view of the significant competence requirements of complex democratic processes, however, such relatively simple techniques may, at best, serve as an introduction to very young learners. The development of democratic competences among older students and grown-ups requires new and more demanding methods.

Debating

Debating as widely practiced within Anglo-American educational contexts is based upon dialectic principles. As a starting point, fixed contradictory positions are rhetorically exposed in order to establish the extremes. After the debate, the motion is put to the vote. Deliberation, on the other hand, is clearly distinguished from such a debate resulting in a vote. Deliberation is characterized by the fact that the participants in a discussion reconsider their own positions and are prepared to engage more fundamentally in a common analysis of a set of problems, an analysis reflecting all the individual points of view in order to uncover their underlying mental dispositions. Processes of deliberative communication overcome the characteristic efforts of debates to display rhetorical brilliance and quick-wittedness and instead focus on mutual understanding and the transformation of opinions.

The Simulation of Parliamentary Sessions

The complex communication processes underlying parliamentary decision procedures are, didactically, difficult to teach and understand. An intensive comprehension of such processes can be achieved by making use of simulations which try to represent real democratic processes. In parliamentary simulations such as "Congress in Action" (practiced at American high-schools) or "Model United Nations" (well known internationally), students are transferred into a democratic "microcosm" in which they take the acting part in a political process over a longer period of time.

The "Congress in Action" program, for example, is carried out with 11th- or 12th-grade students at US high schools. The simulation of Congress runs over a period of several weeks. During this time, the learners play the part of a representative or a cabinet member. By means of authentic material about the function, the centers of interest, the convictions, loyalties and networks of this representative, they prepare themselves to play the representative's part. Each learner is involved in a particular legislative initiative and, in his or her function as a representative, has to elaborate a position paper based on the knowledge acquired. On the basis of this paper, the learner cooperates in simulated committee meetings as well as plenary debates, where he or she represents the representative's position. All the decision-making and voting processes of a real parliament are thus simulated on the basis of actual functioning mechanisms of the US Congress. The pedagogic function of this comprehensive teaching arrangement is to bring about a practical understanding of genuine political processes in a parliamentary democracy.

The National Issues Forum

Since most citizens in modern democracies participate in politics only occasionally—the main opportunities for participation being elections, which take place only every few years—they typically have only limited information on social and political problems. Especially in media-oriented democracies, public opinion seems to be fluent and marked by whatever the dominant headlines are. A democracy which demands little political participation of its citizens does not seem to consider worthwhile the investment of time and effort into a careful discussion of political information. Many political scientists argue that this *status quo* contributes to a widely spread state of "rational ignorance" among citizens.[16]

A method developed with a special view to democratic education is the "National Issues Forum," which seeks to contribute to the training of capacities for deliberation.[17] Following the model of the "New England Town Meetings," one of the essential founding institutions of the American democracy, the National Issues Forum assembles citizens who deliberate on specific topics such as drug abuse, systems of social security, labor market policy, or juvenile de-

---

[16] See, e.g., Bryan Caplan, "Rational Ignorance versus Rational Irrationality," *Kyklos* 54, no. 1 (2001): 3-26.

[17] See www.nifi.org/.

linquency. National Issues Forums take place in schools and universities and are also organized by communities, religious groups or other associations of civil society. The aim of these forums is to give people with different opinions and conceptions of the good life the possibility to find and formulate common aims for political action, through respectful and informed deliberation.

National Issues Forums are structured discussions chaired by trained moderators. The participants need not have any expertise but, before the beginning of the forum, are given comprehensive information material which ought to be as neutral as possible. Based on this material, they weigh up the pros and cons of different political solutions to a problem. They analyze the different alternatives and respective arguments. Guided by the moderators, they try to take their own perspective as well as that of the common welfare into account. The forums have no direct binding effect upon politics, but their results are forwarded to, and discussed with, local and national politicians. Often, a National Issues Forum also becomes the basis for further action to be taken by the citizens of a community.

Deliberative Polling

One method whose potential application in civic education has not been sufficiently researched yet is Deliberative Polling as developed by James Fishkin and his colleagues.[18] The method of Deliberative Polling has aggregative as well as deliberative components.

In Deliberative Polls, a controversial topic is chosen. Then a group of 100 to 300 test persons (typically, a random sample of the population) is selected and, to begin with, the participants are interviewed individually about this topic by means of questionnaires. The second step is a phase of deliberation. The test persons are invited to deliberate on the given topic for one to three days. For their preparation, they are given information materials presenting a balanced view of the two (or more sides) sides which, for general transparency, are also made available to the public. The deliberation phase is now arranged in several steps. In large plenary

---

[18] James S. Fishkin, *Democracy and Deliberation* (New Haven: Yale University Press, 1991); *The Voice of the People* (New Haven: Yale University Press, 1995). See also Robert C. Luskin, James S. Fishkin, and Roger Jowell, "Considered Opinions: Deliberative Polling in Britain," *British Journal of Political Science* 32, no. 3 (2002): 455-87.

sessions, various experts and advocates (as well as politicians) present the different points of view on the issue in question. In smaller discussion groups, led by trained moderators, the participants develop questions which they subsequently discuss with the experts and advocates in larger plenary sessions. Finally, each participant is asked again to fill in the same questionnaire as in the initial poll. In this way, the individual opinions and preferences before and after deliberation can be compared with each other.

Deliberative Polls have already been carried out on a large number of different issues and in different countries, including energy supply in Texas, crime in the United Kingdom, the introduction of the Euro in Denmark, and the constitutional referendum on the abolition of the monarchy in Australia. Fishkin and his collaborators frequently found evidence of a considerable shift of opinions. They also showed that public interest as opposed to private interest often found a more prominent place in the foreground after the phase of deliberation. Moreover, in some Deliberative Polls, the questionnaires contained questions revealing something about the state of informedness of the test persons, such as questions on factual matters. The evaluation of the answers to such questions provided evidence of a higher degree of informedness among the participants after the phase of deliberation.[19]

Deliberative Polls are well suited for testing the hypothesis, mentioned above, that deliberation can bring about a meta-consensus. Data from Deliberative Polls have shown that deliberation cannot, typically, establish complete single-peakedness (as defined above) but a high degree of partial single-peakedness.[20]

While the research interest of Fishkin and his collaborators is obviously centered on the empirical data generated by Deliberative Polls and the more general political-scientific lessons that can be learnt from this data, the method of Deliberative Polling, as Fishkin emphasizes, provides "both a social science experiment and a form of public education in the broadest sense."[21] The latter aspect of

---

[19] For detailed information and references to relevant literature, see http://cdd.stanford.edu.

[20] See Christian List et al., "Can Deliberation Increase Preference Structuration? Evidence from Deliberative Polls."

[21] At www.law.utexas.edu/research/delpol/index.html, accessed in 2002 when the

Deliberative Polling is at the centre of the deliberation project we present here. Unlike most existing approaches to democratic education, Deliberative Polling offers an instrument by which we can evaluate, quantitatively, the effects of deliberation in terms of the data generated before and after participation in the process.

A Deliberation Project in an Educational Context

We carried out a project modeled on Deliberative Polling within the context of a two-and-a-half-week workshop of the German Students' Academy (Deutsche Schüler Akademie).[22] The entire academy consisted of 6 different workshops with 15 participants each. Our workshop was entitled "Democracy and Deliberation: How to Deal with Conflicts in a Pluralist Society." The workshop had a theoretical as well as an empirical aim. The theoretical aim was to elaborate and discuss the controversy between aggregative and deliberative models of democracy. Teaching and learning methods included textual analysis, short presentations by the students and discussions. The empirical aim, which we sought to achieve together with the participants of our workshop, was to plan, carry out and evaluate an entire Deliberative Poll—or at least something as close to a Deliberative Poll as feasible within the given setting. The issue was: "Topical questions of educational policy in Germany." The test persons were the participants and the teaching staff of the other workshops of the academy (94 altogether). Thus, unlike in Fishkin's Deliberative Polls, the set of interviewees was not a random sample of the reference population. The questionnaire developed in our workshop is included in the appendix. The questionnaire contains questions about the financing of university studies, university admission, final

first version of this paper was written, also see James Fishkin, Robert C. Luskin and Roger Jowell, "Deliberative Polling and Public Consultation," *Parliamentary Affairs* 53 (2000): 657-666.

[22] Supported by the Federal Ministry of Education and Research, "Bildung und Begabung e.V." organizes annual summer academies for gifted students of the upper levels of secondary schools in Germany (Gymnasien). Each academy consists of several workshops on different topics. Each participant in the academy takes part in one particular workshop but also has the possibility to participate in a comprehensive extracurricular program within the framework of the academy. In the course of the academy, the students are familiarized with the methods and techniques of academic work.

exams in secondary education ("Abiturprüfungen"), the structure of the school system (a differentiated selective system vs. comprehensive schools), full-time day school vs. part-time day school.

After a first interview of the test persons, a deliberation phase was carried out, consisting of two evening sessions (with a participation of 93 and 85 persons, respectively) and an ensuing second interview. The deliberation phase was modeled after the structure developed by Fishkin. To provide the interviewees with information, after the first round of questionnaires, we distributed material with pro- and counter-arguments to the different aspects of the issue, which had been developed by our workshop. The first, somewhat longer evening session focused on the university issues, the second, shorter one on the school issues. Both evening sessions consisted of three parts each. In the first part, "informed" participants of our workshop acting as experts presented the different viewpoints on the various topics to the 93 or 85 test persons present. Afterwards, the test persons were selected randomly to sit together in small groups and, guided by a moderator from our workshop, to deliberate on the issues of the poll. The third part consisted of another plenary session during which the small groups could ask the "experts" questions. Due to the limited number of participants and the overall organization of the academy, it was not possible to examine an additional control group of test persons who did not participate in the deliberation phase.

As indicated above, unlike in a professional Deliberative Poll, we were primarily interested in the process and less so in the polling data generated by it. Particularly because of the composition of our sample, these data are not representative of a larger reference population. Nevertheless, as we will now show, these data are of some interest: they permit a (descriptive) quantitative evaluation of the deliberation process. Quantitative criteria for the evaluation of the deliberation process were:

- the *degree of informedness* of the interviewees after as opposed to before deliberation;
- the *collective cohesion* of the preferences of the different interviewees in the form of the degree of meta-consensus after deliberation compared to before

We examined the influence of deliberation on the informedness of the interviewees by means of two knowledge-oriented questions:

- Question 2.2: Does there exist, at some universities in the USA, a performance-oriented selection process? (The correct answer is "yes.")
- Question 5.2: In which federal states of Germany is there a centralized secondary school exam ("Zentralabitur")? (The complete correct list is: "Bayern, Baden-Württemberg, Saarland, Thüringen, Sachsen, Sachsen-Anhalt, Mecklenburg-Vorpommern.")

Figure 4.2 summarizes the results of these knowledge-oriented questions. The results show that questions referring to informedness were answered more correctly after deliberation than before. The percentage of interviewees with a correct answer to question 2.2 increased from 49% before deliberation to 81% after deliberation. As to question 5.2, the average number of correctly named federal states with centralized secondary school exams increased from 2 before deliberation to 4 after deliberation. This is consistent with the hypothesis that deliberation leads to the acquisition of information.

We checked the influence of deliberation upon the degree of meta-consensus among the interviewees by means of questions concerning their preferences on the following issues: the financing of university studies (question 1.1), the method of payment of tuition fees if applicable (question 1.2), admission to university (question 2.1), a differentiated selective school system vs. comprehensive schools (question 3), half-time day school vs. full-time day school (question 4.1), decentralized vs. centralized secondary school exams (question 5.1). In answer to each such question concerning preferences, the interviewees could specify a descending preference ordering over different alternative models. For details, see the questionnaire in the appendix.

For a quantification of the degree of meta-consensus before and after deliberation, we calculated—for each question at both times—the share (in percentage) of interviewees with single-peaked preferences with respect to the same left-right axis.[23] In addition to

---

[23] Methodologically, this follows List et al., "Can Deliberation Increase Preference

Question 2.2

Number of interviewees with the correct answer before deliberation: 46 (49%)

Number of interviewees with the correct answer after deliberation: 75 (81%)

Question 5.2

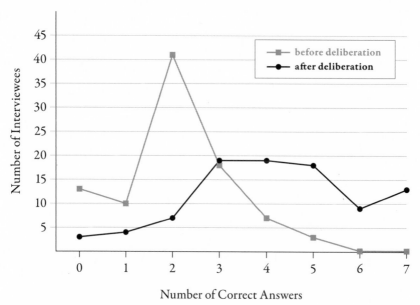

Figure 4.2: Deliberation and knowledge-oriented questions

that, we determined which left-right alignment of alternatives this axis corresponded to (both before and after deliberation). And we also determined the respective Condorcet Winner (both before and after deliberation).

Figure 4.3 summarizes the results of the questions focused on preferences. The results for the university issues (questions 1.1, 1.2 and 2.1) are consistent with the hypothesis that deliberation increases the degree of partial single-peakedness, whereas the results for the school issues (questions 3, 4.1 and 5.1) are not. Given the limitations of our data, however, these findings should only be seen as descriptive of the particular case investigated; they do not support

Structuration? Evidence from Deliberative Polls."

any generalizations beyond this case.

The increase in the degree of partial single-peakedness on the university issues, which suggests an increase of a meta-consensus, may be explained by the fact that the degree of the students' informedness and of their readiness to express their views on university issues before deliberation was comparatively small and unstructured and that the deliberation process was therefore capable of leading to a structuring of preferences.

Question / topic (see questionnaire)	Percentage of interviewees (from a total number of 93) with single-peaked preferences on the same left-right axis		Left-right axis (for the interpretation of the models see questionnaire)		Condorcet Winner	
	Before Del.	After Del.	Before Del.	After Del.	Before Del.	After Del.
1.1 Financing of university studies	43 %	52 % (+)	C A B D E	C A B D E	B	B
1.2 Method of payment of tuition fees	83 %	87 % (+)	A B C	A B C	B	B
2.1 Admission to university	63 %	67 % (+)	A C D B	A D C B	D	D
3 Differentiated selective schools vs. comprehensive schools	90 %	80 % (-)	A B C D	B A C D	A	A

4.1 Full-time day school	95 %	96 % (0)	A B C	A B C	B	B
5.1 Decentralized vs. centralized secondary school exams (Zentralabitur)	91 %	87 % (-)	A B C	A B C	C	C

Del.= Deliberation

(+) = increase in the degree of partial single-peakedness

(-) = decrease in the degree of partial single-peakedness

(0) = no relevant change in the degree of partial single-peakedness

The rather contrary effect on the school issues could possibly stem from the fact that, even before deliberation, the participants already held rather strong (and, moreover, very homogeneous and, in part, almost unanimous) opinions about issues of school policy. The deliberation process may therefore have resuscitated those views by confronting the students with views on the comprehensive schools they had hardly ever heard before. Deliberation also changed the dominant left-right axis of the alternatives regarding the structure of the existing school system. Before deliberation, the mixed system (model B) (a differentiated school system with comprehensive schools as an option) was placed in the centre as a compromise solution (A B C D). After deliberation, however, it moved to the edge of the left-right axis (B A C D). This modification of the left-right axis might be due to the argument put forward in deliberation that, within a mixed system (model B), comprehensive schools may produce worse results than within a system where they are the only type of school.

Another factor which may have contributed to difference between the results on the school issues and those on the university issues is the fact that, due to the different lengths of the two evening sessions, there was less time for the deliberation on the school issues than on the university issues.

As we have pointed out, our deliberation project differed from Fishkin's Deliberative Polls as it was carried out within an educational context and as the group of interviewees was not a random sample from an underlying reference population. Nevertheless, our empirical findings on the effects of deliberation upon the two quantitative criteria considered—the degree of informedness and the degree of meta-consensus—are consistent with the results of Fishkin's Deliberative Polls. As in Luskin, Fishkin and Jowell's paper, we were able to identify an increase in informedness among the participants and, as in List, McLean, Fishkin and Luskin's paper, we were able to identify—at least for some of the relevant questions—an increase in partial single-peakedness.[24]

Conclusion

The results of our deliberation project suggest that Deliberative Polling, when applied in an educational context, is suited to increase democratic competences in several ways.

- Deliberative Polling incorporates aggregative as well as deliberative aspects of democratic processes and creates a "microcosm" in which participants, through personal experience, can develop an understanding of real processes of democratic communication and decision making. The deliberative aspect can promote the capacity for an argumentative engagement with political views.

- Deliberative Polling can lead to an increase in the participants' informedness and thus, at least within the group of interviewees, counteract a situation of "rational ignorance."

- Deliberative Polling can structure problem fields, increase meta-consensus among the participants and thus contribute to the solution of aggregation problems. Given that many of the notorious paradoxes and problems of aggregation can be traced back to a lack of structure or cohesion among individual preferences, the structuration

---

[24] See Robert C. Luskin, James S. Fishkin and Roger Jowell, "Considered Opinions: Deliberative Polling in Britain," and Christian List et al., "Can Deliberation Increase Preference Structuration? Evidence from Deliberative Polls."

processes inherent in deliberation can help to facilitate consistent democratic aggregation.

ACKNOWLEDGMENTS

We thank the participants of the workshop "Democracy and Deliberation" of the Schülerakademie Gaesdonck 2002 without whose active collaboration the project presented in this paper could not have been realized: Laura Birg, Mira Colsmann, Florian Frederico Cortez Kiesow, Anne-Marie Dörnenburg, Andreas Englberger, Tanja Greiner, Corinna Gundelach, Irene Köppe, Fabian Löffler, Frieder Meidert, Richard Peter, Anne Rittstieg, Armin Schmidt, Tim Stoffel, Ulrike Zirpel. We would also like to thank the German Schüler Akademie, Bonn, for enabling the project and all the other participants and collaborators in the Gaesdonck Akademie 2002 for taking part in our polls as well as the deliberation meetings. For very helpful comments, we are very grateful to Volker Brandt and James Fishkin. The terms "Deliberative Polling" and "Deliberative Poll" have been registered as trademarks ™ in the USA by James Fishkin and his colleagues. Special thanks to Klaus Jürgen List for translating the paper from German into English.

BIBLIOGRAPHY

Arrow, Kenneth N. *Social Choice and Individual Values*. New York: Wiley, 1951.

Becker, Michael. "Politik als Verständigungsprozess—Modelle deliberativer Demokratie." *Zeitschrift für Politik* 47, no. 2 (2000).

Black, Duncan. "On the Rationale of Group Decision-Making." *Journal of Political Economy* 56 (1948): 23-34.

Bohman, John and William Rehg, editors. *Deliberative Democracy: Essays on Reason and Politics*. Cambridge: MIT Press, 1977.

Caplan, Brian. "Rational Ignorance versus Rational Irrationality." *Kyklos* 54, no. 1 (2001): 3-26.

Cohen, Joshua. "Deliberation and Democratic Legitimacy." In *The Good Polity: Normative Analysis of the State*, edited by A. Hamlin and P. Pettit. Oxford: Basil Blackwell, 1989.

Dryzek, Jon S. *Deliberative Democracy and Beyond*. Oxford: Oxford University Press, 2000.

— and Christian List. "Social Choice Theory and Deliberative Democracy: A Reconciliation." *British Journal of Political Science* 33 (2003): 1-28.

—. *Discursive Democracy: Politics, Policy and Political Science*. New York: Cambridge University Press, 1990.

Elster, Jon "The Market and the Forum." In *Foundations of Social Choice Theory*, edited by J. Elster and A. Hylland. Cambridge: Cambridge University Press, 1986.

—. Introduction to *Deliberative Democracy*, edited by Jon Elster, 1-18. New York: Cambridge University Press, 1998.

Estlund, David M., Jeremy Waldron, Bernard Grofman, Scott L. Feld."Democratic Theory and the Public Interest; Condorcet and Rousseau Revisited." *American Political Science Review* 83 (1989): 1317-40.

Fishkin, James S. *Democracy and Deliberation.* New Haven: Yale University Press, 1991.

—. *The Voice of the People.* New Haven: Yale University Press, 1995.

—, Robert C. Luskin, and Roger Jowell. " Deliberative Polling and Public Consultation," *Parliamentary Affairs* 53 (200), 657-666.

Gutmann, Amy and Dennis Thompson. *Democracy and Disagreement.* Cambridge: Harvard University Press, 1996.

Knight, Jack and James Johnson. "Aggregation and Deliberation: On the Possibility of Democratic Legitimacy." *Political Theory* 22 (1994): 277-96.

List, Christian, Robert C. Luskin, James S. Fishkin, and Iain Mclean. "Can Deliberation Increase Preference Structuration? Evidence from Deliberative Polls." Paper presented at the Conference of the American Political Science Association, Washington, DC, 2000. Revised in 2006 under the title "Deliberation, Single-Peakedness, and the Possibility of Meaningful Democracy: Evidence from Deliberative Polls." http://personal.lse.ac.uk/list/PDF-files/ DeliberationPaper.pdf.

—. "Two Concepts of Agreement." *The Good Society* 11 (2002): 72-9.

Luskin, Robert C., James S. Fishkin, and Roger Jowell. "Considered Opinions: Deliberative Polling in Britain." *British Journal of Political Science* 32, no. 3 (2002): 455-87.

McLean, Iain and Fiona Hewitt, editors. *Condorcet: Foundations of Social Choice and Political Theory.* Cheltenham: Edward Elgar, 1994.

Miller, David. "Deliberation and Social Choice." *Political Studies* (special issue) 40 (1991): 54-67.

Niemi, R. G. "Majority Decision-Making with Partial Unidimensionality." *American Political Science Review* 63 (1969): 488-97.

APPENDIX

Questionnaire: Topical Questions referring to German Educational Policy

1. The Financing of Studies

1.1 Consider the following alternatives for the issue of the financing of studies:

Model A   No tuition fees whatsoever.

Model B   Tuition fees only above a certain number of semesters (e.g., for long-term students or for research studies).

Model C   Tuition fees from the first semester onwards but with state grants primarily awarded on social / financial criteria.

Model D   Tuition fees from the first semester onwards but with state grants primarily awarded on criteria of academic performance.

Model E   Tuition fees according to a free market-oriented choice of universities.

My preferences for the models are: (Please fill in the respective letter of the model.)

1st Preference	2nd Preference	3rd Preference	4th Preference	5th Preference

1.2 Imagine that tuition fees are introduced. Consider the following alternative proposals for the method of payment:

Model A   Tuition fees are to be paid during studies; there is no state plan for financing.

Model B   Tuition fees are to be paid only after the completion of studies. Students are given a credit on favorable terms.

Model C   Tuition fees are to be paid only after the completion of studies through an income-oriented tax (high payment for a high income and *vice versa*).

My preferences for the models are: (Please fill in the respective letter of the model.)

1st Preference	2nd Preference	3rd Preference

2. University Admission

2.1 Consider the following alternative proposals for admission criteria to university studies:

Model A	No admission restrictions to university studies whatsoever; free matriculation after having passed the Abitur examination.
Model B	The only admission criterion is the average of grades in the Abitur examination ("numerus clauses").
Model C	Selection of students by universities on the basis of subject-oriented cognitive performance tests (e.g., written entrance exams).
Model D	Universities select students on the basis of written applications and personal interviews.

My preferences for the models are: (Please fill in the respective letter of the model.)

1st Preference	2nd Preference	3rd Preference	4th Preference

2.2. Do some universities in the USA select students on the basis of their performance?

Yes: .... No: .... Don't know: ....

3. The Structure of the School System

Model A	Exclusively the existing differentiated system (two or three types of schools: Gymnasium, Realschule, Hauptschule, different in the respective federal states).
Model B	The existing differentiated school system (two or three types) plus the comprehensive school as an alternative option.
Model C	Exclusively comprehensive schools with internal streaming (i.e., students are taught in courses of different performance-oriented academic levels).
Model D	Exclusively comprehensive schools without any internal streaming (i.e., all the students are taught together in courses of the same academic level).

My preferences for the models are: (Please fill in the respective letter of the model.)

1st Preference	2nd Preference	3rd Preference	4th Preference

4. Part-Time vs. Full Time Day School

4.1 Consider the following alternative proposals:

Model A   Full-time compulsory day school for all students.
Model B   Parents and students can choose between full-time and conventional part-time day schools.
Model C   On principle, no full-time day school.

My preferences for the models are: (Please fill in the respective letter of the model.)

1st Preference	2nd Preference	3rd Preference

4.2 Imagine that the compulsory full-time day school is introduced. What do you think of the following proposals for the organization of afternoon courses? (For this question, several proposals may be supported.)

	I object	no opinion	I am in favor
Leisure activities in the afternoon, such as sports or arts			
Individual support / tuition given to weaker as well as strong performers			
Compulsory social engagement of students in the afternoons (e.g., in the form of project work)			
Conventional classes in the afternoon just as currently in the morning			

5. Abitur Examinations

5.1 Consider the following alternative proposals:

Model A   No centralized Abitur examinations; Abitur examinations are arranged internally by the schools.

Model B   Centralized Abitur Examinations at federal-state level.

Model C   Centralized Abitur Examinations at the level of the Federal Republic of Germany.

My preferences for the models are: (Please fill in the respective letter of the model.)

1st Preference	2nd Preference	3rd Preference

5.2 Which federal states of Germany have centralized Abitur examinations?

CHAPTER 5

The Promises and Challenges of Deliberative Democracy in Practice: A Comparative Case Study of Two School Districts

Julie Marsh

Over the years, the model of deliberative democracy has come under attack for being utopian and incompatible with the economic, cultural, and social complexity of modern societies.[1] Some critics argue that citizens lack the interest in politics to motivate participation as well as the skills and abilities demanded by the model.[2] Others claim that most citizens do not possess the information needed to adhere to its principles.[3] Still others note that the process is time consuming and impractical, particularly given the size of democratic societies.[4]

Yet very little empirical research has tested these claims and examined the ways in which deliberative democracy plays out in real-world settings, particularly in educational settings.[5] This chapter

---

[1] Seyla Benhabib, ed., *Democracy and Difference: Contesting the Boundaries of the Political* (Princeton: Princeton University Press, 1996).

[2] Richard A. Posner, *Law, Pragmatism, and Democracy* (Cambridge: Harvard University Press, 2003).

[3] Colin Farrelly, *An Introduction to Contemporary Political Theory* (Thousand Oaks, CA: SAGE Publications, 2004).

[4] Michael Walzer, "Deliberation, and what else?" in *Deliberative Politics: Essays on Democracy and Disagreement,* ed. Stephen Macedo (Oxford: Oxford University Press, 1999).

[5] For exceptions see Anthony. S. Bryk et al., *Charting Chicago School Reform: Democratic Localism as a Lever for Change* (Boulder: Westview Press, 1998); Archon Fung, "Accountable Autonomy: Toward Empowered Deliberation in Chicago Schools and Policing," *Politics & Society 29*, no. 1 (2001): 73-103; Lorraine M. McDonnell and Stephen M. Weatherford, *Practical Deliberation in Local School Districts: A South Carolina Experiment,* CSE Technical Report 520 (Los Angeles: U.C.L.A. Center for the Study of Evaluation, National Center for Research on Evaluation, Standards, and Student Testing, 2000).

attempts to address this gap by exploring the enactment of deliberative democratic principles in two California school districts—two
cases that are best understood as quasi-democratic in nature due to
the selection of participants via appointment not formal election.

In the first district, Highland,[6] one teacher, parent, principal, and
student from each school met with citizens, district administrators,
and board members to develop long-range strategies to improve
districtwide student achievement. Building on a ten-year history
of strategic planning, the district convened a three-day, facilitated
meeting of brainstorming, discussion, and priority-setting that occurred in rotating small and large groups. Guided by professional
facilitators and explicit norms of participation, the group ultimately
agreed upon four key strategies. Following the dissemination of this
plan, the district organized "action teams" to plan for implementation. Over time, the district implemented many of these jointly
constructed ideas and most participants left the experience feeling
empowered and willing to participate again.

In the second district, Mid Valley, the superintendent and board
president appointed a group of community leaders to participate
in the Community Accountability Project (CAP), an initiative to
improve system-wide education through enhanced community involvement. The design of this endeavor was a bifurcated process
in which community leaders (the "Advisory") first met as a group
over the course of a year to generate their own ideas; then shared
and discussed these ideas with the school board and central office;
and ultimately co-constructed action items. In the first year, community advisors met monthly with district staff to develop the goals
and activities of CAP and decided upon four strategies to pursue
jointly with the district. After three tense "Study Sessions" between
community members, the school board, and district leadership, no
actions were taken on the proposed ideas. The investment of two
years and more than $400,000 left participants and observers embit-
tered by the experience.

In the end, these cases present an intriguing puzzle: Why did
two districts with seemingly similar intentions—to engage a repre-

---

[6] To ensure anonymity, pseudonyms are used for the names of all organizations,
initiatives, and individuals in this chapter. In addition, statistics cited about
organizations and communities are approximations, not exact figures.

sentative group of constituents in reason-based decision-making aimed at improving learning for all students—achieve widely disparate results? In this chapter, I seek to answer this question and demonstrate that although the model of deliberative democracy is relevant and "implementable" in contested terrain, its realization is likely to encounter significant obstacles along the way. First, I describe the two school districts and how their deliberative endeavors unfolded over time. I then examine why one district was more successful at achieving its deliberative goals than the other, uncovering a set of inter-related factors that shaped the face-to-face deliberations and actions of participants. In conclusion, I present implications for practice and identify unresolved issues emanating form this work.

This chapter draws on data collected from January 1999 to January 2002.[7] In the Mid Valley School District, I conducted observations and interviews as the initiative unfolded, with additional reflective interviews conducted after the initiative ended. In the Highland School District, data collection focused on an initiative that had already taken place. To address the limits of retrospective data in this district, I interviewed a wide range of individuals to capture multiple accounts of the same events. I also used documents to confirm and disconfirm participants' accounts—including notes and overheads from meetings, facilitators' scripts, handouts disseminated at meetings, and planning documents. In all, I coded and analyzed data from more than 100 interviews and focus groups with key participants and observers (district and school administrators, board members, parents, citizens, teachers, students); observations of formal and informal meetings; and an extensive review of documents and archival records.

Setting the Stage: Situating the Cases

To understand how these endeavors evolved, one must begin with a broad understanding of the local context, history, participants, and timeline.

---

[7] For further details on the study and its methods, see Julie A. Marsh, *Democratic Dilemmas: Joint Work, Education Politics, and Community* (Albany: SUNY Press, 2007).

Local Context

The two study districts resided in the greater Northern California Bay Area, a region famous for its natural beauty and thriving economy (at least at the time of data collection). I selected these districts because they both viewed deliberative democratic engagement of citizens and educators as a valuable part of their work. Both districts were also comparable in size (less than 10,000 students and 20 schools); grade configurations (Kindergarten through eighth grade); and fiscal resources (both spent roughly $6,000 per student and received total revenues of $40 to $50 million a year). They were also both located in mixed urban-suburban neighborhoods with demographically diverse student populations, although Mid Valley enrolled a greater proportion of Hispanic students (two-thirds of their population compared to one-third of Highland's) and of English Language Learners (half of all students compared to one-fourth of Highland's). Finally, both districts benefited from the stability of internal leadership (both superintendents enjoyed a long tenure of approximately ten years) and of positive community-district relations (while citizens were not particularly active in district affairs, they were not seen as adversarial).

History

The history of deliberative endeavors, however, differed greatly in the two cases. Highland's deliberative endeavor built on more than a decade of experience with strategic planning designed around a well-known model adapted from the corporate sector for educational organizations. The model specified many aspects of the process, including who should participate, key guiding principles, the length of the session, and the steps to follow to create the plan and form action teams. In 1988, the district organized the first strategic planning session, which focused primarily on defining the district's mission and solidifying core beliefs. Highland then repeated this process every two to five years, modifying the structure each time (e.g., tightening the timeline so that plans covered two- to three-year periods, including participation by students). By 1998, when the district engaged in the strategic planning sessions examined in this research, the district had adopted a set of parameters governing the process and had narrowed the district's goal to one: 100% of students will meet or exceed district standards. Given the consensus developed in the recent past around the beliefs, mission, parameters, and goals, district leaders decided that the 1998 session would not be "a complete renewal" of the strategic plan, but instead an update, to develop new strategies that achieve the district's goal.

Mid Valley's three-year attempt to carry out an initiative started in 1997 when the superintendent worked with a state legislator to establish a "pilot" accountability program which would allocate financial rewards to districts that made substantial progress toward meeting the goals of locally designed accountability plans. Although the bill was never signed into law, the superintendent remained committed to its underlying concepts and established a new initiative, CAP. In the summer of 1998 he appointed a group of community advisors to design this effort and a full-time district administrator to direct it. The superintendent's original vision was that a committee of citizens would determine benchmarks, annually analyze district data, judge whether the district as a whole made educational progress, recommend financial rewards for evidence of progress, and help develop next steps to improve future student performance. Although the new CAP director and advisors shaped CAP into something quite different over time, throughout the early months of the initiative, many district leaders remained hopeful that the state would ultimately resurrect its original legislation to fund CAP and provide the financial rewards. By mid-1999, it became clear this funding would not materialize. This history nonetheless left an imprint on the minds of participants and observers, as discussed later.

Who Participated

Although both districts made efforts to constitute "representative" bodies to participate, Highland's can be characterized as more participatory while Mid Valley's resembled a more elite representative body.[8] Based on detailed recommendations from school principals (who were given specific criteria intended to ensure diversity of gender, ethnicity, and other characteristics), Highland administrators selected for participation in strategic planning at least one parent, teacher, administrator, and in some cases a student, from each of the district's schools. They also included some district administrators,

---

[8] See Marsh (2007) for a more in-depth discussion of participatory and representative democracy and its application in these two cases.

board members, and community members from a local university, police department, and city government. In total, 62 individuals participated: 31 school educators, 12 parents, 9 district leaders or staff, 3 students, 3 citizens, 2 classified school staff, and 2 facilitators.

In Mid Valley, the superintendent and school board president appointed 13 influential leaders of the community to the CAP Advisory, including elected officials, parent and community activists and respected professionals, many of whom had children in district schools. This Advisory also interacted in later months in Study Sessions with top district administrators and school board members, who comprised another set of participants in the CAP initiative. Despite efforts to secure participation from teacher union leaders, the district did not attain teacher representation. In total, the effort involved 27 individuals: 11 from the community, 14 from the district office and school board, and two school principals.

Timeline of Events

Highland's strategic planning started with pre-planning meetings in early 1998, followed by three days of strategic planning in June and August 1998. Action teams were developed and met on and off from October 1998 through April 1999. The school board formally adopted the strategic plan in June 1999 and implementation of various strategies started in 2000.

In Mid Valley, the CAP initiative occurred from August 1998 to March 2000. The Advisory met monthly throughout this period and joined district leaders in three Study Sessions in April 1999, August 1999, and February 2000. The CAP director resigned in March 2000.

Deliberative Democratic Intentions

Unlike other endeavors examined in this book, leaders in both districts did not explicitly use the terms deliberative democracy when describing their efforts. Yet their intentions and words clearly mirrored the core principles of deliberative democracy. As discussed throughout this book, deliberative democratic model seek to promote the common good and base decisions on reasoned argument and public discourse. While many theorists over the years have adopted various names for the concept of deliberative democracy, they share many of the same basic principles:[9]

---

[9] See, for example, Benhabib (1996); Joseph M. Bessette, *The Mild Voice of Reason:*

- Conversations and decisions are aimed at the common good;
- Decisions are based on reasoned argument and the merits at hand;
- Reasoning must be reciprocal, meaning participants appeal to reasons and premises that are shared or could be shared by fellow participants;
- Reasons given are open and public, and the information needed to assess those reasons are accessible;
- There is a shared understanding that all voices are heard;
- Participants are accountable to all who may be bound by decisions and formal linkages exist to ensure this accountability; and
- Action follows.

Leaders in both districts articulated many of these tenets, in particular a desire to involve participants in improving the good of the district as a whole. In Mid Valley, the superintendent explained that CAP would "help pull [the] community together around a *common vision*." Ideally, he envisioned a district where "different sub-communities articulate, 'these are our interests, these are what we have in *common* and what action steps we can put in place to bring that about together and [be] mutually responsible with the schools.'" Similarly, the CAP director described the initiative as "a collaboration to do joint work with people who share a *common interest* in the quality of life in this community," which is "different from setting up an us/them kind of relationship." Throughout early meetings, district leaders repeated that CAP "isn't just discussion," but intended to generate action around what is best for the district as a whole.

In Highland, leaders pledged to involve educators and non-edu-

Deliberative Democracy and American National Government (Chicago: University of Chicago Press, 1994); Joshua Cohen, "Deliberation and Democratic Legitimacy," in *The Good Polity: Normative Analysis of the State,* ed. Alan Hamlin and Philip Petit (New York: Basil Blackwell, Inc., 1989), 67-91; Jon Elster, "The Market and the Forum: Three Varieties of Political Theory," in *Deliberative Democracy: Essays on Reason and Politics,* ed. John Bohman and William Rehg (Cambridge: MIT Press, 1997), 3-33; Archon Fung and Erik Olin Wright, "Deepening Democracy: Innovations in Empowered Participatory Governance," *Politics & Society* 29, no. 1 (2001): 5-41; Amy Gutmann and Dennis Thompson, *Democracy and Disagreement* (Cambridge: Belknap Press of Harvard University Press, 1996).

cators in deciding what is best for all students "system-wide." As the district organizer explained,

> So [we were] trying to find ways to get them thinking differently than just coming with a narrow view. They're asked to keep their own agenda items outside the door. Everybody comes with no identified roles—no teacher, custodian. Everybody comes in equally. And that's really stressed. And *if you have a particular bias or an issue, that's not why we're here.* We ask people to not attend if they can't feel that they can keep that apart. . . . We all come as just people without district office labels or anything else, *just working for the good of the students and improving our achievement.*

The primacy of common interests over individual needs is made explicit in the district's criteria for team selection. One of the desired attributes of team members articulated on a list sent to principals when soliciting participant nominations was an ability to "subordinate special interests to good of organization."

In both districts, leaders' descriptions of how participants were expected to interact also reflected many of the deliberative democratic principles outlined above. In Highland, the initiators repeatedly argued that strategic planning was a two-way process that involved a wide-range of participants in meaningful decision making. The superintendent emphatically noted the importance of bringing in diverse perspectives to co-construct ideas with district administrators:

> We don't use it [strategic planning] as a PR fluff tool. . . . There have been some wonderful things that have come out of strategic planning from the heads of the people in our community as they look at schools and schooling with a different perspective. We have always felt that that was the most value of the process because, otherwise, we talk to ourselves, and you're doomed to repeat the same dumb stuff you've done before. But people make you look at yourself when you bring them in from outside and have a different perspective.

As discussed later, many of the structures and norms established at the outset were intended to facilitate this deliberative democratic process.

In Mid Valley, the CAP director clearly envisioned educators and non-educators deliberating and developing ideas together. This commitment to equality of voice is evident in his repeated comments throughout the initiative about not directing the process: "Part of my R&D is to find out what happens when I don't try to control those situations and allow an advisory group to speak its mind, even if it's totally off-base." Early documents developed by the CAP director and participants also signaled an intent for CAP to involve reasoned-based decision making and "informed discussions." At the outset, the superintendent also indicated an interest in involving community members as partners in the CAP initiative—ones who take "ownership" and develop a sense of "mutual accountability." He also spoke of the value of "open dialogue," letting community members examine data to develop ideas, working on shared interests, and being involved in a "two-way process." As discussed later, however, other comments and actions by the superintendent signaled a potentially different conception of democratic involvement.

Deliberative Democratic Practice

To what extent did the two districts realize their deliberative democratic intentions? In this section I briefly highlight how the two endeavors unfolded along the core principles.

Conversations and Decisions Aimed at The Common Good

Aside from a few skeptical caveats, Highland participants had a common sense of mission: to determine together where the district wants to go and how to get there. According to one principal, the purpose was "To bring community members, parents, administrators, teachers, all of the different players in the [Highland] District together to create a plan that met the needs of all of the different members of the community—not just the teachers or just the students or students, but everybody involved." The one major exception was Maria, a non-English-speaking parent who understood the purpose as the district *giving information* to participants (I return to Maria later). When probed, most participants also described the discussions as ones focused on the good of the district, instead of individual interests. For example, one student explained, "I thought everyone there was trying to not only improve their schools, or fill their own needs, but they also were willing to help our district as a whole."

141

In contrast, in Mid Valley, the idea of working toward the common good never congealed at the broader level when the community and board came together. Moreover, there was considerable inconsistency in perceptions of the purpose of CAP. Some participants admitted to never really understanding its mission. Others believed community members were brought in under the false pretense of collaboration, but were intended to serve other purposes. According to one district administrator: "[I]t was kind of brought in as a way to bring the community into the schools more so that they would support schools more financially, that it would be more willing to pass bonds or tax overrides or whatever." As examined in more depth later, these suspicions of ulterior motives contributed greatly to pervasive mistrust and the demise of CAP. In the joint Advisory-Board Study Sessions it became clear that participants were not on the same page and were not necessarily working to achieve common ground. As many participants explained, the initiative took on a more interest-based tone over the course of the year and meetings reflected little sense of shared goals. Unlike Highland, Mid Valley leaders did not consistently focus on how to structure the process in ways that lead participants to a shared understanding of purpose or a broadening of private interests.

Decisions Based on Reasoned Arguments

Aside from a few counter-examples, Highland participants consistently described strategic planning as two-way dialogue, intellectual exchange, and people explaining their point of view. According to one citizen participant:

> It was debating but it was not arguing. . . . There were times when people would have different opinions. . . . You'd get some teacher saying, "We don't have enough prep time," and then some parent saying, "I don't care about your prep time; I want you teaching my kid." But it wasn't sort of personal and defensive. And they then sort of talked through, "Well, what does that mean? How do we do that?"

The student described a similar reasoning process: "And then the people who weren't really for that . . . strategy, . . . we asked them . . . what would they want? . . . Yeah, to explain their point of view, since they weren't for the [ideas] that we had." Several structural features facilitated this reasoning process. First, small groups allowed significant amounts of time for in-depth conversation. Second, once all groups presented their priority strategies and these top 10-12 strategies were displayed on poster paper, facilitators gave each participant 30 seconds to present his/her arguments for or against various strategies. This process, called a "30 second whip," publicized individuals' reasons for wanting a certain strategy. It encouraged them to consider the proposed strategies based on their merits instead of who introduced them or which appeared to have more support. Third, the decision rule of "can you live with this?" helped, as one citizen explained, "to get buy-in without getting bogged down in consensus." This rule prevented the decision making process from breaking down in the face of one person whose views were counter to the general will of the group. Moreover, by asking the question "Is there anyone who cannot live with this as a strategy?" facilitators often inspired participants to open up and make their reasons explicit.

In Mid Valley, reason-based decision making characterized most Advisory meetings, but the evidence is more mixed for the broader interactions in the three Study Sessions. Facilitated in part by an extensive review of data (discussed in greater detail under "publicity" below), advisors spent much of the first year learning about and then discussing the performance of district students, how they were instructed and assessed, how teachers were supported, and how schools are funded. Over time, advisors began asking questions and requesting new data to inform the discussions. Ultimately, advisors used these data to articulate the perceived problems and potential solutions. For example, the group's decision to focus on improving teacher quality stemmed from discussions about test scores. Most advisors credit the seeds of this idea to the research of a local education professor who spoke at one of their meetings. Her data linking teacher quality to student performance, along with discussions about teachers' working conditions, convinced advisors that teachers were the linchpin for improvement. It was not the status of any one person that swayed advisors, but instead the merits of this argument: improving the quality of teaching will improve the quality of learning. One advisor explained:

[We were] all very much individual thinkers and we didn't just say okay to everything that they were suggesting. We raised lots of questions. . . . And then we all began to understand the same issues and began to see what the issues were that were important to us. . . . And the teacher quality issue seemed critical to everything. . . . [T]o improve student learning and student achievement we need quality teachers. And how do we do that? We have to pay them more. We have to make sure they can get housing. And we need to provide mentoring for them. Whatever it takes.

This process of open dialogue and reason-based decision making broke down, however, when meetings expanded to include district leaders. Most notably, a debate over "specifics" dominated the first two Study Session. While advisors pushed to get buy-in for broad ideas and goals, two vocal board members, George and Charles, maintained an unyielding focus on implementation details. At points, participants appeared to be speaking *past* each other instead of *to* each other—listening more to their own reasons than those presented by others. For example, when community members introduced ideas of how to support teachers, several board members and district administrators repeatedly appealed to implementation constraints—"we are prevented from letting go of bad teachers"; "All of us would like to do that, . . . but we have CDE [state department of education] saying there are more than four standards. We are given a limited amount of money. . . . All our money is earmarked." One advisor tried to reason with these individuals by offering a solution to the problem. "We know there are restrictions," she stated, "but what if we tried to get a waiver? There are people in the community who want to support the board in taking those risky moves." The board member who was most forcefully pushing the issue of constraints, however, did not respond and the idea of waivers was never addressed.

During the final Study Session months later, district leaders, for the first time, attended to issues of how to structure the meeting to promote reason-based discussions. For example, the facilitator's ground rules asked participants to "listen to each other: avoid side conversations" and participants broke into small and large groups throughout the day to brainstorm and argue for ideas about which they felt strongly. Despite the concrete decisions made and the much-improved process encountered, most participants felt that the final Study Session was a "non-meeting," "a sham," or a "joke" that was unlikely to go anywhere. George and Charles, who appeared to be disengaged and resistant throughout the meetings, later admitted to not buying into the process or ideas generated.

Reciprocity and Equal Voice

Most Highland participants conveyed an understanding that participation in strategic planning required listening to all perspectives and appealing to reasons that could be shared by all participants, not just like-minded participants. When participants disagreed with an idea they were repeatedly asked to explain their reasons. Moreover, the 30-second whip ensured that everyone had an opportunity to speak their mind and hear others' views. Participants' descriptions of the process were peppered with references to the ideals of reciprocity and equal voice. For example, one principal explained, "we made decisions about how do we want to best meet those [district] goals [by] listening to everybody's ideas." More directly, a parent (Lucy) described the importance of *empathy* in this process:

> [S]o everybody's coming from their own vantage point, which is what people need to hear so you can at least understand and be empathetic to what the other person is feeling. If the teacher in the classroom can't buy off on these strategies, then you're lost. 'Cause it starts with them. And if the teacher's not going to buy it, then it's going to be too hard to implement.

According to Lucy and others, the discussions moved beyond "what is best for my kid" to a process whereby participants tried to understand others' views, lives, and needs.

In Mid Valley, principles of reciprocity characterized interactions within the Advisory. For one, participants spent a lot of time in meetings anticipating the needs and interests of the community and board members, for example discussing what evidence the board and teachers would need in order to be convinced of the merits of their ideas. While these interactions suggest reciprocity, they nonetheless fail to fully achieve the ideal because these discussions occurred in isolation of these other participants to whom reciprocity was directed. The bifurcation of the process—which kept board members out of the loop for one year—and the lack of teacher involvement constrained the deliberations from the outset.

The principles of reciprocity and equal voice eroded, however, when district leaders joined advisors at the table. Although district leaders sat interspersed along side advisors in meetings, these actions appeared to be token. As I discuss later, the dominance of board members George and Charles conflicted with the physical image of partners working as equals. And once again, hopes of achieving reciprocity and equality of voice returned in the final Study Session with the inclusion of a facilitator who stated that everyone would have an opportunity to advocate for one or more ideas. She failed, however, to enforce this rule and made no effort during the day to encourage those who remained silent to express their ideas. In the end, most participants characterized CAP Study Sessions as lacking reciprocity. A CAP staffer perceived resistance and lack of reciprocity on the part of several district leaders: "you've got to be willing to accept what the community's going to say to you if you engage them. You can't just engage the community and then say, 'I don't like what you came up with, so be quiet.'"

Publicity

Openness and publicity characterized virtually every stage of Highland's planning process. Facilitators ensured participants opportunities to publicly air their views by writing ideas generated in groups on large poster paper displayed on the walls, changing the make-up of small groups, and utilizing the whip. Aside from a few counter-examples, most participants attested to this open dialogue. In addition, organizers made available information participants needed to make decisions about the district as a whole and to assess the ideas offered by co-participants. The district devoted the first day of planning almost entirely to this purpose—organizing activities (e.g., "jigsaw" in which small groups assigned one member to become an "expert" on a topic and report the information back to the group) and providing a notebook of material describing the district and its policies and programs. Throughout the meetings organizers maintained a keen eye on ensuring access to information. For example, groups were arranged so that at least one well-informed administrator belonged to each group.

Overall, data played a central role in the deliberations. For example, on the second day of planning, participants received a worksheet entitled "District Indicators: What does our data tell us?" In heterogeneous small groups, participants reviewed the material in the binder and filled in the blanks, such as "The average number of years teachers were in the district in 1997 was _____" or "The number of students expelled was ____ over the last three years." After completing the worksheet, participants were asked to discuss in their groups: "What implications might the above information have for student achievement?" In the end, most of the final strategies directly emerged from an examination of data. For example, according to the district organizer, in looking at test scores of students in grades K-2, the group "felt they were not as high as they should be considering we've had a *massive* literacy training in our district for those teachers." The group believed that one primary reason for this problem was the weak language skills of students entering the district. As a result, the group decided that preparation for kindergarten was one strategy to address this problem.

Nevertheless, language issues constrained the district's ability to fully ensure access to information. Despite organizers' effort to overcome potential language barriers by hiring a translator for non-English speakers (clearly a positive indicator of expanding access), there were limits to what the translator could achieve. For example, given the fast pace of discussions, the translator was not able to translate all of the dialogue and the content of posters on the walls. Moreover, as Maria noted, all of the written materials were produced in English—including the notebook of data others found so useful.

In Mid Valley, tension over the issue of publicity persisted throughout the CAP initiative. Within the Advisory meetings, data were critical catalysts for deliberations. During the first eight months, CAP staff brought in speakers and information about education reform, district curriculum and assessment, and student achievement. An advisor reported, "we would just get lots of information, lots of articles, lots of different things. And it just became really obvious that to really make education work there really needed to be some real changes."

Although advisors understood the value of publicity and generally adhered to it within Advisory meetings, the overall structure of CAP nonetheless violated this principle. The two-stage process prevented the board, district leaders, and teachers from knowing what the advisors were discussing in their private meetings. When board members and administrators finally convened with the Advisory, most had not been briefed on the extent and nature of advisors' work. As a result, several district leaders questioned the legitimacy of the Advisory and the extent to which advisors understood the district and its policies.

A telling example of the tensions surrounding publicity came in the final Study Session when one advisor, Mike, called for an Advisory-only caucus to discuss his concern that the meeting was going in the wrong direction. The suggestion to meet privately represented a potential breakdown of deliberative procedures—taking the discussion out of earshot of all participants. Other participants quickly recognized the dilemma. One advisor responded, "Can we do it publicly?" Mike explained that he did not believe the narrowing of topics up for consideration captured the directionand work of the Advisory. Others joined in, trying to identify the concern and resolve it publicly. Although Mike ultimately retracted his suggestion, this impulse to caucus demonstrated once again that those at the table had not developed relationships as partners in a deliberative process.

Accountability and Credibility

In Highland, once again, the structure of strategic planning greatly enforced an understanding that participants were accountable to one another, to certain norms of behavior, and to the overall decisions. Facilitators introduced, and participants added to, a set of process norms that ensured not only accountability to democratic processes (e.g., reasoning, listening to others), but also accountability to individuals and groups outside of the room. For example, the expectation to cast aside personal agendas suggested that participants think about the impact of proposed strategies on everyone who might be affected by or asked to implement those ideas, including those not at the table (i.e., what Gutmann and Thompson call accountability to "moral constituents"). Most participants interviewed recalled these norms being reviewed at the beginning of each day, and believed that they were more or less followed and enforced.

Ultimately, the district published and disseminated a pamphlet with the four strategies agreed upon by the planning team. By codifying and publicizing the work, the district further ensured accountability to the strategies. The failure to publish the plan in Spanish, however, limits the scope of accountability—in essence, removing non-English speaking parents from the community to which this work was accountable. Accountability to the strategic plan was further institutionalized and made credible by formal linkages to the policy system. First, the school board was required to vote to adopt the strategic plan and action plans, which occurred in June 1999. Other formal mechanisms ensuring credibility were understandings that the final strategies guided the district budget and resource decisions and that the superintendent's evaluation was tied to progress at meeting these strategic goals. Nevertheless, there were apparent weaknesses in the district's accountability to the plan in later years. While district leaders paid a lot of attention to the new plan in the first year, monitoring of its implementation seemingly waned in subsequent years (the departure of the superintendent and several top administrators at the end of the 1999-2000 academic year likely contributed).

In Mid Valley, accountability was informally established among members of the Advisory. Over time advisors developed strong ties with and felt accountable to their fellow advisors. For example, Mike considered dropping out early on, but ultimately stayed due to the urging of colleagues. Advisors with very different backgrounds and professions, many of whom did not know each other prior to joining CAP, developed bonds so strong that the idea of leaving the group was virtually unacceptable. The Advisory also devoted a lot of time in its meetings anticipating the needs and interests of others not at the table—particularly teachers and district leaders. As such, they developed a sense of accountability to those moral constituents who would be affected by and involved in implementing their ideas.

This sense of accountability, however, was missing from the larger CAP initiative. During the first two Study Sessions no norms were established up front to ensure accountability to a certain process or set of goals. As noted earlier, even though a facilitator introduced norms in the final Study Session, she failed to fully enforce them. More importantly, there were never any formal mechanisms put in place to ensure that action would be taken on the ideas generated by advisors or in the Study Sessions. The board was not required to vote on the Advisory's plan or to revisit the decisions reached in the final Study Session. Finally, the continual delay on the part of district leaders in setting dates for future meetings signaled little sense of responsibility to the group. As one advisor explained, "we felt like we were being shined on. . . . And by 'shined on' I mean . . . that it would be more convenient if everybody just kind of went away and just quietly disappeared off the face of the earth."

Action Follows

In Highland, there is ample evidence of the district implementing at least some of the ideas articulated in the final strategic plan. Starting in October 1998 and continuing for the next six months, action teams developed detailed plans for each strategy: including an articulation of specific results, actions, individuals responsible, time-lines, and expected costs. Ultimately, the implementation of these plans became the responsibility of district administrators.

Overall, the district made significant strides with two of the four strategies. For example, Strategy #1 "recognitions and interventions" is well-established across district schools. By September 1999, the district had established an intricate promotion and retention policy that directed schools how to identify students at risk of failure and how to support them through a menu of intervention options.[10] Teachers and administrators were trained on how to implement this system and by late 1999-2000 all schools implemented it. In 2000-2001, the district focused on the recognitions portion of this strategy by convening a series of community celebrations of student achievement that included performances by choirs, displays of student work, and a review of test scores. The district implemented Strategy #2 "preparing children for kindergarten" in several ways. Although lack of funding stalled efforts in 1999, the availability of new funds re-ignited activity in early 2001, when district administrators reconvened a task force to consider ways to expand access to preschool across the district. Over the next year the district secured more than $1 million in state, city, and private funds to open at least three new preschools and revamp several existing facilities. The dis-

---

[10] State policy banning social promotion passed in the 1997-98 legislative session required all districts in the state to establish such a system of interventions in 1999-2000. Thus, the district's move to implement Strategy #1 is partly attributable to state policy and incentives. However, it is clear that the district was moving in this direction prior to the state's actions. The state policy did, nevertheless, influence the district's program. One administrator noted that "we probably would not have put as much emphasis on the SAT-9 [as the measure determining promotion and retention], particularly in schools where most of the kids don't speak English."

trict also implemented a new, four-week summer program in August 2001 for 25 Spanish-speaking children entering kindergarten.

Ultimately, in Mid Valley, nothing happened to the four initial ideas proposed by the CAP Advisory or the list of action items agreed upon at the final Study Session. Although community advisors had developed several ideas for improving district education, the board took no action on them. When it became clear to advisors and CAP staff that district leaders would not schedule a follow-up meeting or act on the ideas generated, they unsuccessfully attempted to merge their efforts with a local Collaborative sponsored by city and county agencies to improve the health of the community. In the end, participants left feeling disillusioned and frustrated.

Synopsis of the Cases

Overall, Highland's strategic planning came closer to achieving the principles of deliberative democracy than did Mid Valley's CAP initiative. Organizers in Highland demonstrated more care in how they structured the process. While not all of these structures and norms were successful (e.g., "catching people up" with one day of intensive examination of data was not enough time, "leaving titles at the door" may not have been effective with well-known leaders), they at least made public some of the potential barriers that could disrupt or inhibit the deliberative process (e.g., lack of knowledge, bias of status). Finally, counter-examples in Highland's strategic planning demonstrate that regardless of the structural arrangements, not every moment reflected or every participant embraced the democratic ideals, as discussed further in the next section.

The interactions of district staff and community members with the CAP Advisory provided the only beacon of democratic light in Mid Valley. Once district leaders joined advisors in deliberations there was persistent tension over the purpose of the endeavor and how the initiative was supposed to unfold, with several board members pushing for more details and community members holding out for a more collaborative process. Unlike Highland, it was not until the final Study Session that Mid Valley attended to issues of process in the same way that Highland had done all along.

Explaining the Divergent Cases: Conditions Affecting Deliberative Exchange

Why was Highland and the CAP Advisory more successful than Mid Valley's overall CAP initiative in engaging in deliberative decision making and action? The similarities of these two districts make it almost impossible to dismiss these two divergent stories on the grounds of one district being larger, poorer, more diverse, or less politically stable. Instead, my analysis uncovered a set of interrelated factors and conditions that appear to explain these cases quite convincingly: power, organizational context, and trust.[11] While each may have independently affected the process of deliberation and action, it is the interactions and relationships between these domains that appear to accurately account for the unfolding of democratic endeavors in each district. For example, one cannot fully understand power imbalances without an understanding of the organizational context or climate of trust in each district. Given the practical limitations inherent in writing about a complex and dynamic process, I examine each domain separately. As the following sections illustrate, although both districts struggled with similar tensions around collective deliberation in these four areas, many of these struggles were more acute and ultimately debilitating in Mid Valley.

Participation and Power
In an ideal, deliberative democracy, participants have equal standing. That is, the status, resources, and cultural capital participants bring to the table—be it their gender, positional authority, access to information, or skills—should not affect their ability to participate in and influence the conversation and decisions. Although theoretically power should not play a significant role, the experiences in Highland and Mid Valley reveal the difficulty of keeping power out of the deliberative arena. An examination of who spoke and did not speak, how frequently they spoke, the quality and content of deliberation, and the perceptions of influence over decision making revealed that in both districts certain attributes gave some participants more power than others and that power manifest in both obvious and subtle forms and "faces."[12] In particular, I found that two sources of power intruded in

---

[11] For discussion of a fourth, albeit less salient factor—institutional beliefs and values—see J. A. Marsh, *Democratic Dilemmas: Joint Work, Education Politics, and Community* (Albany: SUNY Press, 2007).

[12] Conceptions of power in both political science and sociology inform this analysis. Decades of work in political theory have yielded a much-debated, multi-faceted understanding of power. The "first face" of power is associated with Robert Dahl

the deliberations of both districts and were particularly acute in Mid Valley: language skills and styles and hierarchical position.

Imbalances Based on Language, Speaking Skills, and Styles

In both districts, individuals who spoke English and were articulate and skilled in logical and rational argumentation participated more frequently and were perceived to be more influential in the deliberative process.[13] While Highland leaders tried to structure the meetings so that all team members were equal participants, the design occasionally faltered along issues of speech and language. For example, most participants interviewed reported that Maria, the non-English-speaking parent, rarely spoke in meetings. Given the limitations of the translator and the lack of materials translated into Spanish, participation was qualitatively limited to those topics made accessible to her. Maria's misperceptions about the purpose of strategic planning (she believed it was an information-giving session on the part of the district) further suggest that this individual did not understand everything that transpired in the deliberations and therefore was not on equal footing with English-speaking participants who had greater access to the content of deliberations.

The language issues in Highland expand beyond this more obvious case of a clear communication barrier. As noted earlier, one criterion for selection onto the strategic planning team was that individuals were "articulate." At the beginning of each session, facilitators and the superintendent conveyed expectations about the kind of talk that was acceptable. As one teacher participant recalled, "it

---

(1957), who defined power as making decisions that affect another person. Peter Bachrach and Morton Baratz (1962) added a second face of power, defined as mobilization of bias in the "non-decision-making" realm (e.g., power manifests when issues are prevented from surfacing or being raised). Steven Lukes (1974) asserted the third dimension of power, in which individuals' or groups' desires and needs are intentionally or unintentionally manipulated. Organizational theory helps flesh out these notions of power, suggesting that power relies on relational attributes: one who possesses more cultural capital or resources relative to others at the table is considered powerful (see Scott 1988).

[13] These characteristics are likely to correlate with socio-economic and educational background. Young (1997b) notes that "speech privilege"—more assertive, confrontational, formal, dispassionate speaking style—correlate with other differences of social privilege (e.g., white, middle-class men tend to have this speech style).

was made clear that . . . this was not to be combative. It was a time to present data and to look at it rationally and calmly." It is therefore likely that individuals who were less articulate or skilled in rational analysis and argumentation may have been at a disadvantage in the planning sessions. For example, one parent, Lucy, admitted that she did not participate as frequently as others who were more persuasive speakers. "I'm a more soft-spoken person. . . . It's harder for us to get our opinions across," she reported. Lucy recalled one principal in particular who possessed those skills she lacked: "she was a very forceful person and would speak with the utmost conviction. And so we ended up going her way." Even those who were "well spoken" concurred that power resided in participants' ability to express themselves. One board member observed, "The ability to articulate something is important. And if you're articulate in this process, you can make your point heard."

In Mid Valley, the speech preferences and biases were less explicit, but equally present. Leaders did not publicize criteria for selection onto the Advisory or any norms of deliberation at the outset. Yet, as the initiative evolved, implicit expectations about acceptable and unacceptable speech emerged. One incident at the second Study Session illustrates this point. At the very end of this meeting, Jose— a Latino advisor who spoke perfect English, but spoke infrequently in meetings—made an impassioned plea for board action. Recalling his daily visits as a doctor of low-income and limited-English-proficient children from Mid Valley's Eastside, Jose confessed to feeling helpless in regard to the educational health and risks they faced at school. He urged the district to be accountable to these groups and to commit to improving teacher quality. Although his speech resonated with several women colleagues, it was not well received by board members. One board member, Charles, quickly responded with hints of resistance: "We all want better teachers. The concern I have is a question of how to make trade-offs?" When interviewed later, Jose expressed deep regret over how he presented his ideas in the meeting. He explained:

> I was just so passionate about what was happening that . . . I almost felt like this was our only chance with them [the board]. . . . But while they [fellow advisors] were all proud about how I did that, I felt like it really didn't get us anywhere. . . . *I almost let*

*my emotions take me over as opposed to just maybe presenting it a little bit
more professionally*. . . . I think maybe they [the board] might have
been more impressed if I had reiterated a lot of the statistics
that we had come across, some of the process that we had un-
dergone to get us where were are. . . . I think I would have done
it differently.

Interviews with several board members confirmed Jose's perceptions of a preference for more rational, logical speaking styles
in governance bodies. In discussing the proper role of community members in district practice overall, one of the two white, male
board members (Charles) commented that people must "do their
homework" before addressing the board. He expected individuals to
define the problem, do their research, think clearly about what they
are proposing and why, instead of just "mouthing off" or "whining."
In the end, participants such as Maria, Jose, and other citizens
and parents lacked resources—the command of English, articu-
lateness, rational speaking skills and political style—valued in the
deliberative arena. As a result, they either participated less or were
perceived to be less influential in the process. The subtle impact of
these biases is perhaps best illustrated by Jose, who no longer valued
his personal style of impassioned speech and was willing to cast it
aside for a more "professional" manner of presentation. Jose—like
potential other individuals from marginalized groups—felt pres-
sured to adopt a new set of styles, and possibly interests, that diverge
from those held previously.

Imbalances Based on Hierarchical Power
Although more traditional power struggles based on one's position in the hierarchy of the educational system or society writ large
occasionally emerged in Highland, they were more pervasive and debilitating in Mid Valley. Despite symbolic efforts to create balance—
for example, when Mid Valley board members started a meeting
by moving off their daises to sit with community advisors at the
table—decisions made by district leaders outside of the shared space
created obstacles for the deliberative process. Regardless of community advisors' status as leaders in the community—many with clout
as elected city and county officials—they were unable to secure commitments from the superintendent or board members on dates for

155

meetings or agreements on future steps. When advisors and district leaders met, they were not meeting on a level playing field. District leaders had complete authority over crucial decisions of when to meet and what to do next, thereby nullifying key terms of deliberative democracy.

In contrast, in Highland, hierarchical power asserted itself primarily before strategic planning process started—in narrowing the scope of planning. The superintendent's decision to leave off the table the district's goal of "100% of students meeting standards" and to focus solely on developing strategies to support the goal represented a more subtle assertion of power—preventing any opportunity to alter the student outcome goals. Several participants objected to this decision and would have preferred to discuss and possibly alter the goal.

Once the Highland deliberations started, however, the process appeared to temper the authority of district leaders. Almost all of the participants interviewed reported that they felt free to state their concerns and believed that participation was fairly evenly distributed. They also widely cited examples where ideas with wide appeal rose above the positional power of participants. For example, one principal introduced a strategy that she knew district leaders did not initially support: providing reading resource teachers in all schools for the purpose of intervening and supporting struggling students. Given that several other parents present (not necessarily from her school) also supported this idea, it eventually made it onto the final list and was implemented in her school. While district leaders may not have supported the idea of spreading these resources to all schools (including schools ineligible for federal funds), the force of the argument and its appeal to a majority of participants advanced the idea to the final list of strategies, where it ultimately received district funds and support.

Mediating Role of Structure

Why did power struggles prove to be more debilitating in Mid Valley? What factors enabled Highland to achieve more of an even playing field? In part, the structure of strategic planning in Highland appeared to mediate some of the potentially inhibiting influences of power. As noted, Highland developed and adapted a set of strategies, norms, and structures with the specific goal of facilitating equal standing and participation. These included: 1) rotating small groups that provided opportunities for individuals who were uneasy speaking in front of large groups—typically individuals with lower status positions and attributes—to contribute in a safe environment; 2) the use of 30-second "whips" guaranteeing each participant an opportunity to state his/her arguments for or against various strategies—potentially enabling voices of those with less power to emerge; 3) a requirement to write down all ideas generated in small and large group discussions and to post them on the wall, ensuring greater accountability to these ideas, making it even harder to silence lower status voices; 4) the use of facilitators who tempered potentially dominant individuals and groups; and, 5) the enforcement of the norms of "leave your title at the door" to further level the playing field (e.g., name tags included first names only and facilitators curbed talk if participants asserted their status into the discussion).

These structural features reflect a specific interpretation of the concept of representation. While they may have facilitated a more egalitarian deliberative process, these features simultaneously prevented individuals from seeing themselves as traditional representatives of particular constituencies and pushed them to appeal to broader reasons that everyone in the district could share. These features also prevented specific group- or role-based positions or platforms from developing. As the literature explains, in any democracy, conceptions of representation range from binding representatives to the will of their constituents (accountability) to allowing them freedom to act on their best judgment (autonomy). These conceptions also weigh the importance of representatives focusing on what is best for a constituent group (particular interests) versus what is best for the community as a whole (common interests).[14]

---

[14] In her classic examination of this topic, Hanna Pitkin identifies a "fundamental dualism" built into the meaning of representation. See *The Concept of Representation* (Berkeley: University of California Press,1967), 9; also *Representation*, 1st ed (New York: Atherton Press, 1969). Over time, theorists and politicians have adopted a range of positions along a continuum of whether representatives should be more independent and autonomous (e.g., Edmund Burke) or more strictly accountable to the mandate of their constituents (e.g., Thomas Jefferson). Many theorists argue that the deliberative model of democracy asks representatives to be independent and autonomous, enabling participants the freedom from strict accountability to reason openly and formulate new positions in the course of deliberations should others convince them to modify previously held positions (McDonnell and Weatherford

Highland's experience suggests that to achieve consensus and level the playing field, deliberative democratic practice may necessitate a conception of representation that emphasizes the autonomous and common ends of the spectra. The norm of "leave your title at the door" helped diminish the effect of status hierarchies and also precluded the possibility of any participant treating strategic planning as a process of bargaining over constituency preferences. Highland participants were expected to be independent thinkers representing not the interests of a distinct constituency but the whole community. The norms and structures clearly inhibited individuals from forcefully defending the interests of particular groups or from using group-based arguments as the basis for decisions.

Organizational Context

Differences in organizational structure, culture, and leadership in Highland and Mid Valley created important contextual conditions for deliberations. In my three years studying these districts—examining their policies and programs, getting to know central office leaders, and closely following the progress of a sample of schools—I found consistent differences in every-day district policies, structures, rules, and attitudes. These reinforcing features had a surprisingly strong influence on democratic efforts: at times directly affecting the process and at other times affecting the power imbalances previously discussed.

Overall, the Mid Valley case illustrates that the features of a bureaucratically entrenched organization—rigid adherence to rules and hierarchy, enforcement of order and uniformity over learning, and centralization of control at the top—appear to conflict with deliberative democratic ideals. Conversely, the Highland case suggests that a more entrepreneurial organization that interprets rules with flexibility, organizes work based on talent and skill, promotes learning over control, and distributes leadership, complements the

2000a; Phillips 1995). Theorists also agree that deliberative democracy pushes representatives to focus on what is common (Sanders 1997; Young 1997a). Many of the same theorists commonly criticize the deliberative model, arguing that this emphasis on commonality is a form of coercive power that perpetuates inequality and undermines the needs and interests of traditionally marginalized individuals (Ibid.).

democratic aims of joint work and might facilitate its enactment.[15] The following sections highlight aspects of organizational structure and culture in both districts and how they influenced deliberations.

Organizational Structure

The formal organization, rules, and procedures of the two districts differed in subtle and not-so-subtle ways, rendering Mid Valley a more rigid bureaucracy and Highland more flexible. Differences in the personnel procedures, division of labor, resource acquisition and allocation, and general rules of the two districts provided very different background settings in which deliberations unfolded. To illustrate, I will examine one of these areas: central office division of labor.

On a broad level, both districts were hierarchical: a superintendent hired by elected board members oversaw the work of lower level administrators, who oversaw staff and school-level employees. However, several subtle differences distinguish the two organizations. In Mid Valley, top administrators repeatedly referred to the district organizational chart that depicted a clear hierarchy of more than six levels. The superintendent oversaw five assistant superintendents, who each oversaw a staff of managers and underlings. The chart also clearly illustrated departments organized around areas of specialization, such as bilingual education, student services, and accounting. In describing the organization of the district, top administrators often referred to the chart, noting their responsibilities for overseeing various departments and specialized staff.

In contrast, Highland central office administrators could not locate an organizational chart. District staff felt strongly that a chart

---

[15] In broad definitional terms, both districts are bureaucracies—well known as hierarchical systems with fixed divisions of labor, levels of graded authority, management that presupposes expert training, and sets of rules that govern official decisions (Weber 1947). Although clearly bound by many bureaucratic features, other organizational arrangements, practices, and values in Highland resemble those of an "entrepreneurial system"—an anti-bureaucratic organizational form defined in the 1990s by scholars, activists, and politicians to alter the purpose, incentives, accountability, power structure, and culture of government agencies. Some features of an entrepreneurial organization include: measuring performance on outcomes not inputs; promoting competition between service providers; defining clients as customers; being driven by mission instead of rules and regulations; decentralizing authority; focusing on preventing problems instead of providing services afterward (Osborne and Gaebler 1992).

could not accurately depict the division of labor and responsibilities of staff. While the central office maintained specialized departments in areas similar to those in Mid Valley, the boundaries between departments appeared to be less defined and more permeable.

In many respects, Mid Valley's central office resembled the prototypical bureaucracy in which "[t]hinking is separated from doing. Doing is compartmentalized by function. Functions are separated into units. Units are broken down into jobs. Jobs are reduced to specific tasks and codified in rigid classifications and descriptions. The tasks are performed by specialists. The specialists occupy cubicles and offices that wall them off from one another."[16] In contrast, "doing" was less compartmentalized in Highland and the hierarchy appeared to be less specified.

Highland's division of labor approximated the model of decision-making called upon by strategic planning and deliberative democracy more broadly, that is, decision-making among equal partners and decisions that seek to promote the common good. The norms of reciprocity and equal voice were consonant with an organization structured as a team of individuals with overlapping functions and jurisdictions. In an environment such as Mid Valley's, in which individuals operated in more isolated, specialized departments, administrators may have been less accustomed to democratic norms, such as interacting with others in and outside of the district as equals or considering how decisions affect individuals outside of one's department. As such, the district's division of labor may have constrained the CAP initiative, which many had hoped would involve outsiders on equal footing with district leaders.

Organizational Culture

In addition to structural differences, there appeared to be related differences in the culture or a "set of taken-for-granted assumptions, shared beliefs, meanings, and values that form a kind of backdrop for action."[17] In repeated interviews and observations, educators' beliefs and attitudes about roles, rules, and data emerged as qualitatively dif-

---

[16] Osborne and Plastrik 1997, 258.

[17] Smircich 1985, 58; cited in W. Richard Scott, *Organizations: Rational, Natural, and Open Systems*, 4th ed., (Upper Saddle River, NJ: Prentice Hall, 1998), 312.

ferent across the two districts, portraying a culture in Mid Valley that valued compliance and order and one in Highland that valued proactive, goal-oriented action, as well as learning. These two backdrops shaped the nature of deliberations in the two districts. The districts' attitudes and beliefs about data help illustrate this point.

While administrators in both districts claimed to be "data-driven," the attitudes and use of data differed greatly. Overall, Highland appeared to be more open to information and used data to improve practice. In contrast, Mid Valley demonstrated a more defensive stance toward data. This difference is perhaps best exemplified by the districts' responses to my research. I presented both districts with a memorandum summarizing the views expressed by teachers and principals in interviews and focus groups, and, in the case of Highland, teacher survey data. For both districts, these memoranda contained a mix of positive and negative information. In Highland, top-level administrators disseminated the memorandum to central office staff and requested that I present the data at the district's cabinet meeting. The district also requested that principals receive copies of the survey results for their schools. While discouraged by some of the negative information, they nonetheless appreciated the opportunity to learn what school-level educators felt and to discuss potential strategies to resolve any concerns. Asked to explain their enthusiasm for seeing the information even though some of it was negative, one top-level administrator replied, "[W]e expect teachers to look at data and make decisions based on that, [so] why shouldn't we?" The memorandum received a very different reception in Mid Valley. Once sent to the superintendent, the memo was never distributed to other administrators. The superintendent never mentioned it and never requested any type of follow-up or discussion.

These contrasting attitudes toward data became direct obstacles for democratic exchange in Mid Valley and facilitators in Highland. For example, in an effort to understand community concerns, CAP staff conducted focus groups with parents throughout Mid Valley. The report of these findings, however, was never disseminated to board members or other administrators. One CAP staffer believed that the superintendent did not want to share the report because it revealed many negative feelings about and much distrust of the superintendent and district. As one CAP staffer commented, the district was "nervous when the skeletons are shown." In contrast, the data-friendly culture in Highland permeated the design and execution of strategic planning. As described, participants were encouraged to carefully examine a wide range of district data, to identify problem areas, and to develop potential solutions. Critical data and "skeletons" were deliberately exposed, examined, and used as the basis for discussion and action. Finally, by definition, a deliberative democratic process calls upon participants to learn and modify their preferences when they cannot defend them in a reasonable discussion—an understanding that clearly resonated more with the organizational culture in Highland than in Mid Valley.

Climates of Trust and Mistrust

Finally, levels of trust[18] set important climates for democratic exchange in both districts. Without the foundation of trusting relationships, participants were not likely to consider co-participants or district leaders partners in negotiating policy for the common good of the district. Overall, I found consistent patterns of mistrust between the various actors in Mid Valley and a set of more trusting relationships in Highland. These patterns hold true for relationships that were *vertical* (between district leaders and other participants) and *horizontal* (among participants and among district leaders). Here I focus on the area of vertical trust.

Patterns of Vertical Trust

In both districts, conversations about the collaborative effort repeatedly focused on participants' perceptions of district leaders who convened the group, as well as district leaders' perceptions of

---

[18] The conception of trust relied on is primarily cognitive and borrows from political philosophy and theory. Trust is defined as "accepted vulnerability to another's possible but not expected ill will (or lack of good will) toward one" (Baier 1994, 99). As such, trusting involves taking a risk: the truster is unable to know for certain that the trusted person or institution will act in a way that the truster expects. More specifically, trust is domain-specific and a "three-place predicate (A trusts B with valued thing C)" (Ibid., 101). Accordingly, one might trust a person with one matter and not with another. This analysis builds on several other bodies of theoretical and empirical literature examining trust (e.g., Bodilly 1998; Bryk and Schneider 2002; Coleman 1990; Fukuyama 1995; Putnam 1995; Putnam, Leonardi, and Nanetti, 1993; Warren 1999). Here I focus on interpersonal trust. See Marsh (2007) for further discussion and analysis of institutional trust.

participants. The contrasting levels of vertical trust in the two districts were most striking with regard to the superintendent. In Mid Valley, community members and administrators who participated in CAP consistently aired suspicions about the superintendent's ulterior motives. As opposed to the superintendent's publicly articulated vision of CAP as an opportunity for educators and non-educators to co-construct new strategies for districtwide improvement, most individuals suspected a hidden agenda to use this community effort to build momentum for another bond measure. Without solicitation, educators and community members repeatedly referred to "ulterior motives," "secret agendas," and "suspicions" of "something other than what they said was going on." It was this pervasive mistrust that led one community advisor to drop out of the Advisory. In the final months of the initiative, even the CAP director hinted at mistrust for the superintendent.

In contrast, participants in Highland conveyed a more positive relationship with the superintendent. The issue of trust did not emerge in conversations in the same way as they did so freely and with such intensity in Mid Valley. Aside from one individual, participants did not gravitate toward this topic and only addressed it when directly asked a series of trust questions at the end of each interview. And the vast majority of participants asked these questions trusted the superintendent to follow through with promises, manage district finances, and involve the community in a meaningful way.

Although the relationship with the superintendent appears to be most salient in both districts, the issue of vertical trust also extended to other district leaders and in both directions. For example, in Mid Valley, many citizens conveyed mistrust for board members, particularly George and Charles. When asked the same set of trust questions mentioned above with regard to George, the board member who had invited them to participate in CAP, advisors and CAP staffers conveyed mixed levels of trust. While all four of the participants asked these questions reported trusting the board member to manage the district's finances, none of them reported trusting him to involve the community in a meaningful way.

How Vertical Trust Affected Deliberations

As the next three examples illustrate, these patterns of trust and mistrust greatly affected the interactions within CAP and strategic planning. The mistrust in Mid Valley played out most visibly in CAP Study Sessions, where community members appeared to be "on guard" and visibly shuttered when the topic of a bond initiative arose. For example, toward the end of the final Study Session, the group attempted to prioritize the ideas generated during the meeting and to outline next steps. In this discussion, one board member, George, suggested, "If you combine them [two items on the list], you have a chronology that naturally develops. We can get a group behind the bond initiative . . . that's something we'll do in the next few months. . . ." A community advisor quickly interjected, "I'd like to keep the bond issue separate from this group. Period." Other advisors nodded in agreement. Throughout the exchange, George's colleague Charles said nothing. Disengaged from the discussions, he continued reading a notebook of personal material in his lap.

Reflecting on this Study Session months later, a community advisor noted that "some trust issues" had not been resolved. These issues came to a head, in her opinion, when George mentioned the bond initiative:

> [W]e had been told "No . . . this isn't about more money." And we were pretty clear in the beginning. We said, "Look, if this is about money, just tell us it's about money, . . . Because some people would have said, 'We want more money? I'm out of here. I'm not doing that.'"

According to the CAP director, it was not only Goerge's comments about the bond that sparked tension and heightened mistrust, but also Charles' withdrawal from the deliberations. This disengagement and perceived "rudeness" not only generated friction, but also signaled a denial of social equality in the deliberative endeavor. By reading while others discussed issues, Charles also denied respect to community advisors, an element critical to deliberation in general and to the formation of trust.[19]

The incidents in the Study Sessions also demonstrated that mistrust extended in both directions. In fact, many CAP advisors and staff members sensed that board members were not entirely con-

---

[19] Anthony S. Bryk and Barbara Schneider, *Trust in Schools: A Core Resources for Improvement* (New York: Russell Sage, 2002).

fident of the skills and vision of advisors. "I don't think they [the board] trusted us," admitted one advisor, "and we weren't sure they knew where we were coming from."

Second, the Advisory presents a contrasting sub-case within the broader Mid Valley story. Over time, the levels of trust between community advisors and district staff in charge of CAP changed dramatically. According to CAP staff, advisors initially approached their work on the Advisory with a tremendous amount of suspicion. As the CAP director explained:

> [Advisors] were leery of this [CAP] because it started with [the superintendent] and their feeling is that he basically just wants more money for the system, that he's not necessarily interested in the reform work. So we spent the several first months just dealing with their distrust for me as the ambassador.

After the first three months of Advisory meetings, however, CAP staff noticed a change among the community members from "distrust to hopefulness." All of the community advisors interviewed agreed that they started with suspicions and gradually developed trust for CAP staffers. When asked to explain this transformation, the CAP director noted that the staff's willingness to listen and act on what they said built trust by demonstrating that "we were really giving them the power to create something."

Finally, in Highland, the development of trusting relationships at the beginning of the process appeared to be a crucial first step in deliberations. Once participants realized that leaders were not "telling [them] what to do" and that co-participants shared similar desires to improve education for all students, they were more able to take the next steps of examining data and brainstorming. As opposed to constantly questioning and discerning the intentions of conveners and co-deliberators, trust enabled participants to channel their cognitive energy into discussing, developing, and agreeing upon improvement strategies.

In sum, mistrust directly lessened participants' motivation to participate and their willingness to invest in the process. While most visible in Mid Valley (e.g., board members disengaged from meeting discussions), the connection also was apparent among a few participants in Highland (e.g., one teacher questioned the legitimacy of the team). Conversely, trusting relationships—those more prevalent in Highland and within the Mid Valley Advisory—appeared to build a sense of shared purpose and helped participants find common ground.

Indirectly, trust and mistrust may have mediated some other potential problems related to power imbalances and organizational context. For example, trusting relationships between district leaders, community members, and school educators appeared to ease struggles to overcome hierarchical power imbalances. A background climate of trust, for instance, may have made it easier for Highland facilitators and district leaders to enforce strict rules about participation intended to level the playing field. Evidence also suggests a connection between the climate of trust and organizational context. For example, as a district leader, being trusted may open up greater possibilities to innovate and experiment with nonbureaucratic strategies that further facilitate collaboration (a situation observed in Highland). When trusting relationships exist, those within the organization may be more likely to give leaders the benefit of the doubt when mistakes or problems arise. Conversely, a district leader lacking trust may feel less able to make mistakes for fear that he or she would further exacerbate mistrust. This leader would be more likely to conform to rules and traditional organizational practices.

Trust and Representation

If trust is so important, then what are its foundations and how might it be cultivated? My analysis indicates that these climates of trust and mistrust often depend, among other things, on perceptions of representation. In Mid Valley, questions about a lack of representation plagued the CAP initiative and further exacerbated the general climate of mistrust. While such questions arose in Highland, most participants had greater confidence in the inclusiveness of the strategic planning team and thus more trust in the process and its leaders. The majority of participants interviewed on this topic in Mid Valley (five out of eight) did not believe that the CAP Advisory was representative of the community. Most noted that the group lacked adequate involvement from site administrators and teachers, and was too small to represent the range of stakeholder groups and interests. In contrast, only a small number of Highland participants (two out of 14) felt the strategic planning team was not representative of the community. The majority felt that the group either involved a sufficient range of participants or was somewhat representative but failed to get enough broader citizens involved.

Comments made about representation in both districts suggest that ensuring inclusive representation is important to deliberative democratic work not only for *substantive* reasons—bringing a diversity of perspectives into the dialogue and ensuring that a full range of knowledge and interests are at the table for decision-making—but also for more *cognitive* and *affective* reasons. Regardless of whether or not those at the table contributed substantively to the discussions, people were more likely to trust the process and those convening the process if they knew that their perspectives were represented, even if it was only in a symbolic way. To many individuals, sufficient representation entailed seeing individuals like themselves participating in the deliberations ("mirror representation"). Others took this one step further, arguing that sufficient representation must be proportionate to the physical makeup of the community at large ("proportionate representation"). As such, if an individual's voice in a deliberative forum is weaker numerically than what would be warranted by the proportion of her constituency in the community, this might further erode his/her trust in the process. Individuals in both districts conveyed these perspectives—maintaining that a similarity of condition (be it role, ethnicity, or gender) ensured fair and sufficient representation.[20]

Most significantly, the perceived lack of teacher representation proved to be one of the biggest obstacles to the CAP initiative. Although district leaders were unsuccessful in securing teachers' union

---

[20] This understanding of representation—or what Phillips (1995) calls "the politics of presence"—contrasts with notions that any person, regardless of physical attributes, can fairly and adequately represent our interests if he/she shares our opinions or beliefs—or the "the politics of ideas." For example, a Highland teacher was highly suspicious of strategic planning and questioned why the planning team included equal numbers of teachers and principals when there were many more teachers in the district than principals. Unlike other participants, he believed in the substantive importance of proportionate representation, noting that only those with lived experience could adequately speak for a constituency. He believed more teachers were needed to interject their own perspectives into the deliberations. As a sixth-grade social studies teacher, he felt unable to speak on behalf of teachers of other disciplines and grade levels.

participation, CAP staff tried to keep the union informed about the initiative. Nevertheless, the Advisory proceeded to meet without involvement of the union or any teacher representatives. Many teachers were outraged that district leaders appropriated more than $400,000 (some perceived it to be more) of the general fund to an initiative that did not directly involve them. Ultimately, union leaders used the CAP initiative as a negotiating tool in salary talks and district leaders could no longer justify supporting the continuation of CAP, particularly while simultaneously asserting that budget and salary cuts were needed.

Ironically, the Advisory had developed strategies that were intended to help teachers. Their priority goal was to "invent new district-and-community-wide systems to support teachers." Moreover, several community members and the entire CAP staff were former teachers. Nevertheless, it was not sufficient that Advisory members took into account teachers' interests or preferences (in the "politics of ideas" sense of representation). Nor was it enough that former teachers participated on the Advisory. Teachers wanted visible evidence of current teachers like themselves at the table in the deliberative process (in the "politics of presence" sense of representation). Due to the pervasive perception that teachers were excluded from the process, CAP was not deemed legitimate by teachers.

In contrast, Highland was very deliberate in involving a wide range of individuals who mirrored the characteristics of broader community stakeholders, including gender, ethnicity, school, roles, and discipline, although not in a proportionate manner desired by at least one participant. District leaders also consciously involved individuals and groups potentially affected by and responsible for implementing the outcomes of deliberations. As such, the majority of participants attested to the inclusiveness of the strategic planning team. These perceptions of representation, in turn, appeared to build a sense of legitimacy and trust among deliberators and potentially among those not directly involved who gained trust in those serving as their ambassadors.

The Paradox of Representation

The importance of mirror or proportionate representation as a precondition for securing trust conflicts with another potential condition for deliberative democracy. Recall that much of Highland's success in balancing power and achieving consensus in strategic planning came from a set of norms that forced participants to "leave their titles at the door" and to act on their best judgment in pursuit of the public good. Accordingly, these cases suggest an interesting paradox: *for deliberative democracy to succeed in practice it must ensure inclusive representation, but representatives must move beyond the very ties to groups and interests that brought them to the table in the first place.* As witnessed in Highland, individuals are invited because they represent a specific constituency or interest group but are then urged to de-emphasize those factional interests in pursuit of broader, common interests.

Implications and Lessons

The experiences of Mid Valley and Highland illustrate both the promise and challenges of enacting deliberative democratic principles in real-world circumstances. While leaders in both districts started with similar goals, they achieved very different results. Highland's strategic planning process involved a wide range of stakeholders in a reason-based decision-making process that yielded several ideas for district wide improvement—ideas subsequently implemented throughout the district. In contrast, the collaboration of district staff and community members within the Advisory provided the only beacon of democratic light in Mid Valley, whose overall CAP initiative devolved into potentially avoidable deliberative failure. Despite the different outcomes, both districts' attempts to initiate and sustain deliberations encountered common struggles along the way. Sitting in a political environment ripe with power imbalances, community-educator collaboration faced a range of obstacles and opportunities. The wider context of organizational culture and social trust further shaped the delicate work of deliberation—providing yet another set of possible constraints and facilitators. Ultimately, the experiences of these two districts generate important practical lessons and raise several unresolved issues and questions.

Lessons for Practice

The two cases suggest that organizers of deliberative democracy seeking to engender confidence and trust in the process and among participants and observers should *pay careful attention to who they involve and how they define the community to be represented.* Organizers might con-

169

sider not only the various stakeholder groups in the community, but also those who might be expected to implement the ideas generated by the group—if they are involved they may be more motivated to carry out its resulting ideas. The aforementioned difficulties of engaging individuals from non-English-speaking backgrounds and/ or born in other countries make it even more imperative for leaders to not only invite a diverse group of representatives, but also take actions that enhance their ability to attend (e.g., providing transportation, child care) and to participate as equals (e.g., translator, translated materials, possible training in advance).

Future attempts at engaging citizens in democratic decision-making should *structure the process to achieve deliberative means and ends.* First, guarantee up front that all participants understand the purpose of the endeavor and agree to the roles they are expected to play. Second, make explicit the rules of engagement—who will facilitate, how communication will occur between the various stakeholders, and deliberative norms—to create an environment conducive to open exchange of ideas. Practices that were especially effective in Highland included the decision rule of "can you live with it?" to help achieve consensus and a focus on the common good, and the use of a 30-second whip to publicize everyone's position on a topic.

Mid Valley and Highland's experiences also highlight *the impor-tance of pedagogy and grouping strategies.* Although CAP staff learned this lesson later, Highland leaders paid great attention upfront to providing a diverse set of activities that enabled participants to re-main engaged and aligned with deliberative norms. In particular, the rotation in and out of small groups appeared to give everyone an opportunity to state their opinion and to facilitate decisions based on reasoned argument and reciprocity. Conversely, Mid Valley's deci-sion to group the community members in exclusive deliberations for more than a year constrained the larger deliberations among district leaders who were not privy to the Advisory-only discussions, ideas, or relationships built over time. Accordingly, practitioners interested in deliberative success may want to balance the need for small group discussions with the need for all participants to reason together in a large group.

These cases also identify the importance of *data as catalyst for deliberative exchange.* Organizers should strategically use data—in these cases, test scores, demographic information, and research—to ensure participants have the relevant information to make reason-based decisions, in particular, to help laypersons judge the arguments given by professionals.

Finally, these cases generate important lessons for leadership. Most importantly, leadership in a deliberative setting implies important *trust-building roles and responsibilities*. Accordingly, a leader's candor and ability to follow through with promises are important foundations for trust. A leader also can facilitate trust by involving a wide range of representatives who might be affected by the decisions made by this group and keeping them informed and acknowledged for their contributions. A leader also can undertake several other trust-building strategies, for example, creating social or informal opportunities to interact with co-deliberators, which Highland and the Mid Valley Advisory did.

In addition, in practical deliberation, there is likely to be a tension between allowing enough time for deliberations to evolve and ideas to crystallize before acting, and not losing the attention and trust of participants and observers by waiting too long to act.

One potential strategy leaders can use to mediate this tension and build trust *during* the process is to accomplish incremental, tangible results or what Karl Weick calls "small wins"—"concrete, complete, implemented outcome[s] of moderate importance" (1984, p.43)—such as encouraging a deliberative body to host a public event or produce a product. These small wins might help enhance participants' trust in the competence of co-participants and possibly enhance the trust of observers who may be viewing the deliberative endeavor skeptically. The increased confidence and trust could further generate a feedback effect on individuals' motivation to continue involvement in deliberations. In Mid Valley, most participants regretted not having accomplished something visible early on in the process. One can only imagine the fate of CAP had advisors succeeded in hosting a community summit as they discussed early on. The experience of coordinating such an event, working together, and gaining credit for this accomplishment could have strengthened the trusting relationships among advisors and possibly built up some semblance of trust between teachers and the district as a whole.

Unresolved Issues

As noted, this study suggests an interesting paradox concerning representation: *for deliberative democracy to succeed in practice it must ensure inclusive representation, but representatives must move beyond the very ties to groups and interests that brought them to the table in the first place.* This paradox might be resolved if one considers each part as accomplishing complementary tasks. The task of constituting a representative body in many ways creates the external legitimacy of the endeavor, convincing the community not directly involved that their interests are safe and will not be ignored. It also enables those directly involved to put some trust in the process because they feel that their constituency group has been acknowledged. The task of creating ground rules for deliberators that disable representation of particular interests serves a different purpose pertaining to the internal, goal-directedness of the process. These rules ensure that participants avoid self-interested bargaining and arrive at workable agreements.

Yet, a resolution of the paradox is not this simple. The task of creating a representative body not only pertains to building legitimacy and trust, but also with meeting a normative requirement of deliberative democracy: that all viewpoints and interests are represented. In other words, a sufficiently inclusive group is necessary to ensure impartiality and a process by which no interest or set of interests are silenced. Given this normative requirement of inclusion, strong constraints on the content of deliberations (e.g., "leave your title at the door") create potentially severe and unresolvable problems, particularly for marginalized groups.[21] In essence, the process may favor the status quo and systematically work against individuals from traditionally marginalized groups who are not politically organized, who lack an associational life, and whose interests are not yet crystallized.

This potential problem is perhaps best illustrated by Maria, who was selected to represent non-English-speaking parents in Highland,

---

[21] As feminist theorists argue (Young 1997a/b, Sanders 1997), by preventing any contributions to the conversation that are framed by participants representing their identity and interests, one may be unfairly biasing the process against individuals or groups whose partial interests cannot be adequately expressed in the current language of deliberation. As Young asserts, "Under circumstances of social and economic inequality among groups, the definition of the common good often devalues or excludes some of the legitimate frameworks of thinking, interests, and priorities in the polity" (1997b, 399).

but was never adequately empowered to do so. Even if she had better understood the process and its purpose, the rules would have silenced her had she introduced constituency-related concerns (e.g., had she commented that a particular district policy unfairly impacted parents like herself). She also may have been coerced into thinking that what was decided in the "common good" embraced her own needs and interests, when it did not. Accordingly, inviting her to attend and providing a translator may not have been sufficient to secure her democratic voice in the process. In deliberative democracy, the common good that emerges is only genuine when it is not systematically biased against any group. If a group is not represented at the table or if an individual assumed to represent that group is at the table, but there is no process whereby that group's interests are articulated or their viewpoints can be brought to the table, then a truly inclusive conception of the common good has not been attained. As such, the paradox of representation raises important dilemmas for substantive deliberation in diverse settings and once again illustrates the challenge of translating theory into practice.

Another related, unresolved issue emanating from these cases are the potential speech biases inherent in the deliberative model and the difficulty of ensuring that all voices within the community are truly embraced in joint work. Despite Highland's relative success in balancing differences in power, both districts failed to fully level the playing field between individuals who were more articulate and skilled in English and individuals with weaker language and speaking skills. Moreover, both districts failed to fully involve members from traditionally under-represented communities, such as ethnic minorities, lower income citizens, and immigrants.

Addressing Unresolved Issues

What could be done to better involve under-represented or marginalized groups and ensure their effective participation once they are at the table? While efforts to provide transportation, child care, and translators are important strategies for removing obstacles to participation for lower-income and non-English speaking individuals, the problem appears to call for even broader social policy and civic engagement efforts. Perhaps one approach to this problem is to concurrently establish greater representation of and role models for marginalized groups in wider civic activities and politics. Some argue that broader structural, economic, and systemic reforms are needed to guarantee every citizen the resources of time, education, and money necessary for deliberation.[22] As such, policies that expand and provide free childcare, employment training, and enhanced education must precede deliberation.

Another important approach to this problem is to cultivate deliberative democratic skills of children in schools. As John Dewey and others have argued, making schools and classrooms more participatory, democratic, and inquiry-focused helps teach civic skills and moral reasoning—building the deliberative capacity of future adults, voters, and communities.[23]

Intermediary and community organizations are other potential "schools" of democracy that can educate children and adults about the American political system and teach them deliberative democratic skills (e.g., how to articulate an argument, how to weigh the merits of one claim against another, how to evaluate evidence). Such organizations can help disenfranchised individuals better articulate their interests and assert their voice in the educational and political systems. These organizations also can help foster an "other looking" outlook among citizens who may approach politics with more interest-based perspectives.

Finally, another approach to this problem is to make available smaller-scale democratic experiences for individuals—ones that are school- and neighborhood-based.[24] Several participants in both districts believed that engaging adults in school-level deliberations would attract a more diverse group and make them more comfortable with the process because they are more likely to know their co-participants, be familiar with the environment, and be drawn to top-

---

[22] Lorraine M. Sanders, "Against Deliberation," *Political Theory* 25, no. 3 (1997): 347-76.

[23] Robert B. Westbrook, *John Dewey and American Democracy* (Ithaca: Cornell University Press, 1991).

[24] Joshua Cohen, "Procedure and Substance in Deliberative Democracy," in *Deliberative Democracy: Essays on Reason and Politics*, ed. J. Bohman and W. Rehg, (Cambridge: MIT Press, 1997), 67-91.

ics that are aligned with their daily experiences. Some theorists also believe that these smaller scale endeavors help individuals discover their true interests,[25] which may in turn make them better participants in a broader deliberative forum.

---

[25] Jane J. Mansbridge, *Beyond Adversary Democracy* (Chicago: University of Chicago Press, 1983).

BIBLIOGRAPHY

Bachrach, Peter, and Morton S. Baratz. "Two Faces of Power." *The American Political Science Review* 56, no. 4 (1962): 947-52.

Baier, Annette C. *Moral Prejudices: Essays on Ethics*. Cambridge: Harvard University Press, 1994.

Benhabib, Seyal, editor. *Democracy and Difference: Contesting Boundaries of the Political*. Princeton: Princeton University Press, 1996.

Bessette, Joseph M. *The Mild Voice of Reason: Deliberative Democracy and American National Government*. Chicago: University of Chicago Press, 1994.

Bodilly, Susan J. *Lessons from New American Schools' Scale-up Phase: Prospects for Bringing Designs to Multiple Schools*. Santa Monica: RAND, 1998.

Bryk, Anthony S., Penny Bender Sebring, David Kerbow, Sharon Rollow, and John Q. Easton. *Charting Chicago School Reform: Democratic Localism as a Lever for Change*. Boulder: Westview Press, 1998.

—, and Barbara Schneider. *Trust in Schools: A Core Resource for Improvement*. New York: Russell Sage, 2002.

Cohen, Joshua. "Deliberation and Democratic Legitimacy." In *The Good Polity: Normative Analysis of the State*, edited by Alan Hamlin and Philip Petit. New York: Basil Blackwell, Inc., 1989.

—. "Procedure and Substance in Deliberative Democracy. In *Deliberative Democracy: Essays on Reason and Politics*, edited by John Bohman and William Rehg. Cambridge: MIT Press, 1997.

Coleman, James S. *Foundations of Social Theory*. Cambridge: Harvard University Press, 1990.

Dahl, Robert A. "The Concept of Power." *Behavioral Science* 2 (1957): 201-15.

Elster, Jon. "The Market and the Forum: Three Varieties of Political Theory." In *Deliberative Democracy: Essays on Reason and Politics*, edited by John Bohman and William Rehg, 3-33. Cambridge: MIT Press, 1997.

Farrelly, Colin. *An Introduction to Contemporary Political Theory*. Thousand Oaks, CA: SAGE Publications, 2004.

Fukuyama, Francis. *Trust: The Social Virtues and the Creation of Prosperity*. New York: The Free Press, 1995.

Fung, Archon. "Accountable Autonomy: Toward Empowered Deliberation in Chicago Schools and Policing." *Politics and Society* 29, no. 1 (2001): 73-103.

—, and Erik Olin Wright. "Deepening Democracy: Innovations in Empowered Participatory Governance." *Politics and Society* 29, no. 1 (2001): 5-41.

Gutmann, Amy, and Dennis Thompson. *Democracy and Disagreement.* Cambridge, MA: Belknap Press of Harvard University Press, 1996.

Lukes, Steven. *Power: A Radical View.* London: Macmillan, 1974.

Mansbridge, Jane J. *Beyond Adversary Democracy.* Chicago: University of Chicago Press, 1983.

Marsh, Julie A. *Democratic Dilemmas: Joint Work, Education Politics, and Community.* Albany: SUNY Press, 2007.

McDonnell, Lorraine. M., and Stephen. M. Weatherford. "Deliberative Democracy and the Rest of Politics: Can Deliberation Share Authority with Self-interested Bargaining?" Paper presented at the annual meeting of the American Political Science Association, Washington, D.C., September 2000.

—, and Stephen M. Weatherford. *Practical Deliberation in Local School Districts: A South Carolina Experiment,* CSE Technical Report 520. Los Angeles: U.C.L.A. Center for the Study of Evaluation, National Center for Research on Evaluation, Standards, and Student Testing, 2000.

Osborne, David, and Ted Gaebler. *Reinventing Government: How the Entrepreneurial Spirit is Transforming the Public Sector.* New York: Plume, 1992.

Phillips, Anne. *The Politics of Presence.* Oxford: Clarendon Press, 1995.

Pitkin, Hanna F. *The Concept of Representation.* Berkeley: University of California Press, 1967.

—. *Representation,* 1st ed. New York: Atherton Press, 1969.

Posner, Richard. *Law, Pragmatism, and Democracy.* Cambridge: Harvard University Press, 2003.

Putnam, Robert. D. "Bowling Alone: America's Declining Social Capital." *Journal of Democracy* 6, no. 1 (1995): 65-78.

—, R. Leonardi, and R. Nanetti. *Making Democracy Work: Civic Traditions in Modern Italy.* Princeton: Princeton University Press, 1993.

Sanders, Lynn M. "Against Deliberation." *Political Theory* 25, no. 3 (1997): 347-76.

Scott, W. Richard. *Organizations: Rational, Natural, and Open Systems,* 4th ed. Upper Saddle River, NJ: Prentice Hall, 1998.

Walzer, Michael. "Deliberation, and What Else?" In *Deliberative Politics: Essays on Democracy and Disagreement,* edited by Stephen Macedo. Oxford: Oxford University Press, 1999.

Warren, Mark E. *Democracy and Trust.* Cambridge: Cambridge University Press, 1999.

Weber, M. "Bureaucracy." In *The Sociology of Organizations: Basic Studies,* 2nd ed., edited by Oscar. Grusky and George A. Miller, 7-36. New York: The Free Press, 1947.

Weick, Karl E. "Small Wins: Redefining the Scale of Social Problems." *American Psychologist* 39, no. 1 (1984): 40-9.

Westbrook, Robert B. *John Dewey and American Democracy*. Ithaca: Cornell University Press, 1991.

Young, Iris M. *Dilemmas of Gender, Political Philosophy, and Policy*. Princeton: Princeton University Press, 1997.

—. "Difference as a Resource for Democratic Communication." In *Deliberative Democracy: Essays on Reason and Politics*, edited by John Bohman and William Rehg, 383-406. Cambridge: MIT Press, 1997.

CHAPTER 6

Building Trust through Inclusion: Reflections on the Practice of Deliberative Democracy

Gregory J. Crowley

In chapter five of this book, Julie Marsh examines why mutual trust among stakeholders is a crucial condition for successful deliberation in the "real" world. In her comparative research on two California school districts, Marsh observes that the most highly engaged community deliberators held a "perception of representation." They felt that the leaders who convened the deliberations had made adequate efforts to engage many different perspectives, including their own, in the process. Such perceptions of representation lead participants to trust and support the process more deeply.

Marsh's case studies show how important it is for those who organize deliberations to ensure that a wide range of perspectives are represented in the process. Only then can deliberation lead to trust in and collective ownership of the process. Marsh's study raises important questions at the heart of deliberative practice. What are the elements of an inclusive deliberative design? What can organizers of deliberation do to ensure that stakeholders who participate, as well as those who do not participate, perceive that their perspectives are adequately represented?

In this chapter I reflect upon experience as a "deliberative practitioner"[1] to illustrate a multidimensional inclusion strategy for building trust in a deliberative problem-solving process. I argue that the question of inclusion does not apply only to considerations of

---

[1] As articulated by John Forester, *The Deliberative Practitioner: Encouraging Participatory Planning Processes* (Cambridge, MA: MIT Press, 1999), the "deliberative practitioner" is one who seeks to show how insightful practice in participatory and deliberative processes can lead to better theory. Forester's premise, which I share, is that students in applied fields can benefit significantly from the insights of practitioners as well as the questions of compelling theory.

"what persons have a rightful claim to be included in the demos"[2] but also to how the process of talking together is itself facilitated and the extent to which deliberation is connected to action. I draw on data collected from April 2006 to August 2009 on an episode of deliberation that I helped organize in the South "Hilltop" area of Pittsburgh, Pennsylvania. My affiliation was the Coro Center for Civic Leadership, whose offices are located on the western edge of nine Hilltop neighborhoods that meander along a bluff overlooking the Monongahela River. The Birmingham Foundation, which serves the Hilltop, awarded a grant to Coro to organize deliberations that would lead to greater neighborhood collaboration in solving shared problems in the Hilltop community.

As stakeholders in the future of the Hilltop, Coro board and staff were aware of the struggles that the neighborhoods had faced in the past 25 years or so, with the rapid decline of the steel industry in Pittsburgh. In the first third of the 20th century, immigrants from Central and Eastern Europe settled in the Hilltop to work in Pittsburgh's growing manufacturing industries. In the second third of the century, stable working-class families benefited from the proximity to downtown, affordability of housing, and overall high quality of life offered by the Hilltop. As Pittsburgh's industrial economy collapsed in the last third of the century, the population plummeted by 50 percent, the quality of schools declined rapidly, crime and violence increased, and a growing number of youth became idle—not in school or work.

With a mission to strengthen leadership for community problem solving and a vision of creating an inclusive democracy, Coro board and staff saw in the Hilltop a need and an opportunity to help move the community forward. Neighborhood identities are very strong in Pittsburgh. Community leaders in the Hilltop had worked mostly with others in their own neighborhoods—through block watches, civic councils and other voluntary associations—to address social problems. Occasionally, groups from different neighborhoods have worked together to take advantage of opportunities in economic development, housing and public safety. Some partnerships such as the Hilltop Housing Initiative have been created to develop housing and

---

[2] Dahl, Robert. *Democracy and Its Critics.* (New Haven, CT: Yale University Press, 1989), 119.

other revitalization efforts in the Hilltop. But no organizational structures were put in place to foster regular collaborative planning among the hundreds of business, government and nonprofit organizations on the Hilltop. Thus the conditions for robust social innovation—cross-sector and multi-neighborhood cooperation—were not in place.[3]

Individual Hilltop neighborhoods suffered from a lack of "bridging social capital"—relationships of trust and reciprocity among different kinds of people who live in various geographic locations and control access to disparate resources.[4] Research on social capital indicates that leaders who succeed in revitalizing economically distressed neighborhoods are those who not only bond with people who are very similar to themselves and live in close proximity but are able to build bridges among people who are likely to be different.[5]

Coro initiated the Hilltop project with the belief that bridging social capital can be built through a formal deliberative process that involves many different kinds of people. When people who do not know each other are presented with opportunities to discuss issues of mutual concern together, they can build a foundation of trust that enables future collaboration. Strategies for including a wide range of perspectives strengthen deliberators' perceptions that the process is broadly representative of relevant stakeholders in the community. Such perceptions of representation motivate further stakeholder participation.

Coro engaged several partners to mobilize diverse stakeholders across the nine Hilltop neighborhoods in various stages of deliberative problem solving. I utilize several sources of data to illustrate the multidimensional inclusion strategy. The first source was 185 interviews with stakeholders living or working in the Hilltop

---

[3] Paul C. Brophy and Kim Burnett, "Building a New Framework for Community Development in Weak-Market Cities," (report prepared for Community Development Partnership Network, Philadelphia, PA, April, 2003). See also Carmen Sirianni, *Investing in Democracy: Engaging Citizens in Collaborative Governance* (Washington D.C.: Brookings Institution, 2009).

[4] On the concept of social capital see Robert D. Putnam, *Bowling Alone: The Collapse and Revival of American Community* (New York: Simon and Schuster, 2000).

[5] See Ross Gittel and Avis Vidal, *Community Organizing: Building Social Capital as a Development Strategy* (Thousand Oaks, CA: Sage Publications, 1998); also Robert Wuthnow, *Loose Connections: Joining Together in America's Fragmented Communities* (Cambridge, MA: Harvard University Press, 1998).

neighborhoods of Allentown, Arlington, Arlington Heights, Beltzhoover, Carrick, Knoxville, Mt. Oliver, Mt. Oliver Borough, and St.
Clair. One hundred forty nine of those interviewed were contacted
through a "door knocking" campaign of randomly selected Hilltop
residential and nonresidential properties. The second source was 62
community meetings attended by an action research team, which included Coro staff as well as faculty, staff and students affiliated with
Carnegie Mellon University's Southwestern Pennsylvania Program
for Deliberative Democracy.[6] The third source of data came from a
day-long "Community Conversation," held by Coro and its partners,
which convened people from across the nine Hilltop neighborhoods.
Forty-seven exit surveys were collected at this event. Additional secondary data sources include the U.S. Census, research reports and
government program information covering the Hilltop.

Inclusion and Deliberation

In his seminal reflections on early American Democracy, Alexis de
Tocqueville observed that when citizens discuss issues with each
other they not only define and learn about the issues but also learn to
understand each other's interests and values.[7] Talking and listening
enables citizens to better understand how issues connect or conflict
from various points of view. Iris Marion Young took Tocqueville's
insight about how people learn through talking together a step further. She argued that if people aim to solve their collective problems
together, "they must listen *across their differences* to understand how
proposals and policies affect others differently situated."[8] Young
emphasized what Marsh calls a "substantive" reason for including
the perspectives of multiple stakeholders in a deliberative process.
By engaging the full range of knowledge and interests in decision-
making, deliberation can lead to better outcomes for the public good.

---

[6] Created in the spring of 2005, the Southwestern Pennsylvania Program for Deliberative Democracy has a mission to improve local and regional decision-making
through informed citizen deliberations.

[7] Alexis de Tocqueville, *Democracy in America,* ed. Richard D. Heffner (New York:
Penguin Books, 1984).

[8] Iris M. Young, *Inclusion and Democracy* (New York: Oxford University Press. 2000),
118.

But there are also "cognitive" and "affective" reasons for making deliberation inclusive, according to Marsh. Regardless of whether deliberators contribute substantively to the results of a discussion, they may be "more likely to trust the process and those convening the process" if they know that their perspectives are being represented. If stakeholders do not believe a deliberative process to be inclusive, they may withhold their trust from the process and bridging social capital may not emerge. When deliberation is used to build social capital as a community revitalization strategy, care must be taken to ensure that perspectives of relevant stakeholders are represented in the process.

The multi-dimensional inclusion strategy in the Hilltop began in the spring of 2006 when Coro formed its "Hilltop Partnership" whose goal was to convene stakeholders across the Hilltop to share their perspectives on common problems, build trust, and begin working together. In addition to Coro, the Hilltop Partnership included the Birmingham Foundation, the Southwestern Pennsylvania program for Deliberative Democracy, the Mayor's Office and the Planning Department of the City of Pittsburgh, the Office of City Council District 3 (representing the Hilltop neighborhoods), and the community development intermediary, the Pittsburgh Partnership for Neighborhood Development (PPND).

There were three dimensions to the Hilltop Partnership's strategy of inclusion that I will illustrate: The dimension of *invitation* focused on including the widest possible range of perspectives in the-deliberative problem solving. The dimension of *deliberation* focused on facilitating dialogue in such a way that diverse perspectives were actually heard and utilized as a source of learning and community problem solving. The dimension of *action* focused on ensuring that deliberation resulted in actions to bring about changes desired by stakeholders.

First Dimension: Invitation

The question of "who participates" is at the heart of modern studies of democracy.[9] Citizens gain the opportunity to participate through a variety of means. The principal way in which citizens come

---

[9] See Robert Dahl, *Who Governs? Democracy and Power in an American City* (New Haven, CT: Yale University Press, 1961).

to participate in deliberative forums is through an invitation that promises something different from the past.[10] Research conducted by Lawrence Jacobs and colleagues suggests that people are much more likely to participate in face-to-face deliberation about a public issue when they are invited to attend.[11] The more that organizers can do to encourage citizens to attend meetings, beyond merely posting a formal announcement, the more people will show up. Intentional outreach efforts are particularly important for engaging people who do not typically participate in public meetings.

Invitations for a preliminary phase of deliberation in the Hilltop were targeted at community leaders—those with experience in organizing others. Leaders routinely show up for public events and often have a keen sense of how to move from deliberation to action on issues. Without inviting leaders to participate, there is little hope that a deliberative process will lead to action on an issue.[12] Connecting leaders from different Hilltop neighborhoods was a top priority of the Birmingham Foundation. Demand for philanthropic investment was rising rapidly against a limited supply of funds in the first decade of the 21st Century. The Foundation established a policy of supporting projects that integrate the work of multiple existing groups for the benefit of the whole Hilltop. From a philanthropic perspective, it made more sense to invest in a few strategically aligned community improvement projects than to support a large number of competing or duplicative projects in different neighborhoods. The Foundation also wanted to ensure that all neighborhoods were represented in any broad improvement efforts. Lessons from past experience taught that community leaders will not support initiatives that fail to represent the perspectives and interests of all neighborhoods affected by a decision.

In March 2006 Jeffrey Koch, a longtime resident of the Allentown neighborhood, won a special election for Pittsburgh City

---

[10] See Peter Block, *Community: The Structure of Belonging*. (San Francisco, CA: Berrett-Koehler Publishers, 2008).

[11] Lawrence Jacobs, Fay Lomax Cook and Michael X. Delli Carpini, *Talking Together: Public Deliberation and Political Participation in America* (Chicago: University of Chicago Press, 2009).

[12] David D. Chrislip, *The Collaborative Leadership Fieldbook* (San Francisco, CA: Jossey-Bass, 2002).

Council District 3. Koch's district covered much of the Hilltop. Faced with shrinking government resources at a time of growing need, Koch was interested in fostering collaboration among voluntary neighborhood associations. He believed that successful government action depended upon neighborhoods working together to decide common goals. As an elected official, he would be able to work more effectively by engaging a single but inclusive group of stakeholders than by working with each group or neighborhood separately. Koch did not want to exclude any groups or neighborhoods from his efforts because he knew how quickly community leaders would become divided if they believed their perspectives had not been represented in an initiative aimed at improvement of the whole Hilltop.

Koch's first major initiative was to invite community leaders on the Hilltop to join a "Hilltop Steering Committee" that would begin the process of fostering collaborative problem solving in the Hilltop. Koch personally contacted approximately 50 leaders, representing active citizens from each neighborhood, to encourage their participation. But he also kept the meetings open to the public and made sure meeting times and locations were well publicized. In November 2006 the Steering Committee held its first monthly meeting. Thirty five leaders representing neighborhoods across the Hilltop attended. The purpose of the meeting was to begin a conversation and build relationships that could lead to a future for the Hilltop that was different from the past. Participants did something that was atypical: They committed themselves to working inclusively to improve the Hilltop as a whole rather than to bring immediate benefits to their own groups or neighborhoods.

Prior to this first meeting of the Steering Committee, in April 2006 the action research team began observing the meetings of community groups across the Hilltop with the goal of identifying the issues of top concern to leaders in different neighborhoods. These observations lasted until late spring of 2007, with a total of 62 meetings attended (including all meetings held by the Hilltop Steering Committee). The team produced a document entitled "Moving Forward Together: A Community Conversation,"[13] which outlined the priority

---

[13] This document is available at www.phil.cmu.edu/caae/dp/polls/spring07/moving_forward_7_07.pdf

185

issues discussed by community leaders across the Hilltop: rising crime, especially violent crime; inadequate opportunities for youth and a rising number of youth at-risk for gang involvement, drugs, prostitution and other crimes; dilapidated housing and infrastructure; and a general disengagement of people from civic life, as measured by declining participation in neighborhood associations and a weak sense of mutual accountability for problems affecting the Hilltop.

"Moving Forward Together" was publicized across the Hilltop, a process I describe later in this chapter. The purpose was to help those leaders working on a neighborhood level to see that their counterparts in adjacent neighborhoods were struggling with similar problems. By describing these issues as topics of major concern not just in Allentown, Beltzhoover, or Mt Oliver, but in all the neighborhoods of the Hilltop, the document linked together multiple separate dialogues into an inclusive dialogue about the need for social change in the Hilltop. Further, the document described the benefits of working together and encouraged people to join a collaborative effort inclusive of all groups and neighborhoods in the Hilltop.

Less active citizens were also invited to participate in the deliberative problem-solving process. Community leaders serving on the Hilltop Steering Committee and active in the neighborhood block watches and civic councils believed that a collaborative Hilltop initiative would not succeed without participation from their less active counterparts. "We need to hear from people who are not at our community meetings," said one Steering Committee member. "We need to get younger people more involved in improving the community," said an Allentown block watch leader. "How can we get people who are beginning to have families on the Hilltop to come out and work with us?" asked a member of a Carrick civic council.

The Hilltop Partnership utilized the protocols of James S. Fishkin's deliberative poll to select less active citizens to be invited to participate.[14] As in the standard opinion poll, respondents in a deliberative poll are selected using probability sampling in order to maximize the diversity of opinions represented in poll results. But respondents in deliberative polls are then gathered together to deliberate upon the issues, which allows each to learn from the diverse perspectives

---

[14] See James S. Fishkin, *The Voice of the People: Public Opinion and Democracy* (New Haven, CT: Yale University Press, 1995).

of others with whom they would not typically discuss issues. When people deliberate they absorb a lot of new information about issues, they can alter their preferences, and they tend to agree more with each other on how to evaluate public choices.[15]

A dozen volunteers, including people from the Hilltop Steering Committee, local libraries and churches, Carnegie Mellon University, and Coro staff, worked together to engage less active people to participate. Individuals were selected through a systematic sample of properties drawn from a geographic information system called the Pittsburgh Community Information System. Volunteers were joined by 25 AmeriCorps volunteers, which Coro engaged through its partner organization, Public Allies Pittsburgh. Volunteers conducted a door-knocking campaign lasting two full Saturdays and four weekday evenings. Door-knockers conducted brief interviews to explore what issues most concerned people. They then invited those contacted to participate in a Community Conversation—a modified deliberative poll consisting of a daylong deliberation focused on the best ways for neighborhoods to work together to address those issues.

Follow-up visits were conducted at locations where contacts were not made in the first round of visits. Additional sampling techniques such as catch sampling outside of a local grocery store were employed as well. Approximately 300 volunteer hours were invested in the door-knocking campaign. One hundred eighty two addresses were visited and 149 people completed interviews. Each was invited to attend the Community Conversation, scheduled for July 21, 2007. One hundred thirty five people expressed interest in participating in the Community Conversation. Each was sent a follow-up letter to reinforce their decision to participate.

The interviews indicated that the less active people contacted through the door-knocking campaign held concerns about their community that were very similar to those articulated by the community leaders. "Moving Forward Together" was updated to include the results of the interviews. It was then provided to the Hilltop Steering Committee. This created a feedback loop between more and less active citizens, thereby strengthening less active stakeholders' perceptions of being represented in the broader Hilltop renewal process.

---

[15] See James S. Fishkin Robert C. Luskin, "Experimenting with a Democratic Ideal: Deliberative Polling and Public Opinion," *Acta Politica* 40 (2005): 284-298.

Monetary support was built into the Community Conversation budget for any individual who needed transportation and/or child-care on the day of the event. This lowered the barriers for participation and thereby created a more inclusive group of deliberators on July 21. In addition to the less active citizens contacted through the door-knocking campaign, every community organization with a known address in the Hilltop was invited to attend. Fourteen "resource partners" were also invited to participate—organizational leaders, from outside and inside the Hilltop, selected because of resources they held that could be used to foster successful collaboration. Resource partners included officials from the Mayor's Office of Neighborhood Initiatives and the Urban Redevelopment Authority, the Birmingham Foundation and several nonprofit intermediaries, including the PPND. One hundred thirteen people attended the July 21 Community Conversation, including 49 people from the door-knocking campaign, 19 community leaders, 14 resource partners and 31 event volunteers.

Second Dimension: Deliberation

The second dimension of inclusion focuses on facilitating deliberation in such a way that diverse perspectives are actually heard and utilized as a source of learning and community problem solving.[16] Two elements of the Community Conversation helped to draw out multiple perspectives in the process of deliberation. First, the agenda for deliberation was generated organically with input from community stakeholders. The protocol for door knockers was to ask, among other things, what issues most concerned people about their communities. Answers to these questions were utilized to construct the agenda for the July 21 event. As mentioned earlier, these items were found to be consistent with topics under discussion in the 62 community meetings.

Agenda items were printed in "Moving Forward Together." People who agreed to participate received the document before arriving on July 21 and were encouraged to suggest modifications or additions to the agenda. After several rounds of feedback on the agenda, the final list of questions that structured small group deliberations

---

[16] See Sam Kaner et al., *Facilitator's Guide to Participatory Decision-making* 2nd edition. (San Francisco, CA: Jossey Bass, 2007).

was: How can we encourage people to get more involved in our communities? What is the best way for us to coordinate the activities of the many groups operating in our neighborhoods? What is the best way for our community associations to work together, along with police, to prevent crimes from occurring? How can we better coordinate existing resources to provide the opportunities that our youth need to succeed? As residents, how can we work together to promote revitalization in our communities?

The second element of inclusion in the Community Conversation was deliberation in small groups of eight to ten people from each Hilltop neighborhood. Small groups were utilized for both the affective and substantive reasons distinguished by Marsh. Affectively, the intimacy of a small circle creates opportunities for mutual recognition and deepens a sense of common identity. Substantively, small groups enable more individuals to participate, and to participate more deeply, than larger groups. For those who are not seasoned public speakers, stepping up to the microphone in an auditorium full of people can be an intimidating experience. To encourage broad participation, facilitators in the Community Conversation were trained to "draw out" less outspoken deliberators and to allow storytelling as well as brainstorming and logical reasoning. Deliberators brought different styles of thinking and communicating to the table. Facilitators honored these differences and helped deliberators to articulate thoughts, feelings and opinions so that others could understand them.

Small-group deliberations were integrated with a plenary session in which deliberators interacted with resource partners. A basic condition of democratic deliberation is that it rely upon reason—"offering evidence, advancing claims grounded in logic and facts, and listening and responding to counterarguments."[17] Resource partners strengthened reason-based deliberation by helping deliberators understand available tools, resources and strategies for collaborative problem solving in the Hilltop. While in their small groups, deliberators developed a wide range of questions that they addressed directly to the resource partners during the plenary session. Examples of questions include, "What can the Urban Redevelopment Authority do to help us revitalize business districts along Brownsville Road and

---

[17] Jacobs et al. (2009), 11.

Warrington Ave?" "What can residents do to support these efforts?" "How can we guarantee that a representative from the police department will attend *all* of our community block watch meetings?" "How do we build a new umbrella organization for the Hilltop that encompasses our neighborhood organizations?" "How can we quickly create a community center for the Hilltop Community?" "How do we strengthen home ownership in our neighborhoods?"

Interaction between deliberators and resource partners helped foster sentiments of inclusion. Face-to-face engagement with people who control access to information and resources helped citizens feel they were being included not only in a conversation but in a broader process of social change.

Third Dimension: Action

The third dimension of the Hilltop inclusion strategy focused on connecting deliberation to action. Unless efforts are made to ensure that talking together leads to collective action, the idea of being represented in a deliberative problem solving process holds no meaning.[18] Many of those invited to participate in the July 21 Community Conversation wanted to know what difference their participation would make. They wanted to be represented in the process of making change in the community, not merely in the discussion. The more active citizens, in particular, had ample opportunities outside of the Community Conversation to speak with and be heard by others. They hoped that the Community Conversation would create a break with the past by establishing a unified voice among neighborhoods and a common point of contact with critical resources.

The Hilltop Partnership viewed the Community Conversation as an opportunity for different stakeholder groups—neighborhood organizations, active and less active residents, public officials, business owners, and community development intermediaries—to form new relationships that could lead to new possibilities for action. These different groups were included not only to ensure that different perspectives and interests were represented in the deliberation,

---

[18] Jeffrey Berry et al. *The Rebirth of Urban Democracy* (Washington D.C. Brookings Institution, 1993), 55; see also Patrick Scully and Martha L. McCoy, "Study Circles: Local Deliberation as the Cornerstone of Deliberative Democracy," in *The Deliberative Democracy Handbook: Strategies for Effective Civic Engagement in the 21ʳ Century*, eds. John Gastil and Peter Levine (San Francisco, CA: Jossey Bass, 2005).

but also to secure the resources and galvanize the collective will to move from dialogue to action.

To bring about action from the dialogue, Community Conversation facilitators documented promising ideas generated in the small groups. During the plenary session, resource partners promoted deeper understanding of issues and offered ways that they could support citizen action. Relationships formed among members of different neighborhood groups. Many of the less active citizens became motivated to get more involved. Approximately 15 participants joined the Hilltop Steering Committee and later became active in that group.

By altering relationships and creating new alignments, the Community Conversation created the opportunity for Hilltop leaders to set a direction on a top priority identified in the Community Conversation: creating an umbrella organization to coordinate the activities of neighborhood-based groups and to serve as a leadership structure for the Hilltop as a whole. The PPND began working closely with Hilltop groups as a direct result of the July 21 event. In the plenary session, the deputy director of PPND stated that her organization could assist interested groups in building an organization with the capacity to create and implement a Hilltop business plan. "If you can take this energy and turn it into a neighborhood plan to address your needs . . . there may be an opportunity for us to work with you in next year."

A post-event survey was administered on July 21 to gauge how deliberation might have shaped the perceptions of participants.[19] It is clear from the results of the survey that deliberators came away with a strong sense of trust in the deliberative problem solving process and its conveners. Eighty eight percent of respondents reported that they definitely (72 percent) or probably (16 percent) would become more engaged in their community as a result of the Community Conversation. Ninety eight percent said they left the Community Conversation with a better understanding of important issues facing their community. Ninety four percent reported the conversation caused them to consider points of view they had not considered before. And ninety eight percent reported the Conversation helped them identify solutions to important issues.

---

[19] Forty-seven participants completed the post survey. Selected results are available at www.phil.cmu.edu/caae/dp/polls/spring07/MFT_Final_Report.pdf

Open-ended survey responses further support the belief that the Community Conversation strengthened people's sense of trust in the process. An 18-year-old female from the St. Clair neighborhood remarked, "Now that I know that people really do care about the community, I would like to participate more." A 25-year-old female from Allentown stated, "The Community Conversation encouraged me to engage more with my community. I am happy to learn that people in my community are willing to participate." A 49-year-old male from Beltzhoover was "encouraged by this conversation at a time when I was ready to sell my home and my business because of rising crime. I do not feel so alone now after this Community Conversation." A 31-year-old female from Arlington believed "the Community Conversation gave people some hope again." A 54-year-old female from Carrick wanted to "see this as a springboard to future conversations and town meetings." And a 29-year-old female from Arlington said simply, "It would be a crime to have this discussion and not go anywhere with it. There should be a follow-up scheduled as soon as possible."

In September 2007 a "Community Conversations Report"[20] was sent to those who participated in the July 21 event and an additional 160 individuals from inside and outside the Hilltop. The report, which documented the results of the Community Conversation, was made available online and in local libraries. Local newspapers and radio stations publicized the report. This raised awareness across the Hilltop about the collaborative efforts and focused people's attention on the priorities emerging from the deliberation. The Steering Committee used the report as a roadmap for working together to improve the Hilltop.

In the spring of 2008 thirteen Hilltop groups enrolled in the PPND's "capacity program," referred to by the deputy director during the plenary session of the Community Conversation. The program qualifies community-based organizations to receive funding for economic development initiatives by providing training and technical assistance in strategic planning, fundraising, board development, financial management and community organizing. After six months of preparation, on September 12, 2008 participants in the

---

[20] Ibid.

capacity program made a presentation to the Birmingham Foundation, the Forbes Funds of the Pittsburgh Foundation, the Urban Redevelopment Authority of Pittsburgh, the PPND and the Mayor's Office of Neighborhood Initiatives. Presenters represented the Allentown Community Development Corporation, Beltzhoover Community Development Corporation, Carrick Community Council, Hilltop Economic Development Corporation, and the Mt. Oliver City/St. Clair Village Border Block Watch. The group proposed to create a 501(c) 3 corporation called the "Hilltop Alliance." The Alliance would not replace the activities of the member organizations but instead "facilitate communication among the organizations on the Hilltop and leverage funding, programmatic and development opportunities that can provide broad benefit to the Hilltop."[21]

Presenters identified the work of the Hilltop Steering Committee and the Community Conversation as instrumental in their coming together to create an umbrella organization. Soon the founding members of the Hilltop Alliance began to work with a local foundation, the Forbes Funds, to create the 501(c) 3. As one active member of the Hilltop Alliance put it, "We've tried a lot of things in the past to make change in our community. This is the first time that I really think we are going to be able to do it."

The Hilltop Alliance developed as a direct result of a deliberative problem solving process. Board members had a great deal of trust in the process, so much so that they have established deliberation as the foundation for problem solving in the Hilltop. The PPND put the group in touch with the national group Everyday Democracy[22], which has provided support to launch a series of community-wide Study Circles focused on moving from dialogue to action on a range of priorities established in the Community Conversation. To the extent that deliberation led to action, stakeholders felt they had been included in not only a well-structured dialogue but a substantive community change process. The focus on action complemented and reinforced the invitation and deliberation dimensions of inclusion.

---

[21] "Hilltop Alliance" (document released September 12, 2008): 2.

[22] Formerly called the Study Circles Resource Center, the organization changed its name to Everyday Democracy in 2008.

Reflections

In this chapter I have illustrated a strategy for how to organize inclusion into three dimensions of deliberative design: the invitation, the deliberation and the action. If organizers of deliberative community problem solving fail to build inclusion into any of these stages, the risk increases that stakeholders will raise questions about the integrity of the process and withhold their support. To be sure, some degree of tension will always surround efforts to engage stakeholders in a complex problem solving effort. Inclusion strategies alone cannot prevent such tensions from emerging. But unlike in the Mid Valley school district studied by Marsh, the challenges surrounding deliberation did not become debilitating in the Hilltop. The multidimensional inclusion strategy contributed a great deal to this positive outcome.

The particular inclusion strategies followed in the Hilltop may be applicable in similar cases of deliberative community problem solving. But more to the point of this study is that inclusion is a challenge to be addressed in more than one dimension of deliberative design. There is no one-size-fits-all approach to building inclusive representation into a complex deliberative process. The choice to utilize a probability sampling strategy for the invitation phase in the Hilltop was based on a perceived need among community leaders to bring "new voices" to the table. For Hilltop leaders an important indicator of inclusion was the number of new faces showing up at the Community Conversation. The door knocking campaign was designed to bring out these new faces. Leaders were satisfied that the process was inclusive to the extent that lots of different kinds of people whom they didn't know—particularly from different neighborhoods—got involved in the community problem solving effort. Leaders were relying on these new people to reinvigorate the ranks of community leadership and provide the energy to move from talk to action.

The Hilltop Partnership initiated a highly open-ended process in which nearly any community issue could have been deliberated. The agenda was created by the diverse voices in the community. The strategy for inclusion was thus not constrained by how the issue was defined.[23] If a more focused issue was under consideration, such as

---

[23] See Frank Fisher and John Forester, eds., *The Argumentative Turn in Policy Analysis*

school district policies for determining school closings, then great care would have to be taken to ensure inclusion of teachers, principals, students, unions, community developers and other stakeholder groups. The literature on applied deliberative democracy will benefit from additional research and reflection on successful inclusion strategies.

and Planning (Durham N.C: Duke University Press, 1993).

BIBLIOGRAPHY

Berry, Jeffrey M., Kent E. Portney, and Ken Thomson. *The Rebirth of Urban Democracy*. Washington D.C. Brookings Institution, 1993.

Block, Peter. *Community: The Structure of Belonging*. San Francisco: Berrett-Koehler Publishers, 2008.

Brophy, Paul C., and Kim Burnett. "Building a New Framework for Community Development in Weak-Market Cities." Report prepared for Community Development Partnership Network, Philadelphia, PA, April, 2003.

Chrislip, David D. *The Collaborative Leadership Fieldbook*. San Francisco: Jossey-Bass, 2002.

Dahl, Robert. *Democracy and its Critics*. New Haven: Yale University Press, 1989.

_____. *Who Governs? Democracy and Power in an American City* New Haven: Yale University Press, 1961.

Fishkin, James S. *The Voice of the People: Public Opinion and Democracy*. New Haven: Yale University Press, 1995.

Fishkin, James S., and Robert C. Luskin. "Experimenting with a Democratic Ideal: Deliberative Polling and Public Opinion," *Acta Politica* 40 (2005): 284-298.

Fisher, Frank, and John Forester, editors. *The Argumentative Turn in Policy Analysis and Planning*. Durham Duke University Press, 1993.

Forester, John. *The Deliberative Practitioner: Encouraging Participatory Planning Processes*. Cambridge: MIT Press, 1999.

Gittel, Ross, and Avis Vidal. *Community Organizing: Building Social Capital as a Development Strategy*. Thousand Oaks: Sage Publications, 1998.

Jacobs, Lawrence R., Fay Lomax Cook and Michael X. Delli Carpini. *Talking Together: Public Deliberation and Political Participation in America*. Chicago: University of Chicago Press, 2009.

Kaner, Sam, Lenny Lind, Catherine Toldi, Sarah Fiske and Duane Berger. *Facilitator's Guide to Participatory Decision-making* 2nd edition. San Francisco: Jossey Bass, 2007.

Putnam, Robert D. *Bowling Alone: The Collapse and Revival of American Community*. New York: Simon and Schuster, 2000.

Scully, Patrick L., and Martha L. McCoy. "Study Circles: Local Deliberation as the Cornerstone of Deliberative Democracy." In *The Deliberative Democracy Handbook: Strategies for Effective Civic Engagement in the 21st Century*, edited by John Gastil and Peter Levine. San Francisco: Jossey Bass, 2005.

Sirianni, Carmen. *Investing in Democracy: Engaging Citizens in Collaborative Governance*. Washington D.C.: Brookings Institution, 2009.

Tocqueville, Alexis de. *Democracy in America.* Edited by Richard D. Heffner. New York: Penguin Books, 1984.

Wuthnow, Robert. *Loose Connections: Joining Together in America's Fragmented Communities.* Cambridge: Harvard University Press, 1998.

Young, Iris M. *Inclusion and Democracy.* New York: Oxford University Press. 2000.

CHAPTER 7

Deliberative Polling in Pennsylvania: From Student Senate to State Senate

Michael Bridges and Joanna Dickert, with Jayna Bonfini

Deliberative polls and related social choice practices are best utilized when they are structurally connected to outcomes that can influence policy formation. The Southwestern Pennsylvania Program in Deliberative Democracy (SPPDD) and its university counterpart, Campus Conversations, has as its mission the goal of instantiating deliberative polling and other forms of democratic dialogue at these regional and university levels. In this chapter, we describe the organizational principles and processes that we have developed and then focus on several case studies. We also note the positive impact that these kinds of practices have on the students and community members who participate in them. This is encouraging news for those who seek a connection between citizenship theory and deliberative democracy. We begin with Carnegie Mellon and end with a collaborative statewide effort involving colleges and universities across the Commonwealth of Pennsylvania.

Campus Conversations

With the certification of the 26th Amendment in 1971, the voting age was reduced from 21 to 18, creating a new opportunity for young people to have a voice in the political process. However, hopes for increased participation from this demographic were short lived as the "turnout rate [for the newly franchised voters] of 48% was the lowest for any age group."[1] in the 1972 presidential election. Statistics from the U.S. Census Bureau confirm that less than half of the

---

[1] Martin P. Wattenberg, *Is Voting for Young People?* (New York: Pearson Education, Inc, 2007): 99.

eligible young voters have voted in every presidential election since the passage of the 26th Amendment. Despite these disheartening numbers, there are reasons for hope. Census Bureau data indicates that voter turnout among 18- to 24-year olds grew from 32.3% in the 2000 presidential election to 41.9% in the 2004 presidential election; data from the 2008 presidential election confirms a further increase to 44.3%, albeit a nominal one. Additionally, as reported by the Pew Research Center for People and the Press, young voters comprised 18% of the total electorate, an increase from 17% in the 2004 presidential election.[2]

The Pew Center report and other current research offer further insight into civic engagement of young people. The Pew Center report on young voter behavior in the 2008 presidential election notes that 28% of young voters in battleground states reported attendance at a campaign event which exceeded similar participation among other age groups.[3] Other data indicates that voting behavior might not be an accurate descriptor of civic engagement among young people, particularly members of the millennial generation.[4] According to a report entitled "Millenials Talk Politics: A Study of College Student Political Engagement" published by the Center for Information and Research on Civic Learning and Engagement (CIRCLE) and the Charles Kettering Foundation, a majority of the college students studied did not find voting to be a vehicle for substantive social change.[5] In particular, they were more likely to volunteer within their local communities[6] or to engage in "civic activities that are

---

[2] Scott Keeter, Juliana Horowitz and Alec Tyson, *Young Voters in the 2008 Election* (Washington, D.C.: Pew Research Center for the People & the Press, 2008), retrieved from pewresearch.org/pubs/1031/young-voters-in-the-2008-election

[3] Ibid.

[4] According to Neil Howe and William Strauss *Millenials Rising: The Next Great Generation* (New York: Vintage Books, 2000) the millennial generation encompasses individuals born in or after 1982. "They are more numerous, more affluent, better educated, and more ethnically diverse. More important, they are beginning to manifest a wide array of positive social habits that older Americans no longer associate with youth, including a new focus on teamwork, achievement, modesty, and good conduct" (4).

[5] Abby Kiesa et al., *Millenials Talk Politics: A Study of College Student Political Engagement.* (www.civicyouth.org/PopUps/CSTP.pdf, 2007), 15.

[6] Kiesa et al., 20.

supportive and consensual"[7] (Olander 2003, 5) such as participating in an event to raise awareness of a cause or funds for a nonprofit organization. While it is important to note that the CIRCLE study of college student political engagement excluded 18- to 25-year olds who are not attending college,[8] the results underline a unique opportunity for institutions of higher education to promote civic engagement among their student populations.

From the founding of Harvard and the other colonial colleges in the United States, colleges have played a pivotal role in the education of individuals who aspire to positions of political and civic leadership.[9] In our contemporary context, institutions of higher education continue to advance their role as the source of professional and community leaders through a variety of curricular and metacurricular experiences as well as the intentional cultivation of partnerships with community constituencies as a means of fulfilling their own obligations of "institutional citizenship."[10]

At Carnegie Mellon University, students have the opportunity to experience the democratic process through the Campus Conversations program. Created in 2005 as a derivative of the SPPDD and initially housed in the Center for the Advancement of Applied Ethics and Political Philosophy, it represented the first systematic use of deliberative polling at the campus level.[11] From its inception, the program has received administrative and financial support at the department, college, and university levels due to its ability to bring together a diverse group of students, faculty, staff and alumni to discuss issues of relevance to the community and when possible, inform policy and decision making. A key component of this support came from the

---

[7] Michael Olander, *How Young People Express Their Political Views* (www.civicyouth.org/PopUps/FactSheets/FS_How_Young_Express_Views.pdf 2007), 20.

[8] Kiesa et al.

[9] See Frederick Rudolph, *The American College and University* (Athens: The University of Georgia Press, 1990).

[10] Nancy L. Thomas, "The College and University as Citizen," in *Civic Responsibility and Higher Education*, ed. Thomas Ehrlich (Phoenix: American Council on Education Oryx Press, 2000), 66.

[11] Since then, The American Democracy Project, an initiative of the American Association of State Colleges and Universities, has added campus-based deliberative polling to its Civic Engagement Action Series. There are currently 29 state colleges and universities participating in this program.

University's Diversity Advisory Council which recognized that "when groups are not in conversation with each other, their misunderstandings and folklore about each other go unexplored and the barriers can grow even thicker and more impermeable."[12] By elevating the level of dialogue above partisan debates that students of the millennial generation perceive to be limiting and ineffectual,[13] deliberative polls on campus have successfully informed the work of student government, the faculty senate and various university committees.

The Campus Conversations program seeks to fulfill three primary objectives. First and foremost, it is an educational process "whereby knowledge is created through the transformation of experience"[14] and is consistent with outcomes for developing "empowered, informed, and responsible learners."[15] The background documents developed and used in the deliberative polling process provide participants with balanced information that encompasses a range of perspectives pertaining to a particular issue, thereby encouraging evaluation and synthesis.[16] Moreover, the process promotes skill building through dialogue as participants articulate their own thoughts, respectfully disagree with others, and collaborate in the formulation of questions for experts. It also encourages critical thinking as participants examine their personal perspective, question any underlying assumptions contained therein, and integrate what they have learned through their experience in the deliberative poll.

Additionally, the Campus Conversations program is designed to promote a commitment to civic engagement and social responsibil-

---

[12] Ann Baker et al., *Conversational Learning: An Experiential Approach to Knowledge Creation* (Westport: Quorom Books, 2002), 8.

[13] Kiesa et al., 4

[14] David Kolb, *Experiential Learning: Experience as the Source of Learning and Development* (Englewood Cliffs: Prentice Hall, 1984), 38.

[15] Association of American Colleges and Universities, *Greater Expectations: A New Vision for Learning as a Nation Goes to College* (Washington, DC: Association of American Colleges and Universities, 2002), ix.

[16] The development of in-house background materials is a significant effort and requires an interdisciplinary team knowledgeable in document design, statistics, and assessment as well as specific content domains. Organizations like Public Agenda, Everyday Democracy, and the National Issues Forum Institute have developed their own sets of issue guides for use by campuses, making it easier for other sites to implement these kinds of programs.

ity. Through our deliberative polls and deliberative loops,[17] participants become active members of a process that not only gives them a voice in decision making but also exposes them to diverse viewpoints. As thoughts are shared and ideas explored, they are engaged in a tangible community building process with other thoughtful and committed individuals. By enabling participants to deconstruct a complex issue and embrace the nuances therein through reflection and dialogue, they not only come to a more thorough understanding of the particular issue in question but also acquire an appreciation of democratic practice and explore the relationship of self to others through shared citizenship within a community. It is a process that actively engages participants and reflects the notion that "in a strong democracy, politics is something done by, not to, citizens."[18]

The final objective of the Campus Conversations program is to encourage substantive interaction among individuals and groups who traditionally do not interact in the context of daily life within the community. Random sampling ensures that participants who differ with respect to race, ethnicity, gender, sexual orientation, ability, and age are part of the conversation. It also ensures intellectual diversity as the composition of the random sample is designed to ensure representation from each of the university's colleges. At Carnegie Mellon, this is a particularly valuable aspect of deliberative polling as the university places a high premium on interdisciplinary collaboration. Moreover, the deliberative process ensures that individuals who report a wide spectrum of political affiliations have their respective voices heard, thereby mitigating the ability of technology via personalized news and weblogs to allow citizens to intentionally and systematically avoid exposure to alternative opinions.[19]

---

[17] A deliberative loop® is a variation of the protocols of deliberative polls. It formally requires that well designed information be given to a diverse group of participants, that these participants engage in a structured conversation about the issues and that a survey or similar data gathering mechanism such as discussion notes be documented in the form of a report or outcome statement. Deliberative loops encompass the work of AmericaSpeaks as well as the protocols of a deliberative poll; it can characterize citizen juries and National Issues Forums as well as participatory strategic planning sessions.

[18] Benjamin Barber, *Strong Democracy: Participatory Politics for a New Age* (Berkeley: University of California Press, 2004), 133.

[19] Cass R. Sunstein, *Republic.com 2.0.* (Princeton: Princeton University Press, 2007).

The Inaugural Conversation:
Campus Diversity and File Sharing

The first Campus Conversation was held on Saturday, November 19, 2005 and focused on campus diversity and moral values in private and public life with an emphasis on file-sharing of copyrighted material. Expert panelists reflected the interdisciplinary nature of Carnegie Mellon and included faculty and staff representatives from a variety of departments including the university's library, philosophy department, graduate education office, and equal opportunity services office. Despite initial marketing and publicity efforts, low turnout from the random sample mitigated overall participant diversity and results could only reflect participants' thoughts as opposed to providing an overall indication of the sentiment of the campus community.

Nevertheless, trends reflected in participant feedback were promising for the future of the Campus Conversations program. Participants assigned high value to aspects of the Carnegie Mellon experience such as being part of a diverse university community and having the opportunity to discuss issues concerning diversity in an academic setting. A majority of participants found the event at least moderately intellectually stimulating and enjoyable and indicated that the deliberative poll exposed them to new or different perspectives to a moderate degree.

Given the positive regard for these aspects of the experience, the Campus Conversations program was established as a viable tool for community development. However, this experience revealed the necessity of supplementing the designated random sample with a convenience sample of interested students, faculty, staff, alumni, and community members. It also underlined the need to initiate and cultivate strategic partnerships with student organizations, faculty, and other campus constituencies in order to ensure short-term success of the individual deliberative polls as well as the long-term sustainability of the Campus Conversations program. One strategy that combined both of these supplemental activities involves working with faculty in courses whose curriculum either dovetails with the process itself (say, a course in political science or a course in survey design) or the subject matter (public art) and arranging for students to receive extra credit for participating as a convenience sample.[20]

---

[20] Convenience samples drawn this way will not only increase the number of participants, but can also be demographically representative and statistically relevant

A final lesson learned was embedded in a commitment to attend to institutional culture as well as the cycle of the academic year, which varies among campus communities. At Carnegie Mellon, undergraduate students in particular report a significant increase in academic commitments in the week leading up to Thanksgiving break. With the first deliberative poll scheduled for the end of that week, it is likely that many students were unaware of the event or even opted to leave campus early once their academic commitments were fulfilled, thereby dramatically impacting participation.

Informing a Debate: Discussing Student Rights

At the same time that the Campus Conversations initiative was being developed, the Pennsylvania State Senate in 2005 formed a committee to investigate liberal bias in state institutions of higher education. The claims of liberal bias and its effect on classroom curriculum and grading had been forcefully made by David Horowitz and was presented on numerous conservative websites. Horowitz proposed both an Academic Bill of Rights and a Student Bill of Rights to address this perception of liberal bias. These documents call for the representation of a broad range of intellectual perspectives in the classroom and for administrative decisions such as hiring, firing, and promotions to be made with no consideration of political ideology. Horowitz invited universities to adopt these documents as policy.

In tandem with this initiative, a student senator at Carnegie Mellon proposed a Student Rights statement for our campus. Debate within the student government focused on the necessity of adopting such a statement given the existing contents of the University's Students' Rights policy and accompanying procedure for the appeal of grades and academic actions, a multi-step procedure guaranteeing full rights to students to pursue grievances to the highest levels of University governance. When the proposal was eventually brought before the Undergraduate Student Senate for a vote, only 40% of the senators voted in favor of the proposed statement. Dissenting senators cited the need for more feedback and clarification from members of the campus community.

Accordingly, a Campus Conversation pertaining to the Student

if analyzed appropriately.

Bill of Rights was designed to provide a mechanism by which to gather this data from students and faculty members. Held late in the spring 2006 semester, resource panelists included faculty and staff from the university libraries, the biological sciences department, the school of drama, and student affairs. Additionally, the chair of the academic affairs committee of student government served as a member of the panel which was the first to include a student. Participation increased due to targeted recruitment of the random sample as well as the inclusion of a convenience sample. Additionally, this Campus Conversation also reflected the benefit to cultivating strategic partnerships within the community. Convenience sample participants were recruited from student organizations and the topic for the deliberation was derived from ongoing debates within Student Senate. The success of this collaboration laid the foundation for future partnerships throughout the campus community.

While the random sample and convenience sample were separated during their deliberations, pre- and post- survey analyses showed that both groups tended to shift their beliefs and perspectives in the same direction. Indeed, the data from the combined samples demonstrated significant shifts in beliefs. Prior to the deliberation, approximately 48% disagreed with the proposed amendment; subsequently, 78% were opposed to the Horowitz amendment. Consistent with the analysis of college students in the earlier study by List and Sliwka, results indicated that the participation in the deliberation increased participants' knowledge and conversancy with the existing Students' Rights policy. With a supermajority of participants opposed to the proposed amendment, the Undergraduate Student Senate was able to conclude that the current policy was sufficient to meet the needs of the students on campus.

As Bridges and Cavalier reported in the Chronicle of Higher Education,[21] during the same period as the deliberative poll at Carnegie Mellon, other campuses were grappling with the issues surrounding the Student Bill of Rights and academic freedom, utilizing different methods for seeking campus feedback and with vastly different results. One such example was Princeton University at which a campus-wide referendum on the Student Bill of Rights was held.

---

[21] Mike Bridges and Robert Cavalier. "Polling for an Educated Citizenry," The Chronicle of Higher Education 53, no. 20 (January, 2007).

Like many such debates, it evolved into a battle waged by campus Democrats and Republicans. At the end of the day, a victory was claimed as the Student Bill of Rights was adopted by the student government on the basis of a 51.8% margin of aggregated votes. After the referendum, tension lingered and for many, the legitimacy of the result remained in doubt with such a slight majority in favor of the proposal. Without making any judgments as to the need for such a policy at Princeton (as policies that address the issues raised by Horowitz and others vary widely among campuses), we do claim that the approaches of the two campuses to this issue differed and that moderated, structured conversations have advantages over mere aggregative outcomes.

Broadening Perspectives:
Deliberating Campus Procedures and Policies

Building on the successful collaboration with the Student Senate, Campus Conversations for the 2006-2007 academic year were designed in collaboration with the Faculty Senate and the University's Public Art Committee. The Fall 2006 deliberation centered around faculty course evaluations (FCE's) and the Spring 2007 Campus Conversation focused on the role of public art on campus. The Campus Conversation on FCE's was designed to inform the work of a sub-committee of the Faculty Senate charged with ascertaining changes being made to the content and delivery method of the FCE's while the deliberative poll on public art sought to provide feedback to the Public Art Committee which had been established by a public art policy that was adopted by the University one year earlier.

The results of the deliberation on the FCE's were presented to the Faculty Senate along with the recommendations of the sub-committee.[22] Aside from many concerns and differences voiced over the general issue of FCE's, which can be a challenging topic under any circumstance, participants also noted the conflated nature of the FCE's as attempting to provide three functions: a mechanism for students to see how courses are evaluated by other students; a means of providing formative feedback to professors for improvements to

---

[22] Results of this and all materials pertaining to Campus Conversations can be found at www.studentaffairs.cmu.edu/dean/conversations/.

their courses; and an assessment of teaching to be used in faculty tenure and promotion cases. These matters continue to influence the ongoing discussions of FCE's on campus and the results from the Campus Conversation mirrored the overall complexity of the issue.

Likewise, the deliberation on the role of public art provided a structure for a conversation about an issue that has been contentiously debated within the campus community. The concerns stemmed from the gifting and subsequent installation of a controversial art piece called "Walking to the Sky." While there were many reasons to address this issue, one in particular revolved around the lack of input from the campus community regarding the work and its location. The results of this deliberative poll helped to inform the work of the Public Art Committee by affirming a general appreciation for public art along with some cautionary notes with regard to the acquisition, placement, and maintenance of public art on campus.

Institutionalizing the Process

Given that the deliberative process not only has the potential to provide campus decision-makers with quality data but also provides opportunities for students to practice the skills needed for citizenship, the various elements of deliberative polls and deliberative loops formed a rationale for institutionalizing this process at the university level. In the case of Carnegie Mellon, this has been at the level of the Office of the Dean of Student Affairs. Here the Dean's Office seeks to systematically incorporate deliberative practice throughout the division of student affairs and utilize subsequent results to improve programs and services that comprise the metacurricular experience on campus. Consistent with the vision of preparing students to be "architects of change" as outlined the University's 2008 Strategic Plan, one of the primary objectives of this initiative is to encourage students to cultivate their skills in ways that promote a sense of social responsibility and assist in their preparation for a life of leadership and impact.

Fine-tuning the Process: Campus Conversations as Beta-Test

In addition to contributing to the educational mission of the institution, deliberative polls and loops at Carnegie Mellon University have also been successfully used to test background materials and survey instruments for use in broader Community Conversations.

Two compelling topics explored in this manner were same-sex marriage and climate change. Here the program reflects the dual purpose of higher education within the broader society.

> Although the modern research university must serve society by providing the educational and other programs in high demand, the university must also raise questions that society does not want to ask and generate new ideas that help invent the future.[23]

Used as beta tests, Campus Conversations not only provide a snapshot of the Carnegie Mellon community perspective for comparative use in subsequent analyses, but also serve as feedback loops to clarify, improve, and amend deliberative poll materials. Adjustments made to the poll materials in this way contribute to the ability to ensure balance in the deliberative process, higher satisfaction among participants in the events, and more insightful data. Taken together, this can enhance the credibility of the results when informing policy and practice.

From Campus to Commonwealth: The Pennsylvania Marriage Amendment

After beta-testing survey instruments and background materials in a November 2007 Campus Conversation on the Issue of Marriage in America, the SPPDD hosted a deliberative poll on a proposed Pennsylvania Marriage Protection Amendment. The House Bill (first proposed in a longer version in 2006 and rewritten as HB 1250 in 2008) reads as follows: "No union other than a marriage between one man and one woman shall be valid or recognized as marriage or the functional equivalent of marriage by the Commonwealth." Leading up to the first-ever state wide deliberative poll on a 'social values' issue, members of our project team worked with Chatham University's Pennsylvania Center for Women, Politics, and Public Policy to solicit strategically located sites for co-hosting the event. We invited organizers from those sites to attend the 2007 Campus Conversation and in the Spring of 2008 we visited each site in preparation for the Sep-

---

[23] Harold T. Shapiro, *A Larger Sense of Purpose: Higher Education and Society* (Princeton: Princeton University Press, 2005), 4.

tember event. The four sites across the Commonwealth of Pennsylvania were Carnegie Mellon University, the Community College of Philadelphia, Shippensburg University, and Slippery Rock University.

With the assistance of the University of Pittsburgh's Survey Research Program and using voter registration rolls from the counties surrounding each of the four sites, we obtained 256 randomly selected individuals. Following deliberative polling protocols, participants joined in small, moderated discussion groups and gathered in a plenary session to pose questions to an expert panel. At the event's conclusion, the participants completed a post-poll survey assessing their views regarding a number of issues surrounding marriage in America. Several months later, in February and March 2009, a follow-up survey was sent to participants to assess their current opinions and to ascertain whether or not their views had changed since the September poll.[24]

Background and Demographics

A number of background and demographic variables were collected to characterize our sample of participants, who were largely middle-aged (mean 54.1 years), with 49% college educated or above and 72% active members of a church. More women participated than men; registered Democrats were in greater attendance than registered Republicans as is representative of the state as a whole. There was substantial variability in the background and demographic characteristics of participants according to geographic site. For example, the proportion of African American participants was higher at the Community College of Philadelphia site (61.1%), while at the Slippery Rock University site, the percentage of participants who identified as white was 97%.

Given that much of the current discussion regarding marriage in America focuses largely on the complex set of issues surrounding the recognition of same-sex relationships, participants were asked to

---

[24] Of the 3358 potential participants contacted, a total of 402 indicated they would attend the deliberative event. This represents a 12% acceptance rate. Of the 402 people who indicated they would attend, 60% were present the day of the event. Thus, the 256 people in attendance represent a 7.6% overall participation rate. The sampling error associated with this number of participants is approximately 6.3%. A summary of the data and findings from the deliberative poll on the issue of marriage in America is located at caae.phil.cmu.edu/caae/dp/polls/fall08/

indicate their views and experiences related to the gay, lesbian, bisexual and transgender (GLBT) community. Our sample data showed that participants were moderately supportive of GLBT issues and reasonably familiar with someone in the GLBT community.[25] For instance, most participants (70%) reported having a GLBT acquaintance and many reported having a GLBT family member or close friend (38% and 39% respectively).[26] In some instances, our participants foreshadowed their complicated pattern of beliefs about same-sex marriage with seemingly inconsistent views. For example, while close to half (45.9%) of the participants reported thinking that homosexuality is morally wrong, 75% reported believing that homosexuals should be allowed to raise children.

Recognition of Same-Sex Relationships

While the broader topic for deliberation focused on the history, meaning and role of marriage in America, a central theme involved the current debate regarding the recognition of same-sex relationships. To better assess our participant's views of this issue, we asked them to provide—in pre- and post-poll surveys—the best representation of their position on the recognition of relationships among same-sex couples: whether or not same-sex couples should be allowed to legally marry, or that same-sex couples should be allowed civil unions but not legal marriage, or that same-sex couples should be given no legal recognition. These choices matched the legal and legislative options described in the background materials (i.e., the decision of Goodridge v. Department of Public Health in Massachusetts, Vermont's Civil Union law, and the proposed Pennsylvania Marriage Protection Amendment).

---

[25] A Harris Interactive report, *Pulse of Equality: A Snapshot of U.S. Perspectives on Gay and Transgender People and Policies,* commissioned by the Gay and Lesbian Alliance Against Defamation (GLAAD) and released in December 2008, found that approximately 19% of U.S. adults report that their views towards the GLBT community have become more favorable over the past five years. The biggest factor for this shift is that more people now know someone who is gay or lesbian. Roughly 73% of adults surveyed personally know or work with a gay, lesbian, or transgendered person.

[26] Participants from the Philadelphia site reported the largest number of acquaintances (81%), while participants at the Slippery Rock site reported the lowest number of acquaintances (60%).

In our post-poll survey, approximately 70% of participants in-dicated that same-sex relationships should receive some form of recognition. In contrast, only 23% believed that same-sex relation-ships should be given no legal recognition.[27] However, this general pattern did not reflect the perspective at all the host sites. Indeed, the pattern of support for same-sex relationships was somewhat re-versed at one site, with nearly 41% of the those at the Slippery Rock site supporting no legal recognition for same-sex relationships. Ad-ditional analyses suggested that support for no legal recognition of same-sex relationships was more likely among those who believed that marriage represents a religious institution as opposed to a civil institution, those who believed that marriage should be governed by religious beliefs and historical tradition and those who supported more conservative positions on issues such as abortion.

While the majority of participants supported formal recognition of same-sex relationships, there was no clear consensus regarding the form that recognition should take. Half of those who supported rec-ognition favored legal marriage for same-sex couples; the other half of those who supported recognition favored civil unions but opposed legal marriage. While both groups indicated strong concerns for civil rights as well as the welfare of children and society, those who sup-ported civil unions over legal marriage were more likely to espouse stronger religious beliefs. For this latter group, civil unions appeared to provide the most balanced solution with regard to the potentially conflicting domains of religious tradition and civil rights.

Participants were also asked to indicate their level of support on the proposed amendment to the Pennsylvania constitution. The responses reflected a dilemma, noted above, that many participants seemed to experience between certain religious traditions and soci-ety's concerns for civil rights. Indeed, slightly over half of all par-

---

[27] Our data here also correlates to the Harris Interactive report on perspectives about the GLBT community. They found that approximately 75% of American adults believe either same-sex marriage or civil unions should be available for gay and lesbian couples. Additionally, only 22% reported that same-sex couples should receive no legal recognition. The Harris report also found that among those favor-ing legal recognition, there was a split on the type of recognition between those in favor of marriage and those in favor of civil unions. It is important to note that the mean age in this report was 45.6, significantly lower that that of our deliberative poll (54.1).

ticipants (52%) indicated support for an amendment to the state constitution that would limit marriage to one man and one woman.[28] Support for this amendment came from both those who opposed any recognition of same-sex relationships and those who favored civil unions but not legal marriages. In contrast, there was much less support for an amendment preventing recognition of civil unions (33.7% support).

In essence, participants seemed to be trying to balance a number of conflicting concerns in thinking about the recognition of same-sex relationships. Many expressed important commitments to historical tradition and strong concerns for religious perspectives. At the same time, they thoughtfully considered the broader issues such as freedom of choice, liberty, civil rights, support for all families and the welfare of children.

In the end, three general positions emerged. For most of the participants, the discussion resulted in an articulated support for same-sex relationships to receive the benefits and protection afforded by legal recognition. For some, marriage appeared to be the best option and those who supported this position tended to oppose any legislation to limit marriage. For others, broadening the constituency of legal marriage to include same-sex couples created a sense of anxiety and discomfort. An observer noted that in his groups these feelings, characterized as caution and concern, were not expressed as anti-gay, but as uncertainty in regard to the future. These participants viewed civil unions as the best option and tended to support legislation to limit marriage to one man and one woman. Finally, a third group of participants, many of whom held strong religious beliefs about the permissibility or morality of homosexuality, opposed any form of recognition. Some felt frustration at the process, especially at one site that had some challenges during the plenary session.[29]

---

[28] While this number is similar to the results of the California referendum, the underlying tendency for legal recognition (70%) as well as the median age and demographics of our sample, show an undeniable movement toward some form of marriage equality, especially in light of the Harris Poll results regarding participants aged 18- 34 (who were 82% in favor of same-sex marriage).

[29] Only two panelists were present during the plenary session and audience members, some of whom were upset by GLBT table literature at registration, questioned them directly about their views. These kinds of wrinkles only highlight the importance of caring for every detail in these events, from soup to nuts.

Participants in this group supported both state and federal legislation to limit marriage to one man and one woman.

Follow-up Survey

Beginning in February 2009, we sent a follow-up survey to the participants in the deliberative poll. We received 150 responses, yielding a high return rate of 54.3% (as compared to more typical return rates of 30-35%). Our response rate at each individual site exceeded 50% as well. This rate of return and a comparison of the participant level data enable us to draw some general conclusions about changes in attitude as a result of the deliberative poll.

As in the post-poll survey administered at the conclusion of the event, we asked the participants to report their answers on what best represents their current, personal position on the recognition of same-sex relationships. It appears that there was a slight movement toward a meta-level agreement in favor of civil unions, even after the deliberative poll. In the post-poll survey, the Community College of Philadelphia and Carnegie Mellon University sites had a majority of participants in support of legal marriage. The follow-up survey results for those sites indicate a movement toward support of civil unions. Most of the movement from the Community College of Philadelphia site was from participants initially supportive of same-sex marriage. The movement from the Carnegie Mellon University site was primarily from participants initially in favor of no legal recognition but the survey also contained a slight movement from participants initially in favor of same-sex marriage.

Additionally, slightly over 40% of the Slippery Rock University participants were in favor of no legal recognition and 6.8% were identified as unsure of their position in their post-poll surveys. However, in the follow-up survey results, a slight majority of Slippery Rock University respondents favor civil unions. The post-poll survey results from Shippensburg University indicated that the participants were roughly broken into thirds among the three options. In the Shippensburg follow-up survey, 50% of respondents were not in favor of any legal recognition of same-sex couples. A closer look at who specifically was responding to the follow-up survey demonstrated that a majority of the Shippensburg follow-up respondents were not in favor of legal recognition in the post-poll survey, did not change their minds, and responded more readily than those holding positions that recognize same-sex relationships.

214

In the follow-up survey, we also asked participants if their position on marriage has changed since the deliberation. Among those responding to the follow-up survey, 19% changed their position slightly while 3% significantly changed their position. As indicated previously, an analysis of the data on the participant level revealed that a slight portion of respondents changed their position of "no legal recognition" towards "recognition of civil union." Conversely, one respondent moved from "an acceptance of legal recognition in some capacity" to "no recognition," while a few others seemed to be more in favor of same-sex marriage, a slight change from a post-poll position on civil unions. At bottom, the tendency in our sample toward broad recognition of legal rights for same-sex couples continued in the months following the deliberations.[30]

Evaluating the Experience

Participants indicated a strong sense of satisfaction with their participation in the deliberative process. In particular, participants reported that they gained a broader understanding of the history of marriage and the issues concerning the current debate concerning marriage and same-sex relationships. Additionally, participants indicated that the deliberative process presented them with perspectives that they hadn't previously considered.

While a number of participants reported frustrations with perceived bias in the background information and site responses varied considerably regarding assessments of the resource panelists, the quantitative and qualitative data regarding the event itself paints a very positive overall picture, paralleling similar levels of satisfaction found in our Campus Conversations. Indeed, responses across all sites in this survey showed that a super majority of our participants felt that the deliberative process was enjoyable, engaging and intellectually stimulating. As one participant wrote: "I just want to thank you for putting this on, and I am very pleased and grateful to have been a part of it. My feelings are strong concerning the common

---

[30] Looking at a partial summary of the data, of the 28 participants who "slightly changed" their position: 15 participants shifted toward civil unions (from varying degrees of opposition), 3 participants shifted toward same-sex marriage, 1 participant supports civil unions but is slightly more supportive of same-sex marriage as a result of the poll, and 2 participants support same-sex marriage but "have a deeper understanding of opposing viewpoints/became less dogmatic."

Rating Deliberative Poll Participation

Question: To what extent did you find participating in the Deliberative Poll...

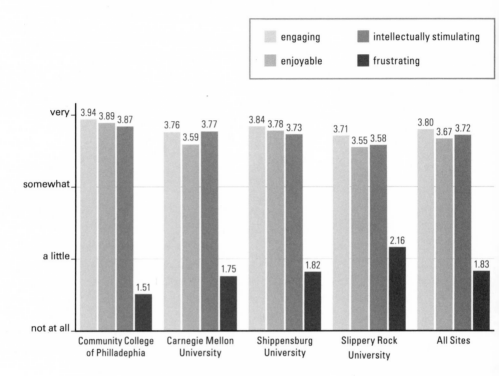

man's involvement in issues like this concerning our country. It's great to be right in the middle of seeing democracy in action."

Influence

In linking this process to outcomes, we contacted local media and local state representatives. Several newspapers, including a Spanish Language one in Philadelphia, published articles on the initial findings. An Op Ed piece appeared in the Pittsburgh Post-Gazette comparing the results of this process with the results and process of California's Proposition 8 referendum. State Representative Dan Frankel, a member of the House Appropriations Committee at a time when the bill in question was being debated, attended the Carnegie Mellon session. At first planning just to stop by, he stayed for several hours, talking to participants at lunch and listening to the

Q&A during the plenary session. At the end of the panel discussion, Representative Frankel thanked the audience for their participation in what he described as an important example of deliberative democracy. Certainly his interest in this process can only increase in light of the 2009 healthcare "Town Hall Meetings."

In June of 2009 State Senator Daylin Leach introduced Senate Bill 935. Referred to the Judiciary Committee, the bill would have the effect of legalizing "same-sex marriage" in the State of Pennsylvania. It offered to repeal previous definitions that limited marriage to a man and a woman, added a section on same-sex marriage, and broadened to definition of "Marriage" to read: "A civil contract between two people who enter into matrimony." Based upon our analysis and in correspondence with him, the Senator saw how the notion of "civil marriage" frames this issue well for those seeking the legal recognition of same-sex couples. The phrase combines the informed opinions of our deliberations. It also draws an important distinction between State and Church by distinguishing the civil side of the marriage contract from that of a religion-based marriage ceremony.

In the Spring of 2010, House Bill 1250 failed to pass committee by a vote of 10 to 6; Senate Bill 935 remained in committee. Regardless of where one stands on the issue and in accord with the need to connect deliberation about policy to influence on policy, the results of this deliberative poll have become one of the tributaries affecting the course of debate in the Commonwealth of Pennsylvania.

Afterward: Deliberative Democracy and the Courts

The concept of deliberative democracy may shed some light on the debate over the role of the courts to determine social value issues like abortion, same-sex marriage and end-of-life decisions. There are those who say that the Constitution is a living document and that the courts have a role in using its basic principles to address, judiciously, new circumstances. Others say that it is a bounded document whose statements are literally restricted and cannot be adjusted according to the times.

Supporting the former position, Supreme Court Justice William Brennan argued that "the precise rules by which we have protected fundamental human dignity have been transformed over time in response to both transformations of social conditions and evolution of

217

our concepts of human dignity."[31] While holding on to the "overarching principles" of the Constitution, it is possible to articulate principles implicit in the intent of the basic law that can serve us in our contemporary setting (like the Right to Privacy).

Chief Justice William Rehnquist disagreed. His disagreement, however, did not imply that social values issues were off bounds, only that they needed to be addressed by the legislative process, not the judicial one. "The brief writer's version of the living Constitution, in the last analysis, is a formula for an end run around popular government. To the extent that it makes possible an individual's persuading one or more appointed federal judges to impose on other individuals a rule of conduct that the popularly elected branches of government would not have enacted and the voters have not and would not have embodied in the Constitution, the brief writer's version of the living Constitution is genuinely corrosive of the fundamental values of our democratic society."[32]

More than 30 years before this contemporary discussion, Justices Frankfurter and Jackson argued in a similar vein. However, their positions issued from the opposite side of the left-right divide. For Frankfurter, the court's intervention in the rights of Jehovah Witnesses to decline reciting the pledge of allegiance in public schools was inappropriate. If the citizens and states want to pass foolish laws, then they deserve foolish laws. Our Founding Fathers believed in the positive freedom of the ancients and Frankfurter too believed that it is up to the citizens to live up to the ideals of democracy.

Of course, public opinion can be easily swayed and writers going back to Schumpeter spoke about the power of advertising, not just to market perfumes, but platforms as well. Yet the way that deliberative democrats value information and discussion could well serve as a tonic against media distortion of issues. And the actual arguments of the courts themselves can become part of the background information that citizens need in order to arrive at more informed opinions. Indeed, the background document used by our participants in

---

[31] Brennan, William J., Jr. "The Constitution of the United States: Contemporary Ratification," (lecture delivered at Georgetown University Law Center. Washington, D.C., October 12, 1985).

[32] William Rehnquist, "The Notion of a Living Constitution," 54 *Texas Law Review* 693 (1976). Reprinted in 29 *Harvard Journal of Law and Public Policy* 401 (2006). Retrieved from www.law.harvard.edu.

the deliberative poll on the Issue of Marriage in America contained the "Voices" of important legal decisions, each with arguments For and Against. And an "argument map" at the end of the document provided a visual overview of the salient features of the legal terrain pertaining to the topic.

So it is possible for deliberative democrats to appreciate both sides of the constitutional debate. In fact, it has been proposed that the 'original intent' of our Founding Fathers was complex, involving not only the document, but the republican ideals that surrounded it and gave birth to it.[33]

In situations like the 2008 California referendum on same-sex marriage, where some argue that the courts may have gotten ahead of the people,[34] the people in turn can listen to the courts as well as themselves in a larger, ongoing conversation.[35] Courts here can play a role in educating the public (in the public reasons they give, both in the decision and the dissent) and informed public opinion can provide a feedback loop regarding the current state of the nation. In a strong democracy, the reasons of the courts and the opinions of the citizens can be part of the same democratic dialogue.

---

[33] See Ralph Ketcham's *Framed for Posterity: The Enduring Philosophy of the Constitution* (University Press of Kansas, 1993).

[34] Jeffrey Rosen, *The Most Democratic Branch: How the Courts Serve America* (New York: Oxford University Press, 2006), 106-113.

[35] This larger, ongoing conversation is part of the thesis in Jürgen Habermas's major work, translated into English by William Rehg, *Between Facts and Norms: Contributions to a Discourse Theory of Law and Democracy* (Cambridge: MIT Press, 1992).

BIBLIOGRAPHY ˙

Association of American Colleges and Universities. *Greater Expectations: A New Vision for Learning as a Nation Goes to College.* Washington, DC: Association of American Colleges and Universities, 2002.

Baker, Ann C., Patricia J. Jensen, and David Kolb. *Conversational Learning: An Experiential Approach to Knowledge Creation.* Westport: Quorom Books, 2002.

Barber, Benjamin. *Strong Democracy: Participatory Politics for a New Age* (20th anniversary edition). Berkeley: University of California Press, 2004.

Brennan, William J., Jr. "The Constitution of the United States: Contemporary Ratification." Lecture delivered at Georgetown University Law Center. Washington, D.C., October 12 1985.

Bridges, Mike, and Robert Cavalier. "Polling for an Educated Citizenry." *The Chronicle of Higher Education* 53, no. 20 (January, 2007).

Fishkin, James S. *The Voice of The People: Public Opinion and Democracy.* New Haven: Yale University Press, 1995.

Habermas, Jürgen. *Between Facts and Norms: Contributions to a Discourse of Law and Democracy.* Cambridge: MIT Press, 1996.

Harris Interactive Public Relations Research Team. "Pulse of Equality: A Snapshot of U.S. Perspectives on Gay and Transgender People and Policies." Report prepared for Gay and Lesbian Alliance Against Defamation, December, 2008. Retrieved from www. glaad.org.

Howe, Neil and William Strauss. *Millenials Rising: The Next Great Generation.* New York: Vintage Books, 2000.

Keeter, Scott, Juliana Horowitz, and Alec Tyson. *Young Voters in the 2008 Election.* Washington, D.C.: Pew Research Center for the People & the Press, 2008. Retrieved from pewresearch.org/pubs/1031/young-voters-in-the-2008-election.

Kiesa, Abby, Alexander P. Orlowski, Peter Levine, Deborah Both, Emily Hoban Kirby, Mark Hugo Lopez, and Karlo Barrios Marcelo. *Millenials Talk Politics: A Study of College Student Political Engagement.* Circle: The Center for Information and Research on Civic Learning and Engagement. John M. Tisch College of Citizenship and Public Service, Tufts University, November 7, 2007. Retrieved from www.civicyouth.org/PopUps/CSTP.pdf .

Kolb, David. *Experiential Learning: Experience as the Source of Learning and Development.* Englewood Cliffs: Prentice Hall, 1984.

Olander, Michael. *How Young People Express Their Political Views.* Circle: The Center for Information and Research on Civic Learning and Engagement. John M. Tisch College of Citizenship and Public Service, Tufts University, July 2003. Retrieved from www. civicyouth.org/PopUps/FactSheets/FS_How_Young_Express_Views.pdf

Rehnquist, William. "The Notion of a Living Constitution." 54 Texas Law Review 693 (1976). Reprinted in 29 Harvard Journal of Law and Public Policy 401 (2006). Retrieved from www.law.harvard.edu.

Rudolph, Frederick. *The American College and University*. Athens: The University of Georgia Press, 1990.

Shapiro, H.T. *A Larger Sense of Purpose: Higher Education and Society*. Princeton: Princeton University Press, 2005.

Southwestern Pennsylvania Program for Deliberative Democracy. Issue of Marriage in America Final Report. Fall 2008. Retrieved from caae.phil.cmu.edu/caae/dp/polls/fall08/

Sunstein, Cass R. *Republic.com 2.0*. Princeton: Princeton University Press, 2007.

Thomas, Nancy L. "The College and University as Citizen." In *Civic Responsibility and Higher Education*, edited by Thomas Ehrlich. Phoenix: American Council on Education Oryx Press, 2000.

United States Census Bureau. Voting and Registration in the Election of November 2000 [Data file]. Retrieved from www.census.gov/population/socdemo/voting/p20-542/tab01.p

United States Census Bureau. Voting and Registration in the Election of November 2004 [Data file]. Retrieved from www.census.gov/population/socdemo/voting/cps2004/tab01.xls

United States Census Bureau. Voting and Registration in the Election of November 2008 [Data file]. Retrieved from www.census.gov/population/socdemo/voting/cps2008/Table%2001.xls

Wattenberg, Martin P. *Is Voting for Young People?* New York: Pearson Education, Inc., 2007.

CHAPTER 8

Citizens Deliberating Online: Theory and Some Evidence

Vincent Price

Introduction

The capacities of ordinary citizens to engage in successful political give-and-take, and thus to participate in meaningful deliberative
democracy, have been debated for some time. Even those espous-
ing great faith in the deliberative citizen, however, have expressed
doubts about the suitability of online, text-based exchanges for
meaningful and constructive political discussion. Some argue that
the impersonal nature of computerized communication renders it
poorly suited to developing meaningful relationships, encourages
uncivil discourse, facilitates diffusion of unverified information, and
ultimately serves to polarize opinions rather than support finding
common ground.

This chapter reviews theory and available evidence bearing on
the functional utility of online "discussion" for political deliberation,
arguing that characteristics of computer-mediated exchanges (viz.,
reduced social cues, relative anonymity of participants, and a reliance
on text-based exchanges lacking non-verbal, facial and vocal cues)
may, under the right conditions, facilitate open exchanges of controversial political ideas. Thus, far from compromising the benefits
of face-to-face group meetings, computer-mediated communication
may prove especially useful for deliberative work.

Data from two, year-long panel experiments in online political discussion are considered in light of these propositions.[1] One

[1] This research is supported by grants from The Pew Charitable Trusts, the Annenberg Public Policy Center of the University of Pennsylvania, and the National
Science Foundation (Grant EIA-0306801) to Vincent Price and Joseph N. Cappella.
Views expressed are those of the author alone and do not necessarily reflect those
of the sponsoring agencies.

223

experiment involved the creation of 60 groups of representative American citizens who engaged in monthly discussions leading up to the 2000 presidential campaign; the second studied 80 groups of citizens meeting several times to debate issues related to health care reform in 2004 and 2005. Both projects gathered extensive survey data from participants, including those in control groups who did not engage in any online deliberation, and recorded the full text of all group discussions for analysis. Main findings largely confirm the value of online deliberation and paint a broadly optimistic portrait of the deliberative citizen online.

The Deliberative Citizen

Democratic theory is of at least two minds about the capacities of ordinary people for rational self-governance. Many express suspicions about the ability of typical citizens to comprehend and decide complicated public issues, and thus doubt the value of mass participation in policy making. Walter Lippmann, for example, finding a number of fundamental inadequacies in both the press and the public, argued for a form of elite, technocratic rule relying on political leaders and technical experts to determine policy and then to organize public opinion for the press.[2] By contrast, other theorists place far more faith in the ability of citizens to deliberate public issues and render sensible judgments about policies. In rebutting Lippmann, for instance, John Dewey argued that modern democracies were threatened less by incompetent citizens than by communication systems that did not adequately serve them, and that with improvements in the means of public discussion, the ends of true participatory democracy were attainable.[3] People are indeed capable, he proposed, though conditions had not permitted them to realize their potential.

The former, dim view of citizen capacities appears to square reasonably well with much survey research over the past several decades, which documents wide swaths of indifference and political

---

[2] Walter Lippmann, *Public Opinion* (New York: Harcourt Brace Jovanovich, 1922), 32.

[3] John Dewey, *The Public and Its Problems* (New York: Holt, Rinehart & Winston, 1927).

ignorance in the American public.[4] A significant number of opinions given in response to public opinion surveys—indeed, by some estimates perhaps as many as a third—may be "top of the head" responses, given rather thoughtlessly and loosely rooted, if at all, in knowledge of the issues at stake.[5] As an input to policy making, mass opinion is thus commonly discounted, in favor of more informed and presumably rational elite opinion. This is not to say that public opinion is accorded no value by such accounts. Rather, it is considered a legitimate input to policy making only in a highly circumscribed and indirect fashion, through periodic elections to accept or reject political leaders, and not as a more direct means of deciding policy.[6] Barber has termed this "weak" democracy.[7] Like others, he argues that a disparaging view of the public underlies the dominant "liberal rationalist" model of democratic government. Citizens are seen as largely ignorant and intolerant, with highly unstable and untrustworthy opinions.[8]

A burgeoning number of political scientists and policy researchers, however, have challenged the liberal rationalist model, arguing that despite claims of being democratic in character, it renders government incapable of adequately reflecting popular interests. They propose instead various forms of "strong" democracy[9] that are built upon direct, participatory, and deliberative engagement of ordinary citizens in ongoing policy formation.[10] While proposals vary widely

---

[4] W. Russell Neuman, *The Paradox of Mass Politics: Knowledge and Opinion in the American Electorate* (Cambridge: Harvard University Press, 1986).

[5] Doris A. Graber, "The Impact of Media Research on Public Opinion Studies," *Mass Communication Review Yearbook* 3, ed. Charles Whitney et al., (Newbury Park: Sage, 1982), 555-64.

[6] Joseph A. Schumpeter, *Capitalism, Socialism and Democracy* (New York: Harper and Brothers, 1942); Giovanni Sartori, *Democratic Theory*, 2nd ed. (Detroit: Wayne State University Press, 1962).

[7] Benjamin Barber, *Strong Democracy: Participatory Politics for a New Age* (Berkeley: University of California Press, 1984).

[8] John S. Dryzek and Jeffrey Berejikian, "Reconstructive Democratic Theory," *American Political Science Review* 87 (1993): 48.

[9] Barber.

[10] C. B. Macpherson, *The Life and Times of Liberal Democracy* (Oxford: Oxford University Press, 1977); Barber 1984; John S. Dryzek, *Discursive Democracy: Politics, Policy, and Political Science* (New York: Cambridge University Press, 1990); David Mathews,

in how best to achieve such strong democracy, they rest on a common set of propositions: that political autonomy grows out of collective engagement in political discussion, and that if people were better engaged in discursive politics they would be transformed as citizens. As Mark Warren puts it, people "would become more public-spirited, more knowledgeable, more attentive to the interests of others, and more probing of their own interests."[11]

The Call for Citizen Deliberation

Echoing Dewey's call for improvements in the methods of public communication and debate,[12] participatory democratic theorists submit that the mass media have transformed politics into a kind of spectator sport. Audiences simply consume political views disseminated by elites through the mass media, rather than function as autonomous, deliberating bodies. The public, which should rightly be a sovereign, reasoning collective, has been displaced by disconnected masses assembled around political spectacle.[13] Opinion polls and popular referenda only amplify shallow mass opinion formed without any meaningful public debate, producing a mere echo chamber for elite debate.

Participatory theorists argue that these conditions are not inevitable, advancing an agenda to engage the electorate, rebuild lost social capital, and reform the press. Proposed remedies for treating the ailing body politic are myriad.[14] However, most emphasize

---

Politics for People: Finding a Responsible Public Voice (Chicago: University of Chicago Press, 1994).

[11] Mark Warren, "Democratic Theory and Self-Transformation," *American Political Science Review* 86 (1992): 8.

[12] Dewey.

[13] Charles W. Mills, *The Power Elite* (Oxford: Oxford University Press, 1956); Jürgen Habermas, *The Structural Transformation of the Public Sphere: An Inquiry into a Category of Bourgeois Society*, trans. Thomas Burger (1962; Cambridge: MIT Press, 1989). Citations are to the Cambridge edition; Benjamin Ginsberg, *The Captive Public: How Mass Opinion Promotes State Power* (New York: Basic Books, 1986); James S. Fishkin, *Democracy and Deliberation: New Directions for Democratic Reform* (New Haven: Yale University Press, 1991).

[14] See Vincent Price and Peter Neijens, "Opinion Quality in Public Opinion Research," *International Journal of Public Opinion Research* 9 (1997): 336-60. See also Price

citizen deliberation and identify in it a number of powerful benefits. Discussion theoretically allows citizens to air their disagreements; creates opportunities to reconsider initial, unreflective impulses; and ideally fosters understanding of alternative perspectives and viewpoints.[15] It is also thought to promote tolerance and understanding between groups with divergent interests, foster mutual respect and trust, lead to a heightened sense of one's role within a political community, and stimulate further civic engagement.[16] The central normative proposition is communitarian in spirit: "When citizens or their representatives disagree morally, they should continue to reason together to reach mutually acceptable decisions."[17]

Calls have been increasingly issued on these grounds for engaging ordinary citizens in structured political deliberations[18] and for including lay citizens in technical policy deliberations.[19] In many such proposals, citizens are selected at random, given incentives to engage in collaborative, face-to-face sessions with their peers, and invited to expert briefings and question-and-answer sessions.[20] A large number

---

and Neijens, "Deliberative Polls: Toward Improved Measures of 'Informed' Public Opinion?" *International Journal of Public Opinion Research* 10 (1998): 145-76.

[15] Hannah Arendt, *The Human Condition* (Chicago: University of Chicago Press, 1958); Jürgen Habermas 1962/1989; Jürgen Habermas, *The Theory of Communicative Action*, vol. 1, trans. Thomas McCarthy (1981; Boston: Beacon, 1984). Citations are to the Beacon edition; Amy Gutmann and Dennis Thompson, *Democracy and Disagreement* (Cambridge: Harvard University Press, 1996).

[16] Barber (1984); John Bohman, *Public Deliberation: Pluralism, Complexity, and Democracy* (Cambridge: MIT Press, 1996); Dryzek 2000.

[17] Gutmann and Thompson, 1.

[18] Fishkin (1991); James S. Fishkin, *The Voice of the People: Public Opinion and Democracy* (New Haven: Yale University Press, 1995).

[19] Frank Fischer, *Technocracy and the Politics of Expertise* (Newbury Park,: Sage Publications, 1990); Frank Fischer, "Citizen Participation and the Democratization of Policy Expertise: From Theoretic Inquiry to Practical Cases," *Policy Sciences* 26 (1993): 165-88; Peter deLeon, "Democratic Values and the Policy Sciences," *American Journal of Political Science* 39 (1995): 886-905.

[20] Peter C. Dienel, *"Die planungszelle: Eine alternative zur establishment-demokratie," Dur Bürger plant seine Umwelt* (Oplanden, Westdeutscher Verlag, 1978); O. Renn et al., "An Empirical Investigation of Citizens' Preferences Among Four Energy Alternatives," *Technological Forecasting and Social Change* 26 (1984): 11-46; O. Renn, et al., "Public Participation in Decision Making: A Three-Step Procedure," *Policy Sciences* 26 (1993): 189-214; Fishkin (1991, 1995).

of other kindred efforts—citizen issue forums, citizen juries, consensus conferences, and the like—have been mounted as well.

Doubts about the Deliberative Turn

Deliberative theory has garnered many advocates and become popular among reform-minded practitioners, but it has attracted critics as well.[21] Bases for criticism are both theoretical an empirical in nature.

First, the argument that group discussion improves the quality of opinion can be questioned in light of much of the research on group decision making. Group discussion has, after all, been known to produce opinion polarization, shifts in new and risky directions, and other undesired outcomes.[22] It entails social-normative pressures that can lead to reticence on the part of those holding minority opinions, contributing to "political correctness" or "spirals of silence" that distort the communication of true preferences.[23]

Second, it may well be doubted whether the core attributes of high-quality deliberation—"egalitarian, reciprocal, reasonable, open-minded exchange"[24]—are reasonably attainable in practice. While the goal of deliberative theory is to embrace all views and empower the disenfranchised, Sanders argues that deliberative encounters likely do just the opposite, discouraging participation by those who lack social or political status (e.g., women or ethnic minorities) or deliberative ability (e.g., the less well educated), thus only further empowering high-status, educated participants.[25] The purportedly egalitarian nature of deliberation cannot be assured merely by invitation; it must be demonstrated in practice by vocal participation, equitably distributed. Also open to question is the degree to which

---

[21] Lynn M. Sanders, "Against Deliberation," *Political Theory* 25 (1997): 347-76. John R. Hibbing and Elizabeth Theiss-Morse, *Stealth Democracy: American's Beliefs about How Government Should Work* (Cambridge: Cambridge University Press, 2002).

[22] Rupert Brown, *Group Processes: Dynamics within and between Groups* (Oxford: Blackwell Publishers, 2000).

[23] Elisabeth Noelle-Neumann, *The Spiral of Silence: Public Opinion—Our Social Skin* (1980; Chicago: University of Chicago Press, 1984). Citations are to the University of Chicago edition.

[24] Tali Mendelberg, "The Deliberative Citizen: Theory and Evidence," *Research in Micropolitics* 6 (2002): 153.

[25] Sanders (2002).

citizen deliberation will be reciprocal, reasonable, and open-minded. People may exchange views, and in some sense argue, without giving reasons for their views; or, if reasons are given, they may simply be ignored rather than given a response.

Third, the vital role accorded disagreement in deliberative theory may be misplaced. People may well find it uncomfortable to disagree, particularly those uncertain of their views, and take political disagreement personally.[26] They may avoid confrontation, and hence real debate. Or, if citizens do air disagreements, the result may prove to be increased animosities rather than mutual respect and trust. And even if disagreement does induce greater political tolerance, it might as well induce ambivalence, and thus come at the expense of political action.[27] For reasons such as these, Hibbing and Theiss-Morse posit that many citizens do not want, and would likely resist rather than embrace, direct involvement in policy making through public discussion.[28]

With the growth of deliberative programs, some of these propositions have been subjected to empirical scrutiny.[29] Still, available evidence has been limited and mixed, so the effects of such deliberative exercises, along with clear understanding of the causes of any effects obtained, is presently difficult to determine.[30] Several studies,

---

[26] Jane J. Mansbridge, *Beyond Adversary Democracy* (Chicago: University of Chicago Press, 1983); Emile J. Pin, *Pleasure of Your Company: A Social-Psychological Analysis of Modern Sociability* (New York: Praeger, 1985); Michael Schudson, "Why Conversation Is Not the Soul of Democracy," *Critical Studies in Mass Communication* 14 (1997): 297-309; Nina Eliasoph, *Avoiding Politics* (Cambridge: Cambridge University Press, 1998).

[27] Diana C. Mutz, "The Consequences of Cross-cutting Networks for Political Participation," *American Journal of Political Science* 46 (2002): 838-55.

[28] Hibbing and Theiss-Morse (2002).

[29] James S. Fishkin and Robert C. Luskin, "Bringing Deliberation to the Democratic Dialogue," in *The Poll with a Human Face: The National Issues Convention Experiment in Political Communication*, ed. Maxwell McCombs and Amy Reynolds (Mahwah, NJ: Lawrence Erlbaum, 1999); Vincent Price and J. N. Cappella, "Online Deliberation and Its Influence: The Electronic Dialogue Project in Campaign 2000," *IT and Society* 1 (2002), www.stanford.edu/group/siqss/ itandsociety.

[30] Price and Neijens (1997); Michael X. Delli Carpini, Fay Lomax Cook, and Lawrence R. Jacobs, "Public Deliberation, Discursive Participation, and Citizen Engagement: A Review of the Empirical Literature," *Annual Review of Political Science* 7 (2003): 315-44. David M. Ryfe, "Does Deliberative Democracy Work?" *Annual*

particularly those by Fishkin and colleagues involving "deliberative polls," indicate that citizens learn from their discussions and sometimes arrive at positions that would not have been registered by conventional means such as a public opinion poll. However, most research has tended toward simple input-output models of deliberation effects and has not tested, for example, whether the content and structure of actual citizen discussions follows normative assumptions, or whether exposure to disagreement from political opponents indeed has the beneficial effects postulated.[31]

The Online Setting

The Internet and World Wide Web have been greeted by some as cause for optimism about a revitalized public sphere.[32] While growing at a fairly rapid rate, however, political "conversation" online remains a rare phenomenon. According to a Pew Research Center study, about 10 percent of those responding to a national survey reported taking part in online discussions about the 2004 U.S. presidential election.[33] Nevertheless, Internet technologies have considerable appeal to adherents of deliberative theory and practice, in that they permit group interactions among geographically dispersed and diverse participants, potentially bringing far greater reach, re-

---

Review of Political Science 8 (2005): 49-71.

[31] Survey-based studies, relying on self-reports of perceived disagreement in political conversations, indicate mixed effects: perceived disagreement predicts greater awareness of reasons supporting opposing opinions (Price, Nir, and Cappella 2002; Mutz 2002); but may also predict lower, not higher rates of political participation (Mutz, 2002). Laboratory experiments do sometimes directly engage research subjects in discussion, for instance, in business decision-making or juries; but analyses have not focused on the tenants of deliberative theory and, moreover, the experimental settings often bear little resemblance to citizen discussion as normally understood.

[32] Mark Poster, "The Net as a Public Sphere," *Communication in History: Technology, Culture, Society*, 3rd ed., ed. David J. Crowley and Paul Heyer (New York: Longman, 1999); Ted Becker and Christa D. Slaton, *The Future of Teledemocracy* (Wesport, CT: Praeger, 2000); Zizi Papacharissi, "Democracy Online: Civility, Politeness, and the Democratic Potential of Online Political Discussion Groups," *New Media and Society* 6 (2004): 259-84.

[33] Pew Research Center, "Trends 2005," Pew Research Center, Washington, DC, 2005, pewresearch .org/pubs/206/trends-2005.

duced cost, and increased representation to exercises in deliberative democracy.

At the same time, some analysts have questioned whether electronic, text-based interactions are well-suited to fruitful political deliberation. James Fishkin argues, for example, that text-based Internet discussions are likely too superficial to sustain sound political deliberation.[34] Robert Putnam also remains skeptical of the Internet's capacities for generating social capital, in part because "computer-mediated communication networks tend to be sparse and unbounded," encouraging "easy-in, easy out" and "drive-by" relationships rather than the close acquaintance promoted by face-to-face contact.[35] Computer-mediated communication is often framed as an impersonal phenomenon that de-individuates participants, rendering it poorly suited to getting to know others, instead encouraging uncivil discourse and group-based stereotyping.[36] Sunstein warns that the Internet, far from encouraging reasonable dialogue over shared issues, merely encourages "enclave" communication among very like-minded citizens, circulating unfounded and often false information, polarizing and intensifying opinions, and contributing to widening gaps between those on opposite sides of public issues.[37] Even if designers of online deliberative programs were able to counter such tendencies, they would still contend with the so-called "digital divide": structural inequities in access to computing equipment, fa-

---

[34] James S. Fishkin, "Virtual Democratic Possibilities: Prospects for Internet Democracy" (presented to the conference on "Internet, Democracy and Public Goods," Belo Horizonte, Brazil, November 2000). Fishkin has since experimented with voice technologies, eschewing the usual text-based "chat" formats characteristic of most online group discussions. Iyengar, Luskin and Fishkin (2003) report that voice-only deliberations (akin to conference calls) produce information gains and opinion changes roughly comparable to those found in face-to-face deliberative polls.

[35] Robert D. Putnam, *Bowling Alone: The Collapse and Revival of American Community* (New York: Simon and Schuster, 2000), 177.

[36] See discussion in Sara Kiesler, Jane Siegel, and Timothy McGuire, "Social Psychological Aspects of Computer-mediated Communication," *American Psychologist* 39 (1984): 1123-34; Ronald E. Rice, "Media Appropriateness: Using Social Presence Theory to Compare Traditional and New Organizational Media," *Human Communication Research* 19 (1993): 451-84.

[37] Cass Sunstein, *Republic.com* (Princeton: Princeton University Press, 2001).

miliarity with its use, literacy and typing ability. The prospects for successful political deliberation online, then, remain unclear.

With each of these potential liabilities, though, come potential benefits. The quasi-anonymity and text-based nature of electronic group discussion, for instance, might actually reduce patterns of social dominance. Studies demonstrate that online discussions are generally much more egalitarian than face-to-face encounters, with reduced patterns of individual dominance and increased contributions by low-status participants.[38] Task-oriented groups generate more unique ideas working in computer-mediated settings than when face-to-face.[39]

Group decision-making experiments generally indicate that online discussions, relative to face-to-face group meetings, generate more open exchanges of ideas,[40] suggesting considerable utility for deliberative work.

Moreover, recent studies suggest that the computer may not be the "impersonal" medium it is commonly made out to be and that, in fact, people find it useful in forming relationships.[41] Experimental comparisons show that computer-mediated discussions produce more questions, greater self-disclosure, more intimate and direct questions, and fewer peripheral exchanges than face-to-face encounters.[42] Other research similarly suggests that people find the

---

[38] Rice (1993); Vitaly J. Dubrovsky, Sara Kiesler, and Beheruz N. Sethna, "The Equalization Phenomenon: Status Effects in Computer-mediated and Face-to-face Decision Making Groups," *Human-Computer Interaction* 6 (1991): 119-46; Joseph B. Walther, "Relational Aspects of Computer-mediated Communication: Experimental Observations Over Time," *Organization Science* 6 (1995): 186-203; A. B. Hollingshead, "Information Suppression and Status Persistence in Group Decision Making: The Effects of Communication Media," *Human Communication Research* 23 (1996): 193-219.

[39] R. Brent Gallupe, Gerardine DeSantis, and Gary W. Dickson, "Computer-based Support for Problem Finding: An Experimental Investigation," *MIS Quarterly* 12 (1998): 277-96; Alan R. Dennis, "Information Exchange and Use in Group Decision Making: You Can Lead a Group to Information, But You Can't Make It Think," *MIS Quarterly* 20 (1996): 433-57.

[40] Stephen A. Rains, "Leveling the Organizational Playing field—Virtually," *Communication Research* 32 (2005): 193-234.

[41] Walther (1995).

[42] Lisa Collins Tidwell and Joseph B. Walther, "Computer-mediated Communication Effects on Disclosure, Impressions, and Interpersonal Evaluations: Getting to Know

lack of physical presence and reduction in social cues to be useful rather than limiting. Bargh, McKenna and Fitzsimmons find that their experimental participants feel better able to reveal their "true selves" online than in person[43]; while Stromer-Galley found a number of people reporting that they felt better able to discuss political disagreements over the Internet than face-to-face, because it felt to them more comfortable and less dangerous.[44] Finally, online encounters may assist people in formulating their thoughts, by requiring greater economy of expression and the conversion of inchoate ideas into text, and by permitting statements to be reviewed and edited prior to posting.

Political discussion online surely differs in fundamental ways from that carried out face to face. Its distinctive features, however, may well prove to help rather than hinder the core attributes of sound deliberation. The reduction in social cues, by restricting the projection of social status, may produce less deferential behavior and so undercut status hierarchies. The ability to input "statements" simultaneously may assist the sharing of ideas, while anonymity should reduce inhibitions and anxieties about expressing one's honest views, particularly when they are likely to be unpopular.

Two Empirical Forays

While by no means resolving these many issues, data from several field experiments help shed important light on the nature of online deliberation. Unique in their design and scale, these two studies—Electronic Dialogue and Healthcare Dialogue—provide unusual empirical leverage on debates over the utility of text-based, electronic group interactions for political discussion. Importantly, neither project aimed at replicating "typical" Internet discussion. Instead, they pursued an experimental logic: What would occur if we were to bring a representative sample of Americans online to discuss

---

One Another a Bit at a Time," *Human Communication Research* 28 (2002): 317-48.

[43] Joseph A. Bargh, Katelyn Y. A. McKenna, and Grainna M. Fitzsimmons, "Can You See the Real Me? Activation and Expression of the 'True Self' on the Internet," *Journal of Social Issues* 58 (2002): 33-48.

[44] Jennifer Stromer-Galley, "Diversity of Political Conversation on the Internet: Users' Perspectives," *Journal of Computer-Mediated Communication* 8 (2003), www.ascusc.org/jcmc/vol8/issue3/stromergalley.html.

politics, or to debate public policy? The results begin to address fundamental questions concerning the putative value of citizen deliberation and, in particular, of airing opposing points of view.

Our review will out of necessity be brief, intended to provide an overview rather than a thorough presentation of findings. After sketching the outlines of each study, we consider evidence bearing on five basic questions. Who attends such discussions? Who talks? How can we characterize the discussions vis-à-vis normative ideals? How do the discussions influence, if at all, knowledge and opinion? And what of their transformative potential: Can we discern any impact on civic attitudes or subsequent engagement?

The Electronic Dialogue Project

The Electronic Dialogue project was a year-long panel study conducted during the 2000 U.S. presidential election. It involved a multi-wave, multi-group panel design, lasting roughly one year. All data gathering was conducted over the World Wide Web. The core of project consisted of sixty groups of citizens who engaged in a series of monthly, real-time electronic discussions about issues facing the country and the unfolding presidential campaign.

The Electronic Dialogue Project: Sample

Unlike many Web-based studies, the project did not rely upon a convenience sample of Internet users. Instead, respondents came from a random sample of U.S. citizens age 18 and older drawn from a nationally representative panel of survey respondents maintained by Knowledge Networks, Inc. of Menlo Park, California.[45]

Details of the sampling are presented in Price and Cappella.[46] Briefly, a random sample was drawn from the Knowledge Networks panel for recruitment to the year-long project. Just over half (51 percent) agreed to participate, and the great majority of those consenting (84 percent) subsequently completed the project's two baseline surveys in February and March 2000. Comparisons of the obtained

---

[45] The Knowledge Networks panel includes a large number of households (in the tens of thousands) that were selected through RDD (random digit dialing) methods and agreed to accept free WebTV equipment and service in exchange for completing periodic surveys online.

[46] Price and Capella (2002).

baseline sample (N = 1684) with a separate random-digit dialing telephone survey and with U.S. Census data indicated that the Electronic Dialogue sample was broadly representative, though it tended to slightly over-represent males, and to under-represent those with less than a high-school education, non-whites, and those with weak interest in politics.

The Electronic Dialogue Project: Design

All baseline respondents were randomly assigned to one of three groups. Those in the discussion group (N = 915) were invited to attend eight online group deliberations, roughly once a month, beginning in April and continuing through December. Members of this group, regardless of whether they attended discussions or not, were also asked to complete a series of surveys, one preceding and one following each discussion event. Participants assigned to the survey-only control group (N = 139) were also asked to complete all the surveys, although they were never invited to attend any online group meetings. The remaining participants were assigned to a project pre/post only condition: They were asked to complete only the baseline surveys and, one year later, the final end-of-project surveys.

Anticipating far less than perfect attendance, sixty groups were formed with roughly 16 invitees per group, in order to produce groups of 5 to 10 participants at each round of discussions. Because of the theoretical interest in the impact of disagreement, three experimental group conditions were created using baseline data: homogeneously liberal groups (n = 20); homogeneously conservative groups (n = 20); and heterogeneous groups with members from across the political spectrum (n = 20). Participants maintained group assignments over the full course of the study.

Discussion groups met live, in real-time, with membership straddling several time zones. Participants logged on to their "discussion rooms" at pre-arranged times, using their Web TV devices, television sets, and infrared keyboards. All discussions were moderated by project assistants working out of the Annenberg School at the University of Pennsylvania, and were carefully coordinated and scripted to maintain consistency across groups. Discussions were not intended to be formally deliberative exercises; instead, group members were simply invited to discuss a number of topics, including which issues ought to be the focus of the campaign; a variety of candidate policy proposals (e.g., in areas of education, crime and public safety, taxes, and foreign affairs), the candidates' qualifications; campaign advertising; and the role of the media. In all, nine rounds of meetings were held. The full text of all discussions, including time-stamps for each comment posted, was automatically recorded.

All respondents to the initial baseline (those invited to discussions, the survey-only control group, and the project pre/post-only group) were contacted again for end-of-project surveys in January and February 2001. Fifty-five percent completed the first survey, and 56 percent completed the second.

The Healthcare Dialogue Project

The Healthcare Dialogue project shared many of the features of the 2000 campaign study, but focused instead on formal policy deliberations about a complex issue: health care reform. It also created online discussions involving health-care policy elites in addition to ordinary citizens. Project objectives included: (a) examining online deliberation as a means of maximizing public influence in policy making; (b) studying the interaction of policy elites and ordinary citizens in online discussions; and (c) testing hypotheses related to group composition and the quality of deliberations and outcomes.

The Healthcare Dialogue Project: Sample

The project again drew upon the Knowledge Networks panel but employed a stratified sampling strategy, such that the final baseline sample (N=2,497) represented both a general population sample of adult citizens, age 18 or older (N=2,183), as well as a purposive sample of health care policy elites with special experience, knowledge, and influence in the domain of health care policy and reform (N=314). The general population sample was further stratified into members of "issue publics" who are highly attentive to and knowledgeable about health care issues (N=804) and ordinary citizens (N=1379). Comparisons of the obtained baseline general population sample to a random-digit dialing telephone sample and to U.S. Census data indicated that the samples were broadly comparable, although project participants were somewhat more likely to be middle aged and to follow politics more frequently.

The Healthcare Dialogue Project: Design

A subset of the baseline panel (262 health care policy elites; 461 issue-public members; 768 ordinary citizens) was randomly assigned within strata to participate in a series of four moderated online group discussions, including pre- and post-discussion surveys, which were conducted over the course of the year. Participants were further randomly assigned to participate in a group that was homogeneous within strata (either elite-only, issue-public-only, or general-citizen-only) or mixed across the three strata. Discussion groups were again scripted to ensure consistency across groups, and short briefing materials were made available prior to each online meeting. The full text of all discussions, including time-stamps for each comment, was automatically recorded.

Because baseline surveys indicated broad agreement that the most pressing problems facing the health care system included the rising costs of health insurance, the large number of uninsured Americans, and the rising costs of prescription drugs, these issues were the focus of the online deliberations. Eighty groups (8 homogeneous elite,12 homogeneous issue-public, 20 homogeneous general citizen, and 40 heterogeneous across strata) met twice in the fall of 2004 to discuss insurance-related issues. A total of 614 project participants (123 elites, 206 issue-public members, and 285 general citizens) attended at least one of the two discussions. The subset of 614 fall discussion attendees was then reassigned to 50 new groups for another round of two discussions in the spring of 2005, focusing on prescription drugs. In this second round, a random half of the participants remained in homogeneous or heterogeneous groups as before, while half were switched (from homogeneous to heterogeneous groups, or vice versa).

Following the four discussion waves—in September and November 2004 and in February and April 2005, with each consisting of a brief pre-discussion survey followed by an hour-long online chat followed by another brief post-discussion survey—an end-of-project survey was conducted in August 2005 (completed by roughly three-quarters of all baseline respondents).

The Evidence to Date

Taken together, these two studies provide observations of close to 800 online group discussions involving more than 1,200 different participants, most of whom attended three or four group meetings over several months. With extensive survey data (19 survey waves in the 2000 project and 10 in the 2004-2005 project), full transcripts of the online interactions, and carefully designed experimental comparisons, we are in a good position to evaluate who attends such discussions, the nature of citizens' online behavior, and the influence of the discussions on knowledge, opinions, and attitudes.

Who Attends?

Rates of participation in the online discussions generally ranged from about 30 to 40 percent of those invited, producing groups averaging around a half-dozen persons each. In both projects, comparisons of attendees to non-attendees found no significant differences in gender, region of the country, or political leanings. However, people who showed up for the electronic discussions were, again in both projects, significantly more likely to be white than those who did not (about a 3-4 percent difference), significantly older (by about 3 years on average) and better educated.

Importantly, data from both projects indicate that attendees were significantly higher than non-attendees in their levels of interpersonal trust, regular "offline" political discussion, political participation and community engagement. Overall, the experience of both projects strongly supports the view that "social capital" goes hand in hand with deliberative participation.[47] Trusting people who are engaged in their communities—even when their activities are not expressly political in nature—were more likely to attend. Those who attended the electronic conversations also scored significantly higher than non-attendees on scales measuring political knowledge and interest in public affairs; and in the Healthcare Dialogue project were also significantly more knowledgeable about health related policy issues and more confident in health care institutions. Multiple regressions consistently show that the most powerful predictor of attendance is "argument repertoire," a count of the reasons a respondent gives in support of his or her opinion on an issue, along with reasons why other people might disagree (which has proved to be a validated and reliable measure of opinion quality).[48]

---

[47] Putnam.

[48] Vincent Price, Lilach Nir, and Joseph N. Cappella, "Does Disagreement Contrib-

Two overall conclusions can be drawn from these analyses. First, robust and predictable differences between project attendees and non-attendees emerge, although most such differences are relatively small in magnitude. The best multivariate models, even those employing as many as 30 predictors, account for only small proportions of variance in participation—less than 20 percent in Electronic Dialogue and less than 10 percent in Healthcare Dialogue. Most of the variability in attendance among invitees, then, appears to be random rather than systematic. Notwithstanding concerns about the difficulty of overcoming the digital divide, both projects managed to assemble samples of discussion participants which, while overrepresenting engaged and knowledgeable citizens, were as a group highly diverse and broadly representative of the general population.

Second, many of the phenomena thought to stem from engagement in deliberation—trust in other citizens, knowledge, the ability to understand reasons on both sides of issues, civic participation—are also predictors of attendance. Any attempt to gauge the impact of deliberation on attitudes, knowledge, or subsequent engagement, then, must carefully account for this fact.

Who Talks?

Bringing a diverse and representative sample of citizens together for discussion is a necessary but by no means sufficient condition for democratic deliberation. We turn, then, to a consideration of what transpired online: How engaged were participants? How egalitarian were the exchanges?

Participants in both projects contributed on average several hundred words per discussion. For example, discounting informal "small talk" at the beginning and end of each discussion and focusing only on the main deliberations, we found that participants in the Healthcare Dialogue project averaged just over 300 words per person. Importantly, "talking" in the online groups tended to be distributed very evenly across participants, with variance across group members typically reaching about 80 percent of its maximum value.[49] Not surprisingly, average words per person declined as groups increased in size.

ute to More Deliberative Opinion?" *Political Communication* 19 (2002): 95-112.

[49] T. Undem, "Factors Affecting Discussion Quality: The Effects of Group Size, Gender, and Political Heterogeneity in Online Discussion Groups" (MA thesis, University of Pennsylvania, 2002).

Multiple regressions predicting individual word counts indicate that older participants—though more likely than younger people to attend discussions—contributed significantly fewer words. In the 2000 campaign study, women contributed significantly more words, but no significant gender differences emerged in the health care deliberations. Typing skills have a discernable though not large effect. The most notable pattern, overall, is the tendency of more politically involved and more knowledgeable participants to enter more words into the discussions: Education, political participation, political knowledge, and especially argument repertoire, had positive effects on the amount of "speaking." Thus, in the Healthcare Dialogue deliberations, policy elites contributed significantly more words than even members of the health care issue public, who in turn contributed significantly more words than ordinary citizens who are less interested in and knowledgeable about the issues.

Despite such predictable biases in favor of more knowledgeable participants, these are small relative to what one might expect from the literature on face-to-face groups. Over all, the word count evidence suggests that the exchanges were quite equitable.[50] Neither project offered any indication that those holding minority views are reticent in the online group environment. Indeed, those whose issue preferences are furthest from other group members, if anything, tend to contribute more rather than fewer words.

The Nature of Citizen Discussion

Deliberation is more than a mere exchange of words. It should be reciprocal, reasonable, and open minded. As noted above, people may exchange views without giving reasons, or they may ignore rather than respond to contrary views. However, both qualitative and quantitative analyses of transcripts indicate that the citizen discussions, while not especially sophisticated in policy terms, were nonetheless substantive and responsive. This is true even of the Electronic Dialogue discussions, which were framed only as talk about candidates and the issues, not as any sort of formal deliberation.[51]

---

[50] Ibid.

[51] See, e.g., Vincent Price, Lilach Nir, and Joseph N. Cappella, "Framing Public Discussion of Gay Civil Unions," *Public Opinion Quarterly* 69 (2005): 179-212; Vincent Price and Clarissa David, "Talking about Elections: A Study of Patterns in Citizen

People freely and frankly exchanged opinions. In the 2000 campaign discussions, for example, people expressed on average 15 statements of opinion, pro or con, with reference to the issues discussed. Moreover, they explained their views. Close to 40 percent of all these opinion statements were coupled with one or more arguments to bolster a position.[52] Almost all groups, even those that were homogeneously liberal or conservative, produced a reasonable balance of both pro and con arguments on most issues. Opinion expression and argumentation both tended to be equitably distributed: Once word counts are controlled for, only strength of opinion showed much relationship to the number of arguments made.[53] Analysis of transcripts and survey responses in both projects suggest that views expressed were diverse, and perceived as such by group members.

Participants had little or no trouble adapting the text format to their discussion aims, and there are many indications that people felt positively about their online experience.[54] Large majorities in both projects reported that the discussion experience was interesting and enjoyable. Liking of the experience was uniform across liberal, conservative, and mixed groups in the 2000 study, while in the health care deliberations, even though policy elites expressed slightly less positive reactions than other citizens, a substantial majority of elites reported liking the experience. Healthcare Dialogue groups, which concluded their deliberations by voting on priorities for health care policy, expressed high levels of satisfaction with their final choices.[55] The vast majority of attendees said that they think "the potential of this technology for good political discussions" is either "good" or "excellent."[56]

Perhaps most important, adverse reactions to disagreement were not much in evidence. To the contrary, exposure to opposing views

---

Deliberation Online" (presented to the annual meeting of the International Communication Association, New York, May 2005).

[52] Price and David (2005).

[53] Ibid.

[54] Price and Cappella (2002); Vincent Price and Jospeh N. Cappella, "Bringing an Informed Public Into Policy Debates Through Online Deliberation: The Case of Health Care Reform," *Proceedings of the National Conference on Digital Government Research*, May 21-24, 2006 (Digital Government Research Center: San Diego).

[55] Price and Cappella (2006).

[56] Price and Cappella (2002).

appears if anything to be an attraction of the online encounters. Open ended survey questions invited Electronic Dialogue participants to identify what they liked and disliked about the experience. Almost half of all coded "likes" referred to hearing others' views, interacting with people from different parts of the country, or learning how much they agreed or disagreed with other citizens. By comparison, just over twelve percent singled out the chance to express their views.[57] Aspects of the discussions that were disliked were fewer in number, and most commonly had to do, not with the substance of personal interactions at all, but instead with technical issues such as logging in or keeping up with scrolled comments on screen.

Impact on Knowledge and Opinion

Analyzing the impact of deliberation is complicated by the fact that, as noted earlier, the best predictors of attendance proved to be precisely those variables usually cast as theoretical outcomes. While this can be interpreted as partly confirming the reciprocal relation-ship between deliberation and good citizenship, it must be taken into account when attempting to gauge the effect of deliberation on attitudes and knowledge. Toward this end, using dozens of mea-sures available from our extensive baseline surveys, we calculated an estimate of each person's propensity to attend and controlled for this propensity score to remove the effects of potential confounding variables.[58] Propensity scoring succeeds in balancing almost all dif-ferences between attendees as a group and their counterparts who did not attend. Particularly when coupled with separate statistical controls for baseline levels of target outcomes and any variables which may remain imbalanced, it enables fair experimental compari-sons to test hypothesized deliberation effects.[59]

---

[57] T. Undem, *Factors Affecting Discussion Quality: The Effects of Group Size, Gender, and Political Heterogeneity in Online Discussion Groups* (Unpublished Master's thesis, Univer-sity of Pennsylvania, Philadelphia, 2001).

[58] Paul R. Rosenbaum and Donald B. Rubin, "The Central Role of the Propensity Score in Observational Studies for Causal Effects," *Biometrika* 70 (1983): 41-55. Ralph B. D'Agostino, "Tutorial in Biostatistics: Propensity Scoring Methods for Bias Reduction in the Comparison of a Treatment to a Non-randomized Control Group," *Statistics in Medicine* 17 (1998): 2265-81.

[59] Vincent Price, Dannagal Goldthwaite, and Joseph N. Cappella, "Civic Engage-ment, Social Trust, and Online Deliberation" (presented to the annual meeting of

Analyses of this sort support several general conclusions bearing on putative increases in opinion quality resulting from deliberation. First, while there are some gains in objective knowledge (e.g., knowing that George W. Bush supported government-funded private school vouchers in the 2000 campaign[60]), gains in issue-knowledge are modest at best. On the other hand, deliberation does appear to produce significant gains in "argument repertoires"—the range of arguments people hold both in support of and against their favored positions. Online discussion attendance significantly and positively predicted scores on this argument repertoire measure, controlling for argument repertoire assessed on the baseline survey and for propensity to attend the discussions.[61]

Second, aside from any influence it may have on the direction of public opinion, deliberation increases levels of opinion holding. Thus, for example, attendance in the Healthcare Dialogue discussions significantly predicted fewer "don't know" responses to a range of policy-opinion questions, again controlling for baseline opinion holding and propensity to attend.[62]

Third, shifts in policy preferences induced by deliberation are usually readily interpretable and appear to reflect the tenor of group argumentation. Although on many topics aggregate levels of support or opposition for the policies discussed remained unchanged, when group-level opinion did shift, the data suggest generally rational movements in keeping with the pattern of group argumentation.[63] In discussing federal funding for character education or school vouchers, for instance, Electronic Dialogue groups tended to produce more opposing than supportive arguments and thus became on average less enthusiastic about such funding.

---

the American Association for Public Opinion Research, St. Pete Beach, Florida, May 2002); Vincent Price et al., "Informing Public Opinion About Health Care Reform Through Online Deliberation" (presented at the annual meeting of the International Communication Association, Dresden, Germany, June 2006).

[60] Price and Cappella (2002).

[61] Joseph N. Cappella, Vincent Price, and Lilach Nir, "Argument Repertoire as a Reliable and Valid Measure of Opinion Quality: Electronic Dialogue in Campaign 2000," *Political Communication* 19 (2002): 73-93.

[62] Price et al. (2006).

[63] Price and Cappella (2002).

Deliberation-induced changes in preferences also seem to reflect movement toward more informed and politically sophisticated positions. Price et al. found that, after controls for propensity to attend, preferences at baseline, and other background characteristics, Healthcare Dialogue attendees were less likely than non-attendees to support tax based reforms and were more supportive than non-attendees of government programming and regulations as a means to cut heath care costs.[64] Importantly, these differences between participants and non-participants parallel those between policy elites and general citizens at baseline. Thus, the impact of deliberation was to move citizens in the direction of elite opinion (even though, since such movements occurred to a greater degree in groups without elite members, they were not apparently the mere product of elite persuasion).

Impact on Citizen Engagement

Finally, what of the transformative potential of online deliberation? Although the estimated effects on civic engagement are small in size, results are consistent across a number of different indicators and across both projects. Online discussion attendees, relative to non-attendees with comparable propensities to participate, score significantly higher in end-of-project social trust, community engagement, and political participation. For example, participants in the Electronic Dialogue discussion reported voting in the 2000 presidential election at significantly higher rates than their counterparts who did not attend, even after extensive controls.[65] While the 2000 project did not find similar increases in personal political efficacy, the later Healthcare Dialogue project did, along with increases in self-reported engagement in health policy related activities such as working for advocacy groups, attending meetings, or donating money to a group pursing health care reform.[66] Thus, the sorts of social and political capital that contribute to participation in online deliberations (see section 5.1 above) are themselves products of discussion

---

[64] Price et al. (2006).

[65] Price and Cappella (2002); Price, Goldthwaite and Cappella (2002).

[66] L. Feldman and D. Freres, "Efficacy, Trust, and Engagement Analyses" (unpublished report of the *Healthcare Dialogue* project, Annenberg School, University of Pennsylvania, 2006).

as well, lending support to claims that social capital and deliberative behavior are mutually reinforcing.

Analyses based on coded transcripts finds almost no evidence that observed gains in social trust or in electoral and community participation were mitigated by encountering disagreement.[67] Estimated effects of Electronic Dialogue participation on post-project community engagement were slightly larger for those who encountered more supportive group members, but there were nonetheless significant, positive effects of discussion even for those who met with substantial disagreement in their groups; and no moderating effect of disagreement was found in connection with either voting or post-project social trust. Thus, although some survey studies using self-reports of perceived disagreement have suggested that face-to-face political opposition can lead to ambivalence and withdrawal,[68] here we find little to suggest that online disagreement disengages.

Taking Stock

As noted earlier, these research findings of themselves do not resolve the many issues raised by critics of deliberative democracy, nor by those adherents of deliberative theory who have questioned the utility of text-based "chat"-type modes of computer mediated communication for productive deliberation. Lacking reasonable experimental comparisons to face-to-face deliberations, we cannot say which if any of our observations are the unique product of the online environment itself. Thus, although we might suspect that participants' openness and tolerance of disagreement resulted from the diminished social cues and relative anonymity afforded by text-based exchanges, such propositions must remain speculative.

Similarly, in the absence of comparisons to other online deliberation programs, or to typical web-based discussions as they now occur naturally, we cannot say how much our findings stem from the particular manner in which these discussions were designed and undertaken (e.g., under the auspices of University researchers with the

---

[67] Vincent Price et al., "Online Political Discussion, Civic Engagement, and Social Trust" (unpublished manuscript, Annenberg School, University of Pennsylvania, 2005).

[68] Mutz (2002).

sponsorship of respected non-partisan and governmental agencies). We make no effort to generalize to other online settings.

Still, these experiments in "online democracy" do begin to address systematically questions concerning the putative value of online deliberation. Randomly selected citizens adapted readily and well to the online environment. They produced reasonably coherent political discussions; showed willingness to debate and engage their opponents; responded favorably to their online experiences; developed opinions and grasped arguments for and against those views; and came away a bit more trusting and civically engaged than comparable non-participants. Though broad stroke, the picture emerging from these analyses of citizens deliberating online shows them, if not quite meeting all the lofty ideals of deliberative theory, certainly coming closer than might have been expected.

BIBLIOGRAPHY

Arendt, Hannah. *The Human Condition.* Chicago: University of Chicago Press, 1958.

Barber, Benjamin. *Strong Democracy: Participatory Politics for a New Age.* Berkeley: University of California Press, 1984.

Bargh, John A., Katelyn Y. A. McKenna, and Grainne M. Fitzsimons."Can You See the Real me? Activation and Expression of the 'True Self' on the Internet." *Journal of Social Issues* 58 (2002): 33-48.

Becker. Ted D., and Christa D. Slaton. *The Future of Teledemocracy.* Wesport: Praeger, 2000.

Bohman, John. *Public Deliberation: Pluralism, Complexity, and Democracy.* Cambridge: MIT Press, 1996.

Brown, Rupert. *Group Processes: Dynamics within and between Groups.* Oxford: Blackwell Publishers, 2000.

Cappella, Joseph N., Vincent Price, and Lilach Nir. "Argument Repertoire as a Reliable and Valid Measure of Opinion Quality: Electronic Dialogue in Campaign 2000." *Political Communication* 19 (2002): 73-93.

D'Agostino, Ralph B. "Tutorial in Biostatistics: Propensity Scoring Methods for Bias Reduction in the Comparison of a Treatment to a Non-randomized Control Group." *Statistics in Medicine* 17 (1998): 2265-81.

deLeon, Peter. "Democratic Values and the Policy Sciences." *American Journal of Political Science* 39 (1995): 886-905.

Delli Carpini, Michael X., Fay Lomax Cook, and Lawrence R. Jacobs. "Public Deliberation, Discursive Participation, and Citizen Engagement: A Review of the Empirical Literature." *Annual Review of Political Science* 7 (2003): 315-344.

Dennis, Alan R. "Information Exchange and Use in Group Decision Making: You Can Lead a Group to Information, But You Can't Make It Think." *MIS Quarterly* 20 (1996): 433-57.

Dewey, John. *The Public and Its Problems.* New York: Holt, Rinehart & Winston, 1927.

Dienel, Peter C. *Die planungszelle: Eine alternative zur establishment-demokratie.* Dur Bürger plant seine Umwelt. Oplanden, Westdeutscher Verlag, 1978.

Dryzek, John S. *Discursive Democracy: Politics, Policy, and Political Science.* New York: Cambridge University Press, 1990.

—, and Jeffrey Berejikian. "Reconstructive Democratic Theory." *American Political Science Review* 87 (1993): 48-60.

Dubrovsky, Vitaly J., Sara Kiesler, and Beheruz N. Sethna. "The Equalization Phenomenon: Status Effects in Computer-mediated and Face-to-face Decision Making Groups." *Human-Computer Interaction* 6 (1991): 119-46.

Eliasoph, Nina. *Avoiding Politics.* Cambridge: Cambridge University Press, 1998.

Feldman, L. and D. Freres. "Efficacy, Trust, and Engagement Analyses." Unpublished report of the Healthcare Dialogue project, Annenberg School, University of Pennsylvania, 2006.

Fischer, Frank. *Technocracy and the Politics of Expertise.* Newbury Park: SAGE Publications, 1990.

—. "Citizen Participation and the Democratization of Policy Expertise: From Theoretic Inquiry to Practical Cases." *Policy Sciences* 26 (1993): 165-88.

Fishkin, James S. *Democracy and Deliberation: New Directions for Democratic Reform.* New Haven: Yale University Press, 1991.

—. *The Voice of the People: Public Opinion and Democracy.* New Haven: Yale University Press, 1995.

—. "Virtual Democratic Possibilities: Prospects for Internet Democracy." Presented to the conference on "Internet, Democracy and Public Goods," Belo Horizonte, Brazil, November 2000.

—, and Robert C. Luskin. "Bringing Deliberation to the Democratic Dialogue." *The Poll with a Human Face: The National Issues Convention Experiment in Political Communication,* edited by M. McCombs and A. Reynolds. Mahwah: Lawrence Erlbaum, 1999.

Gallupe, R. Brent, Gerardine DeSantis, and Gary W. Dickson. "Computer-based Support for Problem Finding: An Experimental Investigation." *MIS Quarterly* 12 (1998): 277-96.

Ginsberg, Benjamin. *The Captive Public: How Mass Opinion Promotes State Power.* New York: Basic Books, 1986.

Graber, Doris A. "The Impact of Media Research on Public Opinion Studies." *Mass Communication Review Yearbook 3,* edited by D. Charles Whitney, Ellen Wartella, and Sven Windahl, 555-564. Newbury Park: SAGE, 1982.

Gutmann, Amy and Dennis Thompson. *Democracy and Disagreement.* Cambridge: Harvard University Press, 1996.

Habermas, Jürgen. *The Theory of Communicative Action,* vol. 1, translated by Thomas McCarthy. Boston: Beacon, 1984. Original work published 1981.

—. *The Structural Transformation of the Public Sphere: An Inquiry into a Category of Bourgeois Society,* translated by Thomas Burger. Cambridge: MIT Press, 1989. Original work published 1962.

Hibbing, John R. and Elizabeth Theiss-Morse. *Stealth Democracy: American's Beliefs about How Government Should Work*. Cambridge: Cambridge University Press, 2002.

Hollingshead, Andrea B. "Information Suppression and Status Persistence in Group Decision Making: The Effects of Communication Media." *Human Communication Research* 23 (1996): 193-219.

Iyengar, Shanto, Robert C. Luskin, and James S. Fishkin. "Facilitating Informed Opinion: Evidence from Face-to-face and On-line Deliberative Polls." Presented to the annual meeting of the American Political Science Association, Philadelphia, September 2003.

Kiesler, Sara, Jane Siegel, and Timothy McGuire. "Social Psychological Aspects of Computer-mediated Communication." *American Psychologist* 39 (1984): 1123-34.

Lippmann, Walter. *Public Opinion*. New York: Harcourt Brace Jovanovich, 1922.

Macpherson, Crawford B. *The Life and Times of Liberal Democracy*. Oxford: Oxford University Press, 1977.

Mansbridge, Jane J. *Beyond Adversary Democracy*. Chicago: University of Chicago Press, 1983.

Mathews, David. *Politics for People: Finding a Responsible Public Voice*. Chicago: University of Chicago Press, 1994.

Mendelberg, T. "The Deliberative Citizen: Theory and Evidence." *Research in Micropolitics* 6 (2002): 151-93.

Mills, Charles W. *The Power Elite*. Oxford: Oxford University Press, 1956.

Mutz, Diana C. "The Consequences of Cross-cutting Networks for Political Participation." *American Journal of Political Science* 46 (2002): 838-55.

Neuman, W. Russell. *The Paradox of Mass Politics: Knowledge and Opinion in the American Electorate*. Cambridge: Harvard University Press, 1986.

Noelle-Neumann, Elisabeth. *The Spiral of Silence: Public Opinion—Our Social Skin*. Chicago: University of Chicago Press, 1984. Original work published 1980.

Papacharissi, Zizi. "Democracy Online: Civility, Politeness, and the Democratic Potential of Online Political Discussion groups." *New Media and Society* 6 (2004): 259-84.

Pew Research Center. "Trends 2005." Washington, DC: Pew Research Center, 2005.

Pin, Emile J. *Pleasure of Your Company: A Social-Psychological Analysis of Modern Sociability*. New York: Praeger, 1985.

Poster, Mark. "The Net as a Public Sphere." *Communication in History: Technology, Culture, Society,* 3rd ed., edited by David J. Crowley and Paul Heyer. New York: Longman, 1999.

Price, Vincent, and Joseph N. Cappella. "Online Deliberation and Its Influence: The Electronic Dialogue Project in Campaign 2000." *IT and Society* 1 (2002): 303-28, www.stanford.edu/group/siqss/itandsociety.

— and Joseph N. Cappella. "Bringing an Informed Public Into Policy Debates Through Online Deliberation: The Case of Health Care Reform." Proceedings of the National Conference on Digital Government Research, San Diego, May 21-24, 2006. Digital Government Research Center, 2006.

— and Clarissa David. "Talking about Elections: A Study of Patterns in Citizen Deliberation Online." Presented to the annual meeting of the International Communication Association, New York, May 2005.

—, Lauren Feldman, Derek Freres, Weiyu Zhang, and Joseph N. Cappella. "Informing Public Opinion About Health Care Reform Through Online Deliberation." Presented at the annual meeting of the International Communication Association, Dresden, Germany, June 2006.

— and Peter Neijens. "Opinion Quality in Public Opinion Research." *International Journal of Public Opinion Research* 9 (1997): 336-60.

— and Peter Neijens. "Deliberative Polls: Toward Improved Measures of 'Informed' Public Opinion?" *International Journal of Public Opinion Research* 10 (1998): 145-76.

—, Dannagal Goldthwaith, and Joseph N. Cappella. "Civic Engagement, Social Trust, and Online Deliberation." Presented to the annual meeting of the American Association for Public Opinion Research, St. Pete Beach, Florida, May 2002.

—, Dannagal Goldthwaite-Young, Joseph N. Cappella, and A. Romantan. "Online Political Discussion, Civic Engagement, and Social Trust." Unpublished manuscript, Annenberg School, University of Pennsylvania, 2006.

—, Lilach Nir, and Joseph. Cappella. "Does Disagreement Contribute to More Deliberative Opinion?" *Political Communication* 19 (2002): 95-112.

—, Lilach Nir, and Joseph Cappella. "Framing Public Discussion of Gay Civil Unions." *Public Opinion Quarterly* 69 (2005): 179-212.

Putnam, Robert. D. *Bowling Alone: The Collapse and Revival of American Community.* New York: Simon and Schuster, 2000.

Rains, Stephen A. "Leveling the Organizational Playing field—Virtually." *Communication Research* 32 (2005): 193-234.

Renn, Ortwin, H. U. Stegelmann, G. Albrecht, U. Kotte, and H. P. Peters. "An Empirical Investigation of Citizens' Preferences Among Four Energy Alternatives." *Technological Forecasting and Social Change* 26 (1984): 11-46.

Renn, Ortwin, Thomas Webler, Horst Rakel, Peter Dienel, and Branden Johnson. "Public Participation in Decision Making: A Three-Step Procedure." *Policy Sciences* 26 (1993): 189-214.

Rice, Ronald E. "Media Appropriateness: Using Social Presence Theory to Compare Traditional and New Organizational Media." *Human Communication Research* 19 (1993): 451-84.

Rosenbaum, Paul R. and Donald B. Rubin. "The Central Role of the Propensity Score in Observational Studies for Causal Effects." *Biometrika* 70 (1983): 41-55.

Ryfe, David M. "Does Deliberative Democracy Work?" *Annual Review of Political Science* 8 (2005): 49-71.

Sanders, Lynn. M. "Against Deliberation." *Political Theory* 25 (1997): 347-76.

Sartori, Giovanni. *Democratic Theory*, 2nd ed. Detroit: Wayne State University Press, 1962.

Schudson, Michael. "Why Conversation Is Not the Soul of Democracy." *Critical Studies in Mass Communication* 14 (1997): 297-309.

Schumpeter, Joseph A. *Capitalism, Socialism and Democracy*. New York: Harper and Brothers, 1942.

Stromer-Galley, Jennifer. "Diversity of Political Conversation on the Internet: Users' Perspectives." *Journal of Computer-Mediated Communication* 8 (2003), www.ascusc.org/jcmc/vol8/issue3/stromergalley.html.

Sunstein, Cass. *Republic.com*. Princeton: Princeton University Press, 2001.

Tidwell, Lisa Collins, and Joseph B. Walther. "Computer-mediated Communication Effects on Disclosure, Impressions, and Interpersonal Evaluations: Getting to Know One Another a Bit at a Time." *Human Communication Research* 28 (2002): 317-348.

Undem, T. Factors Affecting Discussion Quality: The Effects of Group Size, Gender, and Political Heterogeneity in Online Discussion Groups. Unpublished Master's thesis, University of Pennsylvania, Philadelphia, 2001.

Walther, Joseph B. "Interpersonal Effects in Computer-mediated Interaction." *Western Journal of Communication* 57 (1992): 381-98.

—. "Relational Aspects of Computer-mediated Communication: Experimental Observations Over Time." *Organization Science* 6 (1995): 186-203.

Warren, Mark. "Democratic Theory and Self-Transformation." *American Political Science Review* 86 (1992): 8-23.

CHAPTER 9

Deliberative e-Democracy[1]

Robert Cavalier

The rise of "e-democracy" over the past few decades has certainly brought many positive changes. Our access to governmental information has greatly improved and communication between citizens and government officials at the national and local levels has greatly increased. Information technology at the intersection between government and the people has blossomed in a thousand ways through the push of distribution lists and the interactivity of blogs. e-Democracy has revolutionized our political campaigns. But, like regular democratic practice, it has also fallen prey to the worst of politics: manipulation, framing and agenda-setting occur at an incredible pace in the 24-7 news and rumor cycle. And the rise of 21st century pamphleteers, with their threads of often vitriolic commentary, challenge the hopes of enthusiasts. There is, in the words of a member of the British Parliament, plenty of e-talk, but not much e-listening.

e-Democracy

For sure, there are efforts at e-democracy that show promise in terms of sophisticated public input loops. OpenCongress provides real-time access to detailed information on Senate and Congressional Bills, albeit with occasional progressive commentary. And during the 2008-2009 transition period of then President-Elect Obama,

---

[1] Elements of this chapter appear in Robert Cavalier, Miso Kim, and Zachary Zaiss "Deliberative Democracy, Online Discussion, and Carnegie Mellon's Project PICOLA (Public Informed Citizen Online Assembly)" in *Online Deliberation: Design, Research, and Practice*, ed. Todd Davies and S.P. Gangadharan (Chicago: CSLI Publications, 2008).

change.gov sought to engage large-scale online citizen participation in the development of policy ideas and to do so in ways analogous to the input of more traditional advisory groups.

Yet, in "Promising Practices in Online Engagement," the authors point out that while there were over 125,000 participants submitting 44,000 ideas on change.gov, the overall attempt suffered from serious drawbacks. Lack of moderators allowed for too many conflated and confusing comments and anonymity led to flaming as well as agenda packing. They also note "early submission bias," whereby proposals that gain an early lead in the voting tended to rise to the top. This phenomenon, aided by self-selection in the open process, allowed "legalizing marijuana" to rise to the top of the list.[2]

One compelling initiative in government-public feedback is Beth Noveck's Peer-To-Patent, an innovative program that now allows patent office employees to tap into pools of expertise. Given that an individual patent office employee must struggle with the dual demands of an archivist and content expert, it made sense to augment the patent process with a community of enthusiastic experts who could collaboratively investigate a patent proposal.

The wiki is a paradigm for such "collaboratories," an idea Noveck explores in her book *Wiki Government* (2009). Arguing that "democratic theory and the design of governing institutions must be rethought for the age of networks," Noveck went on to become the Obama Administration's Deputy Chief Technology Officer for Open Government. Her first effort, hosted by the National Academy for Public Administration, involved a three-stage process. The first phase solicited a wide range of suggestions for creating a more participatory, transparent government. The second stage invited discussions on the topics selected from the previous brainstorming session. The final stage, drafting, sought to move toward concrete policy recommendations based upon input from the previous stages.

While Peer-to-Patent relied on knowledgeable volunteers, more open forums still suffer from self-selection and agenda setting, often accompanied by misinformation. Developers of these kinds of environments are aware of this. Flagging off-topic posts (like those

---

[2] Scott Bittle, Chris Haller, and Allison Kadlec, "Promising Practices in Online Engagement," *Public Agenda*, Occasional Paper, No. 3 (2009), www.publicagenda.org/pages/promising-practices-in-online-engagement.

wishing to discuss President Obama's birth certificate), adding moderator controls and using mapping tools to help participants visualize where the process is and where it is going help to filter out the uninformed and the irrelevant.

It is clear that the Open Government Initiative in the summer of 2009 chartered new territory in e-democracy at the White House. There were over 900 ideas and 33,000 votes in the brainstorming session. The discussion section elicited more than 1,000 comments in response to 16 topics and the drafting phase, which lasted from June 22nd through July 6th, resulted in 305 drafts by 375 authors, with 2,256 participants voting on those drafts. Many good ideas were brought forth and discussed and the process as a whole was successful.

Challenges remain, however. During the brainstorming session, a fissure appeared between participation and collaboration. A NAPA analysis suggested that participants lacked information or context upon which to construct suggestions.[3] Many of the most well-informed ideas were summaries of position statements (many of which came from the deliberative democracy community). And many of the top vote-getters were basic concepts having little direct relevance to collaboration (e.g., make voting day a national holiday).

The authors of the memo suggest the need for a clearer definition of "collaboration" and one that gives individuals and groups examples to work with—along with the opportunity to participate alongside those with experience in collaboration. Other advice asks, "What can we do to give participants more context and clear targets against which to frame their thinking and comments . . . frame a participatory dialogue around how best to leverage or improve these starting points. Or, put out a menu of policies and proposals already under consideration and seek input on those."[4]

So it's still fair to say that what's largely missing from Wikis and Web 2.0 is a certain type of knowledgeable, engaged citizen-based discourse envisioned by proponents of deliberative democracy. As described throughout this book, such discourse is inclusive, informed

---

[3] Memorandum to Beth Noveck, Deputy Chief Technology Officer for Open Government Office of Science and Technology Policy, The White House from Lena Trudeau, Vice President. The National Academy of Public Administration (June 1, 2009).

[4] Ibid.

and well structured. All the better if there are ways to capture the results of the conversation and present these to stakeholders in such a way as to influence policy and other sorts of practical outcomes.

Deliberative e-Democracy

To implement this kind of environment online is the goal of what could be called "deliberative e-democracy," a phrase that has been evolving as proponents of deliberative democracy enter the arena of e-democracy. Terry Flew, for instance, speaks of "online deliberative democracy" when he refers to multidirectional activity, quoting Stephen Coleman and John Gøtze's models of "citizens as shareholders in power rather than consumers of policy."[5]

Noveck herself was an early proponent of this view, working with Benjamin Barber on Unchat,[6] a text-based version of deliberative e-democracy. Users logging into Unchat found themselves in a semi-circular "seating area" with places for a moderator and opportunities to talk in sequence. Features such as "whispering" and 'shouting' allowed for meeting-like interactions, as when someone mentions something to his neighbor or someone raises her hand to interject a point. Vincent Price's study of online deliberation also used a text-based environment. His chapter discussed in detail the nature of this experiment and its outcomes. And in his assessment, well structured text-forums might actually improve upon face-to-face deliberation by reducing the effects of social cues (such as physical appearance and social dominance). But text-only environments have significant drawbacks. They may systematically exclude citizens with poor typing skills or those embarrassed by spelling and grammatical errors. Real-time interactive chat is challenging not only for participants, but for "moderators" as well. Trying to follow as well

---

[5] See Terry Flew "From e-Government to Online Deliberative Democracy," (presentation to Oxford Internet Institute Summer Doctoral Program, Chinese Academy of Social Sciences, Beijing, July 11, 2005) and Stephen Coleman and John Gøtze *Bowling Together: Online Public Engagement in Policy Deliberation* (Hansard Society, London, 2001). I see no reason why there can't be both collaboration of the kind envisioned in Noveck's *WikiGovernment* and structured deliberation of the kind practiced by proponents of deliberative democracy. Connected to outcomes, both models fit Coleman and Gøtze's definition.

[6] For information about *Unchat* visit www.benjaminbarber.com/unchat.html

as comment upon an ongoing chat is like Lucille Ball trying to control chocolate candies moving by on a conveyer belt in that classic episode of *I Love Lucy*.

So when it came time to compare fact-to-face with online deliberation, Shanto Iyengar and colleagues chose an audio-based online conferencing tool (Lotus Sametime). The study, involving a random sample of citizens participating in a deliberative poll on America's role in the world occurred in 2003, at the cusp of the Iraq War. Aside from survey questions ranging from foreign policy to NAFTA, the environment and the protection of human rights, researchers were interested in certain methodological questions.[7] Specifically, to what extent and in what way does deliberation affect participant opinion in these matters and to what extent and how does the online treatment differ, if at all, from face-to-face deliberation?

In line with other studies of deliberative polls such as those described in chapter seven by Bonifini, Bridges, and Dickert, there was an increase in knowledge of facts and attitude changes tended to move in the direction of expert opinion (assessed through differences in mean between pre- and post surveys). In the face-to-face treatment, statistical changes were noted in seven of nine policy indices. In the online treatment, six of nine policy indices revealed statistically significant changes. Broadly speaking, online and face-to-face results were similar: on four of the nine issues, there was change in the same direction; and none of the nine indices showed statistically significant changes in opposing directions.

The Virtual Agora

Given that outcomes are similar, online modes of deliberation might serve as "social science microscopes" for the study of political deliberation. In 2001 researchers and developers at Carnegie Mellon began a project entitled "Developing and Testing A High Telepresence Virtual Agora for Broad Citizen Participation: A Multi-Trait, Multi-Method Investigation." The software developed specifically for this project made it possible to stage a two-phase experiment

---

[7] Robert C. Luskin, James S. Fishkin and Shanto Iyengar, "Considered Opinions on U.S. Foreign Policy: Face-to-Face versus Online Deliberative Polling," (Stanford Center for Deliberative Democracy Research Papers at cdd.stanford.edu/research/papers/2006/foreign-policy.pdf).

in online citizen deliberation. The first phase involved a controlled comparison of real-time online and face-to-face deliberation. The second phase involved citizens in a combination of real-time on-line meetings and asynchronous deliberations to identify (1) critical issues facing a specific school system, (2) policy approaches to addressing those issues, and (3) a strategy for implementing the participants' preferred policy approach.[8]

We were able to perform this experiment with a genuinely representative sample of over 500 citizens, including many with little or no computer or online experience prior to our study.[9] Preliminary data analysis shows that there was no apparent difference between computer-mediated and face-to-face discussions in terms of the attitudes of the participants changing as a result of their engaging in discussion. Both groups tended to end with participants forming a strong consensus on the issues, always in the direction of the expert opinion. Furthermore, discussants in both conditions also reported higher levels of critical thinking, confidence, and empowerment than did the control group, which read about the issue under discussion, but did not participate in deliberations. Finally, and in line with other studies in deliberative democracy, participants ascribed a very high degree of legitimacy to the collective outcome of their deliberations.

Results like these run counter to the claims put forth by John R. Hibbing and Elizabeth Theiss-Morse (2002) in *Stealth Democracy*. These authors rely on a survey finding that most Americans prefer not to become engaged in pubic debate, preferring a belief that consensus among well-meaning experts is sufficient for our democratic institutions. But as Peter Muhlberger points out, "Hibbing and Theiss-Morse's evidence against deliberation comes from research on public meetings about highly divisive issues and social-psychological

---

[8] NSF Grant No. EIA-0205502. PIs were Robert Cavalier, Peter Muhlberger and Peter Shane. Cavalier's participation focused mainly on discussions of interface design, Peter Muhlberger was the chief social science researcher, and Peter Shane's interests focused on issues relating to the policymaking processes of government agencies. A website, The Virtual Agora Project, contains studies and research relating to this NSF Grant (virtualagora.org/).

[9] Knowledge Networks generated a sample of 6,935 City of Pittsburgh residents. Of these, 22% agreed to participate and 37% of these (568) actually participated in the first phase of the study. Numbers dropped off to a still respectable 230 during the second stage of the study.

experiments, not with research on typical deliberative practices."[10] Such research carried out in the Virtual Agora Project yields different results and different interpretations of the Stealth Democracy thesis. In particular, he argues from the data that deliberation undermines the Hibbing and Theiss-Morse survey data by showing how the public can deal with reasonable disagreement and seek solutions independently of political authority. Muhlberger introduces the notion of "parochial citizen worldviews" as a way to intersect with Hibbing and Theiss-Morse's thesis. There is a sense in which participants' particular views about politics in the studies overlap. But separating these views (such as political disinterest and conflict aversion) and immersing participants in an informed, well structured deliberative process leads to a different conclusion. Indeed, "[d]eliberation in particular could both help clarify that reasonable people hold a diversity of views and exposes discussants to complex processes of decision making . . ." all the while encouraging a sense of engagement, "cultivating a more civically-minded public."[11]

PICOLA

Beginning around 2003, Project PICOLA (Public Informed Citizen Online Assembly) evolved as a parallel development project designed specifically to model the protocols of James Fishkin's Deliberative Poll®. Using local funding, Carnegie Mellon Center for the Advancement of Applied Ethics and Political Philosophy developed a front-end interface that tied together software for both synchronous and asynchronous discussions as well as tools for registration and survey-taking (caae.phil.cmu.edu/picola/). Because PICOLA, like the Virtual Agora, was based on complex programming environment that combined both commercial and open-software tools, we were not able to sustain it past its initial five-year cycle. However,

---

[10] Peter Muhlberger, "Should E-Government Design for Citizen Participation? Stealth Democracy and Deliberation" (www.geocities.com/pmuhl78/dgoStealth-V3P.pdf). See also Muhlberger, "Stealth Democracy, Apathy Rationales, and Deliberation" (Paper presented at the annual meeting of the International Communication Association, Sheraton New York, NY, May 5, 2009), www.allacademic.com/meta/p14489_index.html.

[11] Peter Muhlberger, "The Virtual Agora Project: A Research Design for Studying Democratic Deliberation," *Journal of Public Deliberation* 1, no 1 (2005): 2.

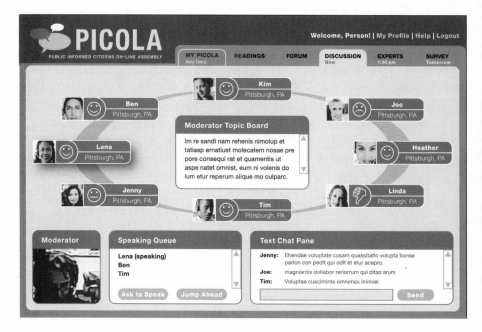

the successful use of the prototype has led us to conclude that the design of PICOLA constitutes a paradigm for these kinds of online tools. It stands as a "regulatory ideal" for high-telepresence, integrated deliberative e-democracy.[12]

The Virtual Agora interface design benefited from online environments like Unchat (for the roundtable), studies like that done by Price (with relevance to text-based asynchronous modules) and tools like those used by Iyengar (for the power of audio). Our research showed that audio-based conversations with video-based moderators (using deliberative practices such as turn-taking, etc.) showed no significant difference from face-to-face deliberations following the same practices. The significance of this outcome is itself far reaching: Well designed and carefully implemented online tools for deliberation can be used alone or in conjunction with face-to-face deliberations to deliver useful results to decision-makers.

At the highest level of Human Computer Interaction, PICOLA embeds in its design the notion of "computers as theatre," first de-

---

[12] Programs like Adobe's Connect and, more specifically, Polimetrix's *Vox Populi* come close to embedding the features of PICOLA and can serve as examples of high telepresence deliberative tools.

scribed by Brenda Laurel in a book of that name. By re-describing the relation of User to Screen along the lines of Aristotle's Poetics, Laurel argues that the user must be brought into the drama of the program and not seen merely as someone outside the screen in need of guidance as to how to navigate the information on the screen. This approach is now apparent in the design of video games, where users can be transformed into a "skier" or "medieval knight." In a similar manner, a user enters PICOLA in such a way as to be transformed into a "citizen" engaged in a community conversation. If successful, this can make the computer disappear, replaced by a virtual public sphere.[13]

In line with many virtual environments, PICOLA had a standard login/registration area, as well as the capability for administrators to add announcements and other information to help orient the participants' understanding of a particular event. Its in its original design, the login area also has a place for picture taking. This allows the program to capture an image of the participant, reduce it to a "picon" and place it next to the person's name in the synchronous roundtable discussion area. It is remarkable how a simplified image of a person lends itself to a sense of presence so important to the "virtual experience" of another human being. But we were far ahead of the easy picture grabbing tools of today and this feature was never fully utilized.

The human voice, however, is also an extremely powerful vehicle for telepresence and thus audio played a key role in our design and should do so in any similar application. In fact, the use of audio levels the playing field for those who lack keyboarding skills. It creates a more inclusive environment and also facilitates a more natural conversation. An asynchronous forum still provides a venue for text-based reflection, but our experience showed that voice-based dialogue is the most useful and civil way to process information in the conversational setting. Finally, both asynchronous and synchronous discussions can be archived for further use in, for example, social science studies or community records.

---

[13] See Brenda Laurel, *Computers as Theatre* (Addison-Wesley, 1991). See also Janet Murray *Hamlet on the Holodeck* (Cambridge: The MIT Press, 1997) as well as Cavalier "The Poetics of Simulation: An Analysis of Programs in Ethics and Conflict Resolution," in *Virtual Decisions: Digital Simulations for Teaching Reasoning in the Social Sciences and Humanities*, ed. Cohen et al. (Lawrence Erlbaum, 2005).

To create a virtual public sphere where the participant truly feels immersed as a citizen in PICOLA's virtual environment, it was necessary to gain an in-depth understanding of the environment that exists for the typical face-to-face experience. This task was an important part of a year-long study in Human-Computer Interaction, using cognitive walkthroughs and think-aloud interviews.[14] The resulting program, "deliberative by design," sought to deliver and support an online conversation that is informed, structured and documented.

As mentioned, a key component of PICOLA is the Synchronous Discussion area. Here participants become fully immersed in the virtual public sphere. We arrived at this immersive environment by studying how these types of discussions happen in real life. Naturally, some positive aspects needed to be maintained, such as the capability for people to carry on brief, side conversations with one another (supported by a text chat box); allowing for immediate, nonverbal responses to various points (supported by the inclusion of emoticons for each participant); and having one focal point where important issues and questions for the expert panel can be displayed (supported by the moderator's whiteboard). On the other hand, we included a speaking queue to add a level of order to the conversation (and to prevent one person from monopolizing the discussion or interrupting other participants continuously). We also had a clock feature to indicate a certain upper limit to each participant's "turn at the microphone" (while this is variable, two or three minutes seem to work well).

Mobile PICOLA

The telegraph, like the Internet . . . transformed social and business practices, but it could be used only by skilled operators. Its benefits became available to the public at large only when the telegraph evolved into the telephone—initially known as the "speaking telegraph. . . ." The mobile phone promises to do for the Internet what the telephone did for the telegraph . . . the

---

[14] The study ultimately employed four analysis methods: Contextual Inquiry and Design, Heuristic Evaluation, Cognitive Walkthrough and Think Aloud Interviews. The investigators were Alex Darrow, Peter Jones, Jessica Smith, Greg Vassallo, and Sam Zaiss. Elements of this study have been incorporated into the design of PICOLA.

262

mobile Internet, although it is based on the same technology as the fix-line Internet, will be something different and will be used in new and unexpected ways.[15]

In 2004, South Korea underwent a political crisis when an impeachment movement was started against then President Roe. Almost 70% of Koreans were against these impeachment procedures and citizens soon became actively engaged in heated online discussions—on the bulletin boards of major portals, in Internet cafes and web-zines, and through their blogs. This active participation via digital media resulted in a national protest when as many as 2,200,000 (4.2% of the population) citizens gathered on the streets throughout the country. As the result, the parties that led the impeachment movement lost by a great margin in the election that followed. In 2009 a similar phenomenon appeared in Iran, this time with the addition of Twitter but with less than successful initial outcomes.

In Smart Mobs: The Next Social Revolution (2003), Howard Rheingold investigates what the media has called the Mobile Future. He notes how often the meaning of these technological transformations only becomes recognized once "the street" figures out how to use them. In line with the examples above, he describes the way Filipinos used an innocuous promotional feature, Short Message Service (SMS), to bring down the presidency of Joseph Estrada in 2001. The message that bought tens of thousands of citizens to a central location called "Edsa" was "Go 2EDSA, Wear black." Rheingold uses this example and many others to analyze the sociological phenomena now known as "Generation Txt." We might expand beyond his thumb-tribes by adding the audio-video features of smart phones, allowing the "secondary orality" of today's generation to come to the fore.[16]

With these mobile technologies, a yet another "public sphere" is emerging and a new civic forum is being created. Perhaps this demo-

---

[15] Tom Standage, "The Internet Untethered," *The Economist*, October 13, 2001.

[16] See Walter Ong, *Orality and Literacy: Technologizing the Word* (New York: Routledge, 1982).While primary orality is characterized as "a culture totally untouched by any knowledge of writing or print," secondary orality pertains to a literate culture that is augmented by technologies that include multimedia.

cratic mobile movement can also be made deliberative and hence stronger in its use and impact. To see how this might come into being, we worked with a doctoral student in design to explore the integration of PICOLA functionality into cell phone/PDA devices (Mobile PICOLA). How people will eventually use the tools that we prototyped for Mobile PICOLA can only be guessed at—but the advantages of these features could already be seen in our beta-tests.[17]

The audio-based synchronous roundtable in PICOLA is the best example of the high-telepresence that we have sought to achieve. Once people enter the roundtable and have made all the necessary adjustments to their sound and headset components, an effortless conversation ensures. But here's a problem: people are not always at their computers when we are ready to start, they need to check the current set up (has the audio control panel been left on mute by the previous user?), and many times they need us to reschedule. Cell-phone/PDA devices may be able to close the gap between user and machine. The advantages of cell-phone/PDA devices include mobility (anytime, any place), identity (cell phones are customized by each individual user and are part of their apparel, so to speak), and accessibility (I can join a PICOLA roundtable even as I walk about town). These advantages may breakdown the barriers to the use of PICOLA-like environments and they might do so in a way that can enhance its impact qualitatively.

Institutional Infrastructure and Democracy 3.0

Aside from the careful design and development of any kind of software, the most important test of its value will be its usefulness. The key here lies in placing an online tool for deliberation within an existing infrastructure that in turn provides a basic infrastructure for the online environment itself. Institutional or organizational settings can also be the source of topics selected for their timeliness and relevance.

The use of the Virtual Agora and PICOLA was supported by a university environment, the former for research purposes, the lat-

---

[17] Miso Kim was lead designer. Her advisors at Carnegie Mellon's School of Design have taken a keen interest in this kind of work as it highlights applications that are capable of having a social impact ("design with a conscience").

ter for development and field-testing. To move from a university setting to a community setting will be challenging, especially for the kinds of deliberative tools envisioned here. Yet in many ways, Barack Obama's 2008 presidential campaign came close to developing this organizational infrastructure. It certainly represented the best integration of Internet and community up to that point. Expanding upon the political party style of these sites, we can see the groundwork for a more deliberative use of online tools combined with actual local, state and national community conversations.[18] In this, we can also see the groundwork for Democracy 3.0 (seamlessly combining the most robust features of face-to-face and online democratic practice).

We might imagine, for example, a Regional Visioning project that will unfold in multiple stages. After government officials and community leaders come to see the need for the functional consolidation of regional efforts and the economic advantages of speaking with a unified voice, they might embark on a well-funded initiative to educate the public on and gain public input into the proposal. Traditional "public forums" and blanket surveys are proving more and more inefficient and uninformative, even lacking in legitimacy.

With background materials developed out of white papers and other forms of research, Study Circles such as those sponsored by Everyday Democracy might be established across the region. Facebook-like tools are used to organize these events and keep track of developments. A Regional Wiki might be set up to grow in size and depth as participants in the Learning Circles (and any other individuals) add content to the Regional Envisioning Statement. At some point, an AmericaSpeaks 21st Century Town Hall meeting might be held in one of the county seats. Participants from the more than thirty Learning Circles would be solicited as part of the convenience sample. Maybe a deliberative poll might be held later on with a random sample discussing the results of the 21st Century Town Hall meeting and lending added legitimacy to the outcome. Perhaps public libraries could host PICOLA-like online discussions of the issues for those who can't join the Learning Circles or other forums due to

[18] Community Builder, a Facebook environment hosted by E-Democracy.org, is an example of efforts to create a non-partisan environment for citizen conversations. The online aspects of AmericaSpeaks' Electronic Town Hall meetings and other similar efforts are also striving to provide structured citizen online discussions that can be linked to face-to-face meetings.

time constraints. Others could join these multimedia deliberations from their home or the local coffee house. Stakeholders would be involved throughout the process and policy makers outcomes would be sure to pay heed to the recommendations of the entire deliberative process.

Throughout all these applications of deliberative democracy—face-to-face and online—the tasks of representing issues, getting good samples, creating the conditions for well-structured conversations, and conducting useful surveys are enormous. The resources needed in terms of time and personnel are daunting. In short, the task of doing democracy, of making democracy stronger, is incredibly hard. Yet this is not only technically possible, but politically important for our democracy. Speaking as a constitutional lawyer and independently of any political affiliation or the nature of his policies, President Obama himself said that our Constitution is less like a blueprint for a house, than a home for a conversation. We are, in the manner of Madison, a "deliberative democracy."[19]

---

[19] ". . . the framework of our Constitution can . . . organize the way by which we argue about our future. All of its elaborate machinery—its separation of powers and checks and balances and federalist principles and Bill of Rights—are designed to force us into a conversation, a 'deliberative democracy'. . . ." Barack Obama, *The Audacity of Hope* (New York: Crown Publishers, Random House, 2006), 92.

BIBLIOGRAPHY

Bittle, Scott, Chris Haller, and Allison Kadlec. "Promising Practices in Online Engagement." *Public Agenda Occasional Paper* no. 3 (2009), www.publicagenda.org/pages/promising-practices-in-online-engagement.

Cavalier, Robert. "The Poetics of Simulation: An Analysis of Programs in Ethics and Conflict Resolution." *Virtual Decisions: Digital Simulations for Teaching Reasoning in the Social Sciences and Humanities,* edited by Steve Cohen, Kent E Portney, Dean Rehberger, and Carolyn Thorsen. New York: Routledge, 2005.

—, Miso Kim and Zachary Zaiss. "Deliberative Democracy, Online Discussion, and Carnegie Mellon's Project PICOLA (Public Informed Citizen Online Assembly)." *Online Deliberation: Design, Research, and Practice,* edited by Davies and S.P. Gangadharan. Chicago: CSLI Publications, 2008.

Clift, Steve. "E-Government and Democracy." Publicus.net: Public Strategies for the Online World, www.publicus.net/e-government.

Coleman, Stephen, and John Gøtze. *Bowling Together: Online Public Engagement in Policy Deliberation.* London: Hansard Society, 2001.

Flew, Terry. "From e-Government to Online Deliberative Democracy." Presentation to the Oxford Internet Institute Summer Doctoral Program, Chinese Academy of Social Sciences, Beijing, July 7-21, 2005.

Hibbing, John R. and Elizabeth Theiss-Morse. *Stealth Democracy: Americans' Beliefs about How Government Should Work.* Cambridge: Cambridge University Press, 2002.

Laurel, Brenda. *Computers as Theatre.* Reading: Addison-Wesley, 1991.

Muhlberger, Peter. "Should E-Government Design for Citizen Participation? Stealth Democracy and Deliberation," www.geocities.com/pmuhl78/dgoStealthV3P.pdf.

—. "Stealth Democracy, Apathy Rationales, and Deliberation." Paper presented at the annual meeting of the International Communication Association, New York, NY, May 5, 2009, www.allacademic.com/meta/p14489_index.html.

—. "The Virtual Agora Project: A Research Design for Studying Democratic Deliberation," *Journal of Public Deliberation* 1, no 1 (2005).

Murray, Janet H. *Hamlet on the Holodeck: The Future of Narrative in Cyberspace.* Cambridge: The MIT Press, 1997.

Noveck, Beth S. *Wiki Government: How Technology Can Make Government Better, Democracy Stronger, and Citizens More Powerful.* Richmond: R.R. Donnely, 2009.

Obama, Barack. *Audacity of Hope.* New York: Crown Publishers, Random House, 2006.

Ong, Walter. *Orality and Literacy: Technologizing the Word.* New York: Routledge, 1982.

Rheingold, Howard. *Smart Mobs: The Next Social Revolution,* New York: Perseus, 2003.

Shane, Peter M., Peter Muhlberger, and Robert Cavalier. "ITR: Developing and Testing a High Telepresence Virtual Agora for Broad Citizen Participation: a Multi-trait, Multi-method Investigation." *Proceedings of the 2004 Annual National Conference on Digital Government Research*, Seattle, WA, May 24 - 26, 2004. dg.o 262 (2004), portal.acm.org/citation.cfm?id=1124214.

Standage, Tom. "The Internet Untethered" *The Economist*, October 13, 2001.

CONTRIBUTORS

S.M. Amadae is a member of the Political Science Department at Ohio State University. She is author of *Rationalizing Capitalist Democracy: The Cold War Origins of Rational Choice Liberalism* (Chicago, 2003), which won the American Political Science Association's J. David Greenstone book award for the best book in Politics and History for 2004.

Benjamin R. Barber is a Distinguished Senior Fellow at Demos and Walt Whitman Professor of Political Science Emeritus, Rutgers University. His publications include *Strong Democracy* (University of California Press, 1984, 2004), the international bestseller *Jihad vs. McWorld* (Times Books, 1995; Ballantine Books, 1996) and *Consumed: How Markets Corrupt Children, Infantilize Adults, and Swallow Citizens Whole* (W.W. Norton & Co., 2007).

Mike Bridges, Joanna Dickert, and Jayna Bonfini, are involved in deliberative polling projects at Carnegie Mellon University. With backgrounds in philosophy, psychology and education respectively, they've worked on both campus and community initiatives.

Gregory J. Crowley, Ph.D. is Vice President, Program Development and Evaluation at the Pittsburgh Coro Center for Civic Leadership. Author of *The Politics Of Place: Contentious Urban Redevelopment in Pittsburgh* (University of Pittsburgh Press, 2005), he has sought to integrate deliberative practices at the neighborhood level.

Christian List is Professor of Political Science and Philosophy, Departments of Government and Philosophy, at the London School of Economics. He is the author of numerous articles on voting theory and judgment aggregation and has worked with James Fishkin and Robert Luskin on assessing deliberative polling protocols. Anna Sliwka is Professor and Program Director for Research, International Relations and Diversity at the Heidelberg University of Education.

Gerry Mackie is Associate Professor of Political Science at the University of California, San Diego. He is a political theorist who works on contemporary democratic theory, especially voting, and the ethics of collective action. His *Democracy Defended* (Cambridge University Press, 2003) won the Gladys Kammerer Award from the American Political Science Association. Prior to his academic career he was an elected leader of a large workers' cooperative in Oregon.

Julie Marsh received her Ph.D. in Administration and Policy Analysis, Stanford University and is currently a researcher at RAND, Santa Monica Office. Her publications include *Democratic Dilemmas: Joint Work, Education Politics and Community* (SUNY Press, 2007).

Vincent Price is Steven H. Chaffee Professor of Communication and Political Science at the University of Pennsylvania. He has published extensively on mass communication and public opinion, social influence processes, and political communication. He is author of *Public Opinion* (Sage, 1992) and was editor-in-chief of *Public Opinion Quarterly* from 1997-2001. His current work focuses on the role of online political conversation and deliberation in shaping public opinion.